C^{apt.} Joshua Slocum

C*apt.* Joshua Slocum

THE LIFE AND VOYAGES OF
AMERICA'S BEST KNOWN SAILOR

by Victor Slocum

SHERIDAN HOUSE

Published by
Sheridan House Inc.
145 Palisade Street
Dobbs Ferry, NY 10522

First paperback edition 1993

Library of Congress
Cataloging in Publication Data:

Slocum, Victor.
Capt. Joshua Slocum: the life and voyages of
America's best known sailor.

Reprint of the 1972 ed.
Includes index.
1. Slocum, Joshua, b. 1844. 2. Voyages and travels.
3. Seaman–United States–Biography. I. Title.
VK140.S6S6 1981 910.4'5'0924 {B} 80-28525

ISBN 0-924486-52-X

Printed in the United States of America

To All Those
Who Sail upon the Deep

FOREWORD

This book is expected to supplement my father's book in which he gave an account of his voyage in the *Spray,* entitled *Sailing Alone Around the World* (New York, 1900). In his book he introduced just enough of his family background and previous seagoing experience to suit the purpose of *Sailing Alone,* and not to make it top-heavy at the start. That was according to his lights nearly fifty years ago. Since then, there has been a growing demand on the part of a certain travelling public to know more about the man. That is where the present book is supposed to fit in.

This has been a task for a mere seafarer who all his life has had more to do with a marline spike and a belaying pin than with a typewriter. My main standby is an early life experience stemming from a seventeen-year turn at sea with my father:— from the time of birth until becoming first mate of the *Aquid-neck.* I was on board of that bark on her loss in South American waters and assisted in the *Liberdade* venture which ended at The Battery in New York. The following account, therefore, though largely biographical in its nature, perforce contains much of history.

In gathering this scattered material and in bringing it into form suitable to merit the reader's attention, the writer must plead competent and sympathetic assistance from friends. First among these is genial Tom Davin of Sheridan House. He has helped me to clear the decks, fore and aft, so that the reader

7

may venture forth upon the work without jamming his toes against the ringbolt of ambiguity or tumble down the hatchway of misunderstanding.

The writer acknowledges his indebtedness to Appleton-Century-Crofts, Inc., for their kind permission to reproduce the drawings of Thomas Fogarty and George Varian from The Century Co., 1900 edition of *Sailing Alone Around the World* which adorn my account of the voyage of the *Spray* herein. I am thankful to *Yachting* for permission to reprint biographical material which first appeared there and to *Rudder* for permission to quote from Mr. C. Andrade Jr.'s article on the lines of the *Spray* which first appeared in that magazine.

My thanks are also due to my accomplished niece, Catherine Woodruff, for her painstaking work in the reproduction and revision of the manuscript. To Mr. W. M. Williamson, a great chronicler of the sea, goes my special gratitude for verifying many historical and geographical details in the book.

I should like to give my thanks to my marine artist friends, Mr. Charles R. Patterson and Mr. Charles Rosner, for their excellent ship portraits of the great *Northern Light* and other commands of Captain Joshua Slocum including the present jacket design of the diminutive *Spray*. The silhouette of the *Spray* on the title page is the work of my old friend and artist, J. Warren Sheppard.

VICTOR SLOCUM

CONTENTS

C^apt. Joshua Slocum

CHAPTER 1

The Return of the *Spray*

O<small>N A DAY</small> in June in 1898 a sea-battered sloop from the direction of the West Indies reached the southern edge of the Gulf Stream, having passed Bermuda. The trades had been good to her, but now clear skies and fresh and dependable breezes were changed to lowering clouds and fitful squalls from the nor'west. One man only could be seen on deck to work the vessel. The sloop with the lone mariner was headed towards New York.

As the sloop approached the southern edge of the Gulf Stream, she was met by typical Gulf Stream weather. In the newly rough sea she jumped like a porpoise, and under the sudden shock her well-worn rigging and gear began to give out. First the mainsheet strap carried away, and then the peak halyard block went. On the following day the gale increased in force while the fitful cross sea increased in height and confusion. Then her hull gave a thud as though she had hit a rock. The jib stay, one of the main supports of the mainmast, had parted. With it, the jib had fallen into the sea. With great presence of mind, the lone mariner on board, who comprised the entire crew, gathered the sail on the deck before it had a chance to trail underneath the vessel and get lost. The rolling and pitching of the sloop in the seaway made the mast switch like a reed, but this the lone mariner clambered up with a single block and the end of a gantline hooked in his belt. A gun-tackle was then got up and the jib stay again tautened from the masthead.

All this was a superhuman feat in singlehanded seamanship. It demonstrated not only cool-headedness but also great agility and strength. This in a man who had been three years at sea by himself. He was 54 years of age.

A winterish storm then broke upon the sloop from the north-west. Hailstones pelted and lightning poured down from the clouds; the lightning, not in flashes alone, but in almost continuous streams. This tornado was the climax storm of a long voyage. The sloop took it all snug and under bare poles. When the tornado first struck, she shivered and heeled over on her beam-ends; but rounding to with a sea anchor out ahead she righted to face out the storm. She had seen one storm like this near Madagascar, but in intensity it was not like this one. Here the lightning kept on longer and thunderbolts fell into the sea all about.

When all was over, the sloop made sail. She reached in for the coast of Long Island to make for a quiet harbor to think things over. Although originally bound for the port of New York, now being to leeward of New York, any port would do.

About midnight Fire Island light could be seen and by daylight the dark green sea had changed to light green. Then a thin line of the Long Island coast, east of Fire Island, hove into sight. Under close reefs the sloop stretched along to the east-

14

ward. Her intention now was to enter the first port to be found at hand and that was Newport, Rhode Island.

The weather, after the furious gale, became remarkably fine. The sloop rounded Montauk Point early in the afternoon. Point Judith was abeam at dark and Beavertail came next. The strange sloop, once past the lightship, came into the beam of the guardship, for Newport was still mined against the Spanish War.

The lone mariner heard a friendly voice from the *U.S.S. Dexter* hail, "*Spray, Ahoy!*" for such it was, and the lone mariner on her deck was Captain Joshua Slocum. It was shortly after midnight when the *Spray* cast anchor, after a cruise of more than forty-six thousand miles around the world after an absence of three years and two months.

Next morning in Newport's inner harbor, the *Spray* swung to her anchor like a seabird resting its wings from a storm. Though seaworn, the new arrival in port was high-headed and buoyant. From a long and constant acquaintance with the wash of the oceans, her sides and decks were bare of paint. The sails were bleached and yet glistening with brine. The hull was encrusted with barnacles and the headgear was yet fringed with ribbons of gulfweed. The running gear was chafed and in most places worn to a frazzle.

Lashed to her rail was a smaller and, if possible, a still more primitive and exotic ship. It was a dugout outrigger canoe which might at some time have run the combers of a South Pacific atoll.

On the sloop's deck were the shells of the great tridacna which could only have been brought from a far sea. Three tons of these were in the sloop's hold as well as other varieties of shells and feathery corals that could only have been collected on a voyage along the equator in the Pacific.

15

Nothing disturbed the Captain's short stop in Newport except a telegram from the New York press inquiring the "object" of his voyage. The object was love of world travel and adventure, but he responded somewhat irrelevantly that he hoped he had "done nothing that an American sailor should be ashamed of."

The new arrival in Newport had performed a feat never equalled in maritime history and had put himself, without knowing it, in the line of the sea kings of all time. His voyage was more than a feat in seamanship; it was a demonstration to fellow mariners that the world was not so large as they thought it was.

After a day or so in Newport to dry sails and gear, the *Spray* continued her way homeward to Fairhaven, Massachusetts. Entering the Acushnet River, she tied up to the very same stake at Oxford Village she had been tied to when she was launched. All agreed that a vessel could not get any closer home than that. Whaling captains again worked over the Acushnet bridge and this time looked wonderingly at the phenomenon: a small and brine-soaked hull which put them in mind of a *kraken* come from the depths of the sea to land.

My brother Garfield and I had come from Boston at the first tidings of the sloop's arrival in port. My father's first hail was, "Vic, you could have done it," and looking at me significantly, "but you would not be the first." My father had at different times, while we were at sea together, complimented me on my seamanship, which from him meant something, but this last to me was the most pleasing. He had advised me not to shave things as closely as I had seen him do, but to wait until I had more experience. Our voyage from Brazil in the *Liberdade* had been a good school, and on her he knew that we had both learned a lot about small-boat sailing on tall water. His wife, Henrietta, was, of course, waiting in Boston for the skip-

16

per to report personally. So he left Garfield and me to discharge
the *Spray's* cargo and to answer the multitude of questions
asked by the constant stream of visitors that came to look and
to watch us work.

The *Spray*, careened, de-barnacled, and re-copper-painted,
began to look more like herself. As soon as it could be arranged
for, a lecture on the *Spray's* voyage was announced, to be
given in the auditorium of the New Bedford city hall. It was
jammed to the carlins; the old salts very expectantly occupying
the front seats long before the appointed time. Garfield ran the
projector for the pictures, while it was my job to preside over
the box office with satisfying results.

The lecturer was very curiously scrutinized by the old salts
in the first few rows at the front; they did not miss a gesture
or an allusion. The lecture recalled places and scenes that they
were familiar with. That particular part of the house knew what
the lecturer was talking about, which made the situation agree-
ably responsive. They liked the reception given to the *Spray*
in Gibraltar by the great battleships. The Strait of Magellan
was the greatest thrill, and how she escaped the Milky Way,
the worst death trap in the seven seas. They were interested in
the expedient of the tacks to make the savage Fuegians hop
around, but they did not think it was as funny as most people
seemed to think it was, for they themselves had been forced to
do the same thing in the South Seas to keep off sure enough
man-eaters. Tacks to step on, to them, were realistic.

The pounding surf and the highland of Juan Fernandez
brought back to many the memory of a wood-and-water party
while whaling. Some of them declared that they had seen the
forebears of the very same goats that were in the picture, or at
least there was a very striking family resemblance. They were
disappointed at there being no pictures of the Nukahiva

17

beauties they had heard about; but became reconciled when the lecturer explained that while passing Nukahiva in the Marquesas there was a strong, fair wind blowing, and he was so contented with his palm and needle repairing the ravages of Cape Horn that he felt little inclination for shore society until reaching Samoa.

Leaving the *Spray* in Fairhaven, my father journeyed by land to New York and then to Washington, where he again fell in with Captain Clark of the *U.S.S. Oregon,* who had passed him to exchange signals at the equator some months before. During their gam in the Navy Department, the Secretary, the Honorable John D. Long, came in. Upon my father being introduced to the interested Secretary, the latter immediately said, "The President wants to see you, and we will all go over to the White House." It was "Teddy" himself.

As they clasped hands shortly, Mr. Roosevelt said, kindly: "Captain, our adventures have been a little different."

"That is true, Mr. President; but you got here first."

When the *Spray* came to lay in Erie Basin, South Brooklyn, visitors were puzzled by her appearance. They expected to see something unusual, but this was a ship of another kind. There were none of the refined appurtenances of a yacht about her decks. Everything was plain and business-like; no varnished teak nor shining brasswork. To them she looked like a fishing boat. Her bows were as round and as full as an old English billyboy's and her breadth of beam ran aft with a slight taper to a broad flaring transom on top of which the fourteen-inch bulwarks stood plumb, with her name—*Spray*—and hailing port—*Boston*—painted in bold black letters.

The rugged and stocky yawl had a stumpy little mast and a stumpy bowsprit. The jiggermast, stepped aft on the transom, was supported by a heavy arched beam over the stern. The mainsail was an ordinary gaff sail, but with the boom shortened to clear the jigger. The mizzen was a lug sail with the yard slung in about the middle and was loose-footed, shooting out to an outrigger that projected aft. On deck there were two deck houses, neither of which had lights of any kind for the sea to smash in. A peep into the forward house, entered by a companion slide, revealed a small square of floor with curios of all kinds stowed around the sides. Everything bore a massive look, and showed that strength had been one of the principal factors in her construction.

The after cabin had the top rounded over on the two sides, and this was also entered through a companionway aft by the wheel. A stanchion in the middle of the cabin provided against the top being smashed down by seas. Around the base of the stanchion a circular table was built so you could sit on the transom or bunk and reach it easily. The Captain's bunk was on the starboard side. And it was interesting to see the little teak handrail along each quarter which the Captain had put up in Australia, and to hear him describe the satisfaction it gave him to see it there, like the monkey rail on the poop of ships he was used to.

My father's life upon the sea, from start to finish, was that of a pioneer, and most of his voyaging was off the beaten track. He was never disposed to think that just because a thing had never been done before, it could not be. He acquired this trait during his early upbringing in the Maritime Provinces of Nova Scotia.

From the time he first took to deep water, at the age of sixteen, his voyages were all foreign. From England he sailed to China and the Moluccas. Rounding Cape Horn he established

19

himself on the Pacific Coast and thenceforward became an American citizen with San Francisco as his personal hailing port. After some adventurous experiences on the Columbia River, a spell at fur hunting in British Columbia, and sailing a California grain coaster for a month or so, he was put in charge of a pioneering Alaska salmon expedition. In command of the bark *Washington*, he was the first American to enter Cook Inlet when the Russians left after the Seward Purchase.

His next adventure was in the eastern Pacific. He visited Easter Island to view its huge and mysterious idols; he visited Nukahiva and the Hawaiian Islands. Sailing from San Francisco again he engaged in the Australia-China trade, having brushes with Malay and Chinese pirates.

China trading formed the base of two other original enterprises: the building of a steamer on Luzon for an English merchant trader; and the purchase of the sixty-ton schooner *Pato* in Manila, whence he sailed via Hong Kong to the Okhotsk Sea, and then to Portland, Oregon, skirting the Kuriles and having sport with grizzly bears on the way. The schooner *Pato* adventures were more like my father than anything else he ever did. It was fishing, sport and trade, the latter not without its profits. The *Pato* wound up in other hands as a South Sea trader.

Back in San Francisco, the Captain bought a bark suitable for the Luzon-China timber trade. When the Chinese demand for Luzon timber declined, he took over, in Hong Kong, the command and part ownership of the ship *Northern Light*, of the house of Pinckney and Benner, New York. This was one of the finest and largest of America's sailing vessels, and for three years he sailed her between New York and Far Eastern ports. Up to this point, my father had made rapid progress both in professional prestige and in prosperity.

On the transfer of the *Northern Light* to a foreign flag, my father bought outright a small Baltimore bark called the *Aquidneck,* which he sailed in the South American trade for three years and which he finally lost through a quarantine altercation he had with Brazilian officials. Leaving the dismantled wreck of the *Aquidneck* in Brazil, he and his family sailed the 5000-mile distance home in a 35 by 7½ foot homemade canoe. It was a sea adventure which intrigued the Captain to such an extent that a few years afterwards, in Fairhaven, Massachusetts, he built with his own hands a nine-ton yawl and sailed it single-handed around the world. The voyage of the *Spray* was a feat never equalled in maritime history; other mariners had girdled the globe in vessels of small tonnage, but no one had ever attempted the voyage alone.

By this exploit, undertaken through pure love of adventure, the Captain achieved the hitherto impossible on the sea, created an enthusiasm in blue water yachtsmen for long distance cruising, and thereafter became America's best known sailor.

CHAPTER 2

Early Days on Brier Island

Joshua Slocum, Master Mariner, born in Wilmot, Annapolis County in Nova Scotia, was descended from a long line of maritime forebears. There had been sailors for generations on both sides of his family. For those interested in Captain Joshua's antecedents, I have put down my findings about our family in an appendix to this book entitled: "The Slocums before Joshua."

When John Slocombe (Slocum), Joshua's father, was about twenty-three and sailing around Brier Island in the Bay of Fundy from Port George to Yarmouth, he became acquainted with Sarah Southern, the daughter of the lightkeeper of the Southwest Light at Westport. Her father was a retired naval man, a veteran of long service on the King's ships. John and Sarah were married and returned to live on the Slocombe farm at Wilmot where Joshua was born.

For the first ten years of their married life, John and Sarah lived on the Wilmot farm, which they concluded was sterile and unproductive. Their eyes turned back upon Sarah's home,

Brier Island. There, Westport was a thriving town where there was demand for a boot shop. That was one of the Nova Scotian industries which had begun to be specialized. John Slocombe, devout and stalwart, was typical of the people. He was a man of narrow sympathies, and in the interpretation of life he was but a slight improvement upon his ancestors who first battled the wilderness. He was possessed of a patriarchal attitude toward his growing family nor spared he the rod so far as disciplining the boys was concerned.

In 1852, John and Sarah returned to Westport, bringing with them little Joshua who by this time was eight. But though young in years, he was already advanced in usefulness. Between scanty school periods he had learned to steer the old grey horse that towed the harrow. The horse was blind in one eye but it could see more with the other than most horses could with two good ones, and it never missed the dinner bell. It turned out, later in his life, that the young driver knew how to shoe a horse, an un-nautical accomplishment he must have acquired by observation during this period and which mystified his later-day admirers.

Again in Westport John Slocombe, who had always been a capital hand at a camp meeting, was elected deacon of the Methodist church. He was physically as well as spiritually equipped to be a deacon on Brier Island, being six feet, two hundred pounds, and muscular. His younger brother Joel, the Mount Hanley judge, was six feet three and tipped the scales at two hundred and twenty-five pounds. He was also muscular. Only Uncle Joel, unlike his brother John, was of a jovial nature and very likable. John was of the old-fashioned Methodist type, a convincing speaker and a powerful exhorter of the sinful, as though there was any temptation on Brier Island to worry about.

24

In spite of the serious side of life, Westport had its diversions and one of these, once in awhile, was provided by some young buck fishermen who used to anchor over Sunday in the snug cove. A certain playful element of the crews used to think it smart to show off to the girls by pulling off some horseplay at meeting, to break it up. The Deacon was known to have kicked two of these yokels off the meeting house porch with one application of the side of his ample cowhide, thus proving that he was as effective as a bouncer as he was fervent in prayer.

John Slocombe had exchanged his Wilmot farm for a boot shop in Westport for the manufacturing of fishermen's cowhides. There was nothing fancy about these fishermen's boots, which were of domestic tanned cowhide. Sewn and pegged together, they were both water-tight and well-nigh indestructible. A fisherman could not get on without them. Thick of sole and coming to the knee of the wearer, they defied salt water, snow, and gurry. In the construction of a cowhide boot the top part was hand-sewn together and then the formidable sole was fastened to the top by wooden pegs. The whole, drawn over a last, was held between the boot pegger's knees as he sat on a low cobbler's bench with bent back, wielding his cobbler's hammer—a percussion instrument of peculiar shape and usable only by a shoemaker.

The boot pegs were small and square and when a package of them was opened it looked something like a carton of the breakfast food we get nowadays. The *modus operandi* for driving a peg was first to drive in the awl and follow up by driving home the peg, this being done by one smart blow and then following it up with several lighter taps of the short-handled, round-faced hammer. The pegs being half an inch apart, and there being three or four rows of them around the sole of each boot, it may be readily surmised what kind of job it was to sit for ten hours, humped up on a bench, pegging cowhides. Besides pegging, there were other chores like tending the soaking tub for softening the leather so it would yield to being pulled over the last.

Was the sewing of the tops done on a machine? Not much! If there were boot sewing machines in 1850, they had not reached Nova Scotia. They used waxed ends, which means that the end of the thread was tipped with a hog's bristle held in place by wax. The waxed end acted as a needle. There were two ends, each inserted into an awl hole, one opposite the other. Having inserted the two waxed ends, the sewer dropped his awl and, seizing the ends between thumb and forefinger of each hand, drew the stitch together. That was one stitch. There were many stitches in a pair of cowhides and each stitch had to be water-tight. A pair of hand-knitted woolen socks went inside the cowhides and that meant health and comfort for the wearer.

In this shop, which looked out into the Cove, Josh was duly set to work, his thrifty father having declared that at the age of ten he was capable of earning his own living. And that was the last of his schooling, in Westport or anywhere else. He became an expert at pegging boots, a task which he hated. If there were anything he hated worse than pegging boots, it was the sight of the soaking vat. If he could have done so, he would have emptied it into the sea and let the gulls drag off the leather. Since he so despised the boot shop, he began to whittle ship models and to contemplate voyages. For these dreams he had abundant material. Tall and stately ships, built in Yarmouth and destined for world trade, passed Brier Island to St. John to be sent to sea.

When Josh was about twelve he found home and shop conditions intolerable, and the final break between him and his father occurred when he received a thrashing for being caught down cellar putting the finishing touches on a ship model which had taken many furtive moments to make. It was a fine piece of work and the last ship model he was ever to make. His father burst in upon him in a fury, seized the precious work of art (and hope) and dashed it to the ground, smashing yards and masts and utterly destroying the whole thing.

On his first attempt to run away to sea he was caught and again thrashed for his delinquency; but later he managed with more success to get away on a St. Mary's Bay fishing schooner. The strange part of all this cruelty on the part of the elder Slocombe was that it was never greatly resented by his son Josh who rather regarded it as a just exercise of parental authority. However, he regretted the smashing of the ship model more than he did the castigation. I have heard him tell his mates about it at the cabin table. They thought it was pretty rough.

The open sea was to be his future and the first step was to go on a St. Mary's smack as cook. On small hand-liners it was customary for the youngest member of the crew to stir up the fire for the constant mugups. He fished over the side like the rest and did not get anything extra for neglecting his line and diving below at every growl to "put the kettle on." After the first time out he demanded a higher rating and got it. He was four years on St. Mary's Bay and his experience was reflected in his love of small fore-and-afters during the following years of his sea life.

The Bay of Fundy is a great funnel-shaped indentation between the peninsula of Nova Scotia and the coast of New Brunswick, through which the tide pours with irresistible force into the harbors and estuaries of those parts. Its unusual tidal nature was first noticed by a Portuguese explorer who likened it to a *fondo,* which in his language meant a funnel. In no part of the world is there greater tidal hazard for small craft than here. The rise and fall of the waters is so great (fifty feet) that the tide starts flooding before the ebb has ceased. This overfall of the heads of the waters causes a tidal phenomenon called a bore. The flood thus overrides the ebb, and its resurgence is a

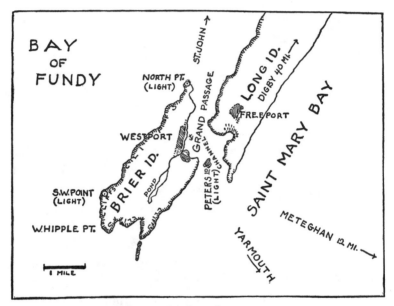

Brier Island and environs

thunderous roar of incoming sea. When the tide is completely ebbed, it is as if the Bay had run dry; nothing but dry flats for mile after mile. The very pigs, having ventured far out for clams on the flats left bare by the outgoing tide, hear the bore first, and at once start back, at full speed, squealing for life and higher land. It was also hazardous for boats and one of the extra perils to be watched for, especially when the farmers first took to small dories on the Bay.

Brier Island, at the entrance to the Bay of Fundy, may be considered to have been the starting point of the *Spray* voyage for there the idea was born. It has been said that an idea is half of the accomplished fact and in this case it was so. On Brier Island was nurtured the future lone circumnavigator in his early boyhood and there he dreamed the dreams that were to shape his life; to impart to him a growing love of the sea; to imbue him with a thirst for adventure,—the springboard of the idea which was many years developing to be at last accomplished.

Impressed as one may be by the aspect of Brier Island by the sea, it is even more imposing by land. In the early days when there were no roads and only paths through the bush it was out of all contact with the main part of Nova Scotia.

To try out the impression of remoteness the writer recently travelled by car from Blomidon Head, south along North Mountain, Digby Neck, Long Island and finally to Brier Island. For forty miles there was a great variety for getting about. The writer admits that he is not very good at navigating an automobile, but on this trip he had a good hand at the wheel. Of course, after leaving Halifax the first objective was Wilmot where my ancestor, the original John Slocombe, had a farm. We identified Wilmot by the sign on the little railway station we found. In the cemetery there were the names of two or three families allied to the Slocombes but no Slocombes. One Slocombe was still living in Wilmot and on the original farm as far as I knew. Caleb was the given name but his wife told me that he was back of the house, haying, and at that, a mile away. That was interesting, and saying something about stopping on the way back from Digby, we ascended the grade over the mountain and looked over the Bay of Fundy to the shore of New Brunswick. It was a grand view. Descending to the rocks which lined the shore we came to Port George and Reagles Cove, names which once had some meaning in the history of the fisherman-farmers who had inhabited the rude hamlets interspersed along.

In Mount Hanley we found the school still standing which little Joshua attended while his family were yet in Wilmot. It was growing late so I did not go in but it was still used as a school for Mount Hanley. The route to Brier Island was so unknown to us that we did not want to risk darkness before getting there and it was as well that we did not loiter by the way. Getting along to the end of Digby Neck we came upon the first outpost of the unknown, a farm with an ox cart and a pair of oxen resting at the door of the barn. The farmer was affable and at once interested in our project of reaching Brier Island. We had begun to think that the nearer we got the further it was away by the vague way they spoke of it.

Our affable friend went to the telephone, contacted the ferryman, who said the tide was just right and to push along. In a few moments we were at the edge of Petit Passage and looking across a mile of water to Long Island whither we were to go. We made a steep descent to the foot of the cliff and found a decked punt just big enough to get the car onto and a motor boat ready to tow the outfit across. Captain Blackford and his helpers were very expert in embarking and unloading on the other side, showing that the process had become a matter of habit. Considerable skill was shown in making a long sweep (a detour in auto language) to offset the velocity of the tide, which here had a rise and fall of twenty feet. On Long Island we had a drive of eight miles until we came to the next dividing strait between the two islands. That was the Grand Passage, evidently named by the early French who used it in sailing from the southern end of Nova Scotia to Bay of Fundy waters. It all had a smack of something foreign.

At last we could look across and see the end of the journey. Getting across was a repetition of the ferrying of Petit Passage, and of course there was the consciousness of having to do the same thing all over again on the way back. What struck us about the ferrying was the hard and honest work the ferrymen did for a very little money. I won't say here how little they charged but if ever I go again I hope they will charge twice as much. I would feel better about it. They should take a lesson or two from the regular tourist channels of travel. But I think there is hope for them for as I went back over the last lap they told me that if I did not come next year, why, to send the toll anyway for they needed the money. I think they meant it. It was low tide which meant there was a long ramp to ascend when we debarked. I stepped on the shore of Brier Island with reverence.

It had been the home of my father in the very formative period of his life. When he started on his voyage around the world in the *Spray,* he stopped at Westport and he was delighted to reach it. He found it charming to be among old schoolmates again. The very stones of Brier Island he was glad to see and said that he knew them all. The little shop around the corner, which for thirty-five years he had not seen, was the same, and he was sure that it wore the same shingles. Lowry the tailor lived there. In his day he was fond of a gun. He always carried his powder loose in his coattail pocket, and in one evil moment put his lighted dudeen in his hind pocket along with the powder. Mr. Lowry, my father said, was an eccentric man.

My father could not forget his good friend, the deacon, who while listening to the sermon, reached his hand out over the

31

door of the pew to jig drowsily for imaginary squid. Bait was the thing uppermost in the deacon's mind. The *Spray* had a good time in Westport before sailing on to Yarmouth. When I arrived for the first time on Brier Island it had been forty-four years since the *Spray* was there and I met quite a few who remembered it but nothing further of the Captain's history; except one, a worthy woman who knew both Joshua and his oldest sister, my aunt Elizabeth whom I had never seen.

My father's eldest sister, Elizabeth Slocombe, was "Aunt Elizabeth" to the whole island while she lived and ministered to the wants of her neighbors. She had the only loom on the island. The wool came already carded from the mainland but the weaving of blankets and the knitting of guernseys, mittens and socks was the work of her own industrious hand. That was not all, either. Many a young Brier Islander first drew breath as she got there just in time if there was a head wind for the stork. And when they grew up during her latter years there was an annual expression of gratitude at the church on the hill in the way of a benefit for Aunt Elizabeth.

This same lady also related to me some of the pranks of the time when boys *would* be boys. One was a youngsters' feud which culminated on the bridge that divided the settlement socially as well as geographically. They were the "Snobtowners" and the "Irishtowners." Joshua was on the "Irishtown" side and at the head of the faction of underdogs who gathered in force to repel an invasion which was reported coming. They were armed with pitchforks and other weapons which could conveniently be had and the clash would have been serious had it not been for the oldsters who put an end to the foolishness. My father was always a pretty fair pugilist and I could gather that Westport was the place to first learn howling and fighting,

(Above) The boot shop at Westport where young Joshua worked as his father's apprentice.

(Below) The Slocombe house which was moved to the government pier for use as a wharf house.

One of the first enterprises of Joshua Slocum in the
United States was designing and building his own
gill-net boat for salmon fishing in the Northwest.
Illustration by Charles Rosner.

The Washington, moored in Cook Inlet where she was later stranded in a gale. Eskimo umiaks in the foreground. Illustration by Charles Rosner.

A view of Westport Harbor, Brier Island, with the brigantine Sophia, Captain Charles Bailey, in the foreground. She was a typical coastal packet. Painted by Mr. C. H. Payson in 1885.

as the song went. The kids were not the least afraid of each other and they grew up that way.

Brier Island is only four miles long. Some people by the name of Welch were the first settlers. They lived in log houses near the shore. They owned their own vessels, fished, and carried the fish to England, bringing back supplies. They lived practically unknown to the rest of Nova Scotia until, in 1784, the island was granted to Major Thomas Hunggerford and others.

While in Westport I explored the island and found that I could walk from one end to the other in three hours. It is about ten miles around. On the seaward side it is buttressed by basaltic cliffs of bold and forbidding aspect. Westport, the unspoiled fishing settlement which nestles in a bight of the Grand Passage, had a protected anchorage in a few fathoms of water. Here could once be seen the fleet of small craft that worked mostly in St. Mary's Bay as well as an occasional brig trading to the West Indies. These last were of about a hundred tons and several were owned in Westport. They were the vessels that traded the island's surplus fish products for molasses, which in turn became good Medford rum. Before the Wilberforce Act which was to the prejudice of the slave trade, that same good Medford rum was known to reach Africa. Trade goes in circles, anyway, so who was to blame. I found that while the island was all rocks around the outside, the center was all farms chiefly given up to the raising of hay for the oxen, the only draft animals I saw. I learned that the local preference for oxen was that oxen could live on grass and hay while a horse had to have grain which could not easily be raised.

There are three lighthouses on Brier Island, or correctly speaking, two on the island itself and another on Peter's Island, a rock at the eastern entrance to Grand Passage and the harbor

33

of Westport. The principal light is Southwest Point, standing on a cliff and looking out over the dangerous ledges extending to sea. This is the light once kept by John Southern, retired naval man. A light of less importance is the one on North Point. The lightkeeper's little girl, a tot of five, showed me how the fog bell worked. She thought it was fun to live in a lighthouse, but her papa would only let her strike the bell when there was fog, which she did not think was fair. My chief interest in lighthouses, however, was the one on Southwest Point for in that I had a family interest. Until 1925 all of the three lights were either kept by John Southern or his descendants.

My father says in his book that on both sides of his family there were sailors and in this statement he refers to the elder John Southern, the keeper of Southwest Light. As a Pensioner, John Southern had come in for this berth. He was of the regular deepsea sailor type. As a young man he had heard the guns of Nelson's fleet in action and he had served on the *Bellerophon* to help take Napoleon to St. Helena. There was a strong tradition around the lighthouse perched on the cliffs of Southwest Point looking out upon the sea. At the lighthouse establishment John Southern raised a brood that was as akin to the sea as the gulls which winged and screamed in the storm. One of these was Sarah, whom John Slocombe was to make his bride and take to North Mountain.

On her stone in the burying ground of Westport I found the date of her death, 1860, the year that Joshua Slocum left the island for good and went deep water. The coincidence might have meant something.

CHAPTER 3

Around the Horn Twice

To sail out of St. John on his first foreign voyage was Josh's first step towards the great adventure. It made no difference to him if his first ship was only a deal droger bound for Dublin. He, and a chum from Brier Island who had joined him, wanted to see Dublin. It was a start. A deal droger was a lumber carrier, clumsy and slow, and in more or less contemptuous disrepute among seamen, especially on the Western Ocean, as the North Atlantic was then called by all true seafarers. My father always called it the Western Ocean.

For the information of the unenlightened, a "deal" in the British parlance was a stick of dimensioned pine or spruce and a cargo of deals was one that could not be damaged as long as it was afloat. The term, droger, invented by sailors, also meant an ill-found, ill-fed and leaky vessel. Sailors despised a leaky ship, not because they were afraid it would sink but because they did hate to hear the mate bawl out, "Man the pump," as soon as they were mustered at the change of the watch at midnight. They would much rather, after the relief of the wheel and the lookout, sprawl under the lee of a deckhouse and have a smoke. The leaky part was not apt to disturb the owner as much as it did the crew, for a ship loaded with deals would never sink. The deck load of deals was held to the ship with chains which went all around the whole business, holding ship and load together until they could get across to the other side of the pond. Furthermore, the term "droger" carried with it a tinge of salty but mild opprobrium, like the Portland Pier horse which, killed by curses and sore abuse was salted down for sailor's use; it was thoroughly despised to the moment the bottom of the cask containing its bony remains was reached.

But for all her disrepute a deal droger could always get a crew. And our two Brier Island boys were among them. Their experience in small fishing vessels along the Fundy coast had done no harm to their seamanship, for on the smaller craft was the place to learn. More initiative and less routine and "soldiering."

The big ship sailor was very smug in his own opinion of himself and fond of relating yarns which illustrated how little the fore-and-after knew about seamanship. There is quite a literature of these stories and they would make a very interesting collection for the seabook shelf. One of the stories was about the schooner captain who became the captain of a ship with yards across her masts but he did not know how to put her about and depended upon his mate, who was used to the rig. One day the mate fell over the side and the captain tried to save him by tacking the ship himself. The ship got in irons and would not swing either way until another ship came along and wanted to know why he was hove to with his main topsail aback.

"Come aboard," the schooner man hailed, "I've lost my

square-rigged mate overboard and I can't get her around, no-how."

With my father, admiration for and confidence in small vessels was a part of his religion. It was a love that lasted him all of his life. Familiarity with small vessels developed self-reliance and of that quality he was in great abundance. He did not need to read Ralph Waldo Emerson. He emulated his own father whom he said was the kind of a man, who, if wrecked on a desolate island, could find his way back if he had a jackknife and could find a tree. That went also for Joshua Slocum.

He and his chum were more amused than disturbed by the events of sailing day. They did not join through the shipping office—they both knew better—and saved their advance wages to send home instead of contributing to the gin mill. They were on board first and had their dunnage stowed before the main crew gang were driven down the dock in the shipping agent's wagon. The crew were perched on top of their belongings, most of them roaring drunk. My father says that this was the first time in his life that he saw men in liquor and he did not think much of it. Nor of tobacco either.

Those of the happy ones who were too far gone were tossed into their bunks by the crimps, who assured the mate that they were good men and it would be all hunky when they came to. The mate had been all through that, before. The rest of the crew paid attention to the mate's orders, getting heavy stores aboard and loosing sails. In time the stupor rolled off the others and they became ready for duty without recourse to the "leather" which Nova Scotia mates were very handy about using to bring back consciousness. That kind of rough stuff was not intelligent and was sure to breed resentment and lead to trouble for the rest of the voyage. The writer has experienced a mutiny which was started by a bucko mate trying too hard to

37

make the newly-shipped crew haul in the towing hawser. It cost the mate his life.

Joshua and his chum were in earnest about going to sea. So earnest indeed that they were the only two foremast hands fit to take the wheel when they sailed. They were, long afterwards, to meet in an East Indian port, each the master of his own ship. The writer was present at the meeting. The "chum" was to become Captain Cheny of the ship *Antelope.* That was when we had the ship *Northern Light.* The recognition of worth on the sea is very sure, no doubt because of so little competition.

On entering Dublin, when the pilot called for the best man on board to take the wheel, Josh was very proud when he was sent aft. The craft yawed excessively owing to her build and trim and it took an alert eye to meet her when the course was changed much. Josh had the knack and he liked it. The pilot was more careful than that other Dublin pilot, who, when the captain asked him if he knew all rocks, replied: "Shure and I do, and that is one of them now," he explained as the ship rammed into it and stuck fast.

Out to see the world and with no idea of turning back, Joshua left the droger in Dublin and took the packet to Liverpool, the meeting point of ships from everywhere, going everywhere. In Liverpool he received his first impression of great ships and great voyages. He became acquainted with the British seaman and admired his style. Then he settled down for two weeks to study his ways and to look for an East India ship. He was not interested in the packet rats, a degenerate type of seaman who swarmed on the emigrant and clipper ships of the Western Ocean. They were well described in the shanty of the day—

> "The tinkers and tailors and shoemakers all,
> Who ship as prime seamen aboard a Black Ball."

His first voyage from England to China was as ordinary seaman on the British ship *Tanjore*. He regarded that as a regular
voyage as it took him around the Cape of Good Hope. He did
not then sight Table Mountain, for it was customary for sailing
ships running the easting down to keep well to the southward
when entering the Indian Ocean and rounding Australia,
bound for Canton.

The *Tanjore* next sailed for Batavia, and there young Josh
was left in a hospital with a fever. There he found a good friend
in Captain Airy of the steamship *Soushay*, who rescued him
from that pest hole of the Dutch East Indies. The route of the
Soushay was through the Torres Strait, from the direction of
Batavia to Brisbane. It included a trip back to Amboina in the
Moluccas; then to Manila, Hong Kong, Saigon and Singapore
and back to Batavia. The experience on the *Soushay* gave the
young seaman an inside acquaintance with the Far East, a region he was to know more of later on. Captain Airy would have
been glad to have him accept a permanent berth but the fever
was still in his bones and the islands were no place for him at
that time.

In the matter of technical training for the profession of Navigator, my father was entirely self-learned, or self-educated. He
was studious in his habits and widely read in science as well as
in literature. During his first two years at sea he prepared
in spare moments for his Board of Trade certificate as second
mate. And the sea is still the best place to learn Celestial Navigation, for nine-tenths of it is facility with the sextant in all
sorts of conditions as well as the practical application of the
problems taken from the book. His first Epitomy of Navigation
was a Norie, published in Liverpool in 1860. That and an ebony
"pig-yoke" with an ivory scale (arc) constituted his first navigational equipment. By results they answered very well. As he

advanced in practice, he was required to assist the captain and the chief mate in making lunar observations for longitude. Three observers, working simultaneously, took the sights. The captain, as senior navigator, took the lunar distance angle of arc.

After two years of deep water, and while on a second voyage from Liverpool to the East Indies, Joshua received his promotion to second mate, at the age of eighteen. This he regarded as the most decisive step in his career. It was graduation from the hardest school on the sea, and a recognition of his ability in seamanship and skill in handling men. During this period there existed, in British ships, a sharp line of demarcation between the foremast hands and the apprentices who were appointed by the company in consideration of a premium, and who were, by the mere serving of time, destined to become officers. They were of the "brass-bound" and "cheesecutter" type, toward which he felt a mild contempt. He was proud of reaching the quarter deck through the hawse-pipes and not through the cabin windows, and of having made himself in spite of adverse circumstances.

In our family album we had a tintype of my father taken in Liverpool at about this period, showing a husky youth, rigged out in checkered flannel shirt and with trousers tucked into cowhide boots, the very kind used on the Bay of Fundy to this day. With an aptitude for leadership, he was already second mate and, according to his own emphatic statement, he *was* a second mate, for resolute and hard-fisted men were then to be found on both ends of the ship, as well as good sailors. He weighed 180 pounds, which backed up a will of iron.

After rounding the Horn twice as Chief Mate on British ships in the coal and grain trade between Cardiff, San Francisco and Liverpool, my father decided to cast his lot on the Northwest

Coast and to make San Francisco his hailing port with the view to obtaining command of a vessel under the American flag in the China trade. He finally did. This was in the early sixties.

While ashore in San Francisco he fell in with the energetic, rough-and-ready life which still pervaded his adopted land. Everywhere about him there was enterprise, and the foundations of fortunes were being laid with small capital plus great initiative. As compared with the East it was easier to start in business.

Here he met a Mr. Griffin who built gill-net boats for the salmon fishery on the Columbia River. Being something of a boat builder himself, and a draftsman as well, Josh became interested in the industry, little dreaming how far it was going to take him. Many of these boats were built at San Francisco, but a large number were also constructed on the Columbia River. He made a design for one of these boats, which was an improvement on the existing type, and this model was bought on sight by a cannery owner in Astoria who had boats built from it at his own establishment.

With few exceptions the boats were owned by the canners, and rented, with the nets, to the fishermen. Deciding to go in for the fishing, he joined another enterprising spirit and, as all the boats were then rented, they determined to work the river and build a boat at the same time. This the partners actually did by borrowing a punt from which to drift their net while they worked at boatbuilding between tides. It was hard work, but they were equal to it. The boat proved a good job and sold for the market price at the end of the season. She is worth a word of description. A double-ender, carvel-built and fitted with a centerboard, her dimensions were, length 25 feet, beam 6 feet, depth 2 feet 6 inches. She was decked for about three feet at each end and had a washboard along each side. A single 16-foot mast, to carry a spritsail, was stepped in the eyes of the boat, making her suitable for short explorations as well as for "shooting twine" on the river. With the mast for a ridge pole, the sail could be spread as a tent when the crew had to remain out on the river more than twenty-four hours. In such cases they would anchor their boat out of the way of passing steamers. Sometimes they would sleep in the daytime, since it often happened that they drifted all night with their nets. As they were always provided with an oil stove, a coffee pot, a slab of bacon, and a shot gun, the prospects were never bad.

With a good season's work on the salmon run behind them, including the proceeds of the boatbuilding venture, the partners next turned their attention to sea otter hunting at Gray's Harbor. At the time a considerable number of those valuable animals were shot in the surf off the beach by both white and Indian hunters, but they were becoming wary, and to make a hit the keenest shot was required. It took a number of tides to wash out the scent of a human footprint in the sand before an otter would dare to come out of the water. A large male otter is about four feet long. Otter hunting was profitable. The pelt was valuable at any season of the year and brought from $50 to $350 on the market.

Sea otter once had a range from Kamchatka to the southern extremity of Lower California. Its story is the story of the Russian settlement of Alaska and the earliest development of the Northwest Coast. China was the market for furs, and fortunes were made by traders from New York and New England, who rounded the Horn in small vessels, traded for furs on the coasts of Oregon, Vancouver Island or the Charlotte Islands, and then exchanged them for teas and silks at Canton. It was due to this trade that Captain Robert Gray, with the ship *Columbia,* discovered the great river and the important harbor which now bear, respectively, the name of his ship and of her captain. With the *Columbia*, Captain Gray finished his trading voyage, returning to Boston on August 10, 1790, the first commander to take the American flag around the world. Profits in the trade were 700 percent.

My father kept a journal covering this period spent on the Columbia River, Gray's Harbor, Puget Sound, and British Columbia, but I remember only parts of it. It was wonderfully rich in accounts not only of his own camp life but that of his mates, with many references to the sea otter and the smaller fur-bearing animals. The diary had humorous allusions to some of his mates. One of these who seemed to interest him very much was Bill Gordon, expert as a trapper and very independent of mind. They hunted for a trading post, and whenever Bill became freshly disgusted with a deal handed out to him by the manager of the post, he would polish up the telescope of his rifle and snuffle through his broken nose. "I smell sea otter." At a period when they were changing their grounds, one of the party turned to trapping in an entirely unexplored region which he reported in a letter to be "full of links and wolfmarines." Thither they all migrated, living on bear meat. The "wolfmarines" were there, and so were the "links" and the unorthographic hunter promised them a "tame goose" for Christmas. It was not very clear to the others just how he was going to procure the "tame goose" but that it would be ahead of bear, they all felt sure. They had faith, however, until it was blasted at the feast by the discovery of a charge of buckshot.

In the journal also were interesting observations concerning the Makah and Vancouver Island tribes of Indians, for whose seamanship he had the greatest respect, and whose canoe seamanship made a decided impression upon him. This was to come out in a tangible way later. Here was the Stone Age Man and here were boatmen working at building almost as it was done in the very beginning. These people were dependent on boats for the necessities of life and the dugout canoe was the nearest approach to a boat that their culture would allow. But they made a good job of it, and produced craft as suitable to use, graceful and as true to line as the white man with more convenient appliances and efficient tools. The main difference was time, the savage taking months to the civilized man's weeks. But this was a factor which did not count.

When a group of coast Indians wanted to build a new canoe, they went to the woods and picked out a tall cedar about fifteen feet around, and as many men as could get around it with their stone hatchets, chipped at it, like beavers gnawing, until it fell. Then they gnawed it again to a suitable length, though no measurement of any kind was made. The log was then split near the widest part, with wedges, and the shaping process started. This was a process of locally charring the wood, first outside and then inside, so that the material could be scraped to shape with their clamshell chisels. If the canoe was not wide enough after it was first dug out, they fixed that in an ingenious manner, showing ample knowledge of the nature of wood. They boiled it by filling the canoe with water and throwing in red hot stones. The wood then became soft enough to yield to spreaders.

But the lure of his inshore adventure did not last long, though it was not without its profits. My father's real ambition was the command of a ship, which he had promised himself when first coming ashore in San Francisco. Resuming the sea, he was put in charge of a coasting schooner carrying grain from San Francisco to Seattle, with a return cargo of coal produced from an inferior vein in that region. That was in 1869. This trade was something like the "coal out and grain home" voyages between Cardiff and San Francisco, on one of which my father first saw the West Coast. One of the first questions the owner of the schooner asked him when he applied for the berth was whether he had ever carried grain. Yes, he had had "considerable experience with grain" but nothing was said at that time about Cape Horn.

On the Coast the grain was carried as a deckload, and to prevent this from becoming damaged or wet from spray required experience and care. By sharp application and observation, the peculiar knack of taking advantage of all weather conditions close under the land was soon acquired by the Captain, who was always quick at learning a new technique. It meant constant vigilance and hard work. In two years of this employment he won the confidence of more important shipowners, which was to lead to his later Pacific experiences.

CHAPTER 4

The *Washington:*

A Honeymoon to Cook Inlet

P UGET SOUND always seemed to my father the most beautiful place in the world. To him, nature there was in tune with human necessities and demands. Next to the scenery, and because he was always a shipbuilder, the virgin forests of fir which grew to the water's edge attracted him. On the shores there were sawmills with capacity for working out timber long enough to plank a ship from stem to stern without a butt. The shipways could be placed alongside of the sawmill itself, which resulted in great efficiency in handling materials. If a plank 200 feet long was required, it could be produced.

A number of vessels were thus built, on the edge of the Washington forest, including the bark *Washington* (332 tons), owned by Merrill and Bichard. She became the Captain's next ship. In December 1870 the *Washington* sailed from San Francisco for Sydney, Australia, with a general cargo. From there she was to go to Cook Inlet, Alaska, on a salmon fishing voyage. For this work the ship was especially provided with lumber and supplies for building boats and a camp, as well as with gill-nets, with which the Captain had become familiar on the Columbia. In fact, it was due to his experience there that he was selected for this Alaskan expedition, making him one of the pioneers in that industry.

Upon his arrival in Sydney the Captain married an American girl. She was Miss Virginia Walker, the eldest daughter of Mr. and Mrs. William Walker, formerly of New York but now prominent members of the American colony of their newly adopted city.

Virginia was heard to remark that as soon as she saw Josh she knew he was just the kind of a man she wanted, not the stuffy sort she saw in conventional Sydney society. She was also intrigued with the idea of going to Alaska in the *Washington,* whither the 27-year-old Yankee skipper was next bound. Virginia was 21, and like most travelling Americans, keen about the great out of doors. Like everything else he did in his life, Josh, as he was known to all of his intimates, lost no time with his courtship and wedding.

Mr. Walker, who was of a pompous disposition, planned to give his daughter away at a formal church affair, but that was too much fuss for Josh who had ideas of his own of how the gear of matrimony should be coiled down for running. Quiet arrangements were therefore made with the dominie at the Christ Church rectory, with full consent of the bride, who was a strictly brought up Anglican. Mr. Walker, on getting wind of what was going on, hailed a carriage and dashed up to the altar just in time to be in at the finish. He was greatly chagrined and never quite forgave the couple. Virginia, who was to become my mother, enjoyed the adventure hugely, and I once heard her tell some of her women friends that it "looked just like an elopement." She was fond of her home and of her surroundings and liked Sydney, but nevertheless entered with enthusiasm upon her new life upon the sea and to which she was devoted to the day of her death.

As my mother's family grew at sea, she often told incidents of her life in Sydney and she was never tired of telling about her father, and his doings. Mr. Walker was an unusual man. First of Albany and then of New York City, he became a California "forty-niner" and soon after voyaged in a packet directly from San Francisco to the Australian gold-fields, where he did as well as he could have wished. He then established a stationer's business on Pitt Street, Sydney. That was his line in America. He was genial and a good mixer; interested in amateur theatricals, he could repeat any speech in Hamlet if given the first line. But his favorite role was Coriolanus, which better suited his declamatory style. When quite young, my mother was allowed in the wings of the stage to watch the actors. Once there was trouble. Tullus, the general of the Volscians, just as the curtain was to rise, unfortunately tumbled over on his beam-ends with the lumbago. Couldn't move. Conspirators, citizens and tribunes gathered around and tried to get him on his feet in time but it was "no go." Coriolanus, in helmet and armor, suddenly appeared with a redhot poker. One quick and skilful application of the end of the poker brought the Volscian to his feet with a bound. The curtain rose and the play went on. Grandpa Walker seemed always to know what to do and he was fond of a practical joke. It was in 1854 when he began to reside in Sydney. He became interested in the volunteer fire brigade, my mother said, and their cockatoo got so it would scream out at any time of the night, "Fire, fire, Walker, fire," without ever being punished for pulling a false alarm.

49

My grandfather's extra activities were merely a continuance of those when he was in New York. There he was a member of the Manhattan Fire Engine Company, Number Eight, with a firehouse on Nassau Street. According to a faded yellow "order" in the writer's possession, Mr. Walker was in 1846 made Second Lieutenant in the Ninth Regiment, N.Y.S. Artillery, so he was a sure-enough New Yorker, but of Scotch extraction. And from being a popular citizen of Sydney he was expected to have, at least, a judicious leaning towards "Scotch." Speaking of Mr. Walker's leaning towards the practical joke brings one to the writer's mind that illustrates his noble loyalty to his daughter, expressed in a rather playful way. Before Josh appeared, Virginia had a suitor who was a bore and she did not know how to get rid of him. She used to receive her unwelcome caller under a tree in the yard where there was a bench. Mr. Walker got a rock, she said it was so big and heavy that she did not know how he ever managed to handle it. But that was no matter, that rock got hoisted up in the tree, and at a proper moment, down came the rock, which hit the earth with a thud. The fellow thought it was thrown at him. He made an undignified departure, never to appear again at the Walker homestead.

There is nothing that cements Americans together in a foreign port so much as the sight of their flag on an incoming man o' war. Even the most pacifist among them must feel at least a tingle. But when a battle-scarred veteran comes in, enthusiasm for their country reaches its greatest height.

The U.S.S. *Kearsarge,* the one that fought and sank the Confederate raider *Alabama* in the English Channel during the Civil War in America, came into Sydney in 1869. The *Kearsarge* had been detailed to an official reconnaissance of the South Pacific Islands with orders to extend her cruise to eastern

Australia. And that is where they were all glad to see the famous fighting ship, though by that time hardly any of the actual participants of the action were on board. Visitors were thrilled by the sight of the patch on the corvette's smoke-stack through which a shell had passed and they listened very attentively when the grizzled and briny gunner's mates explained the workings of their great pivot gun, amidships, which had given the enemy the final coup de grace and sent her to the bottom.

Mr. Walker arranged for a grand ball in honor of the officers of the *Kearsarge,* and with his daughter Virginia, costumed as "Columbia," led the grand march. As toastmaster, with eclat and wit, he presided at the spread ("tuckout" they say in Australia) and reception which followed. Of course there were exchanges of photographs and no doubt there were hearts in Sydney that followed the visiting ship back to her base port in Callao. In my mother's time there was still the red plush album with its collection of cherished portraits, family and otherwise. In ours were a number of the uniformed visitors to Sydney, and I noticed that my father always put on a bored and disinterested look every time they were shown to callers on our ship. Certain anecdotes heard in childhood never fade and one in particular sticks. The name of the young gentleman in shoulder straps must have been either Nickerson or Nicholson, for he wrote "Young Nick son of Old Nick" in the album of a girl acquaintance of my mother's who pestered him too much for his autograph. The autograph fiend thought that he was real mean. She was mad.

On leaving Sydney for Alaska, my mother's young brother, George Walker, went with them. He was then a lad of twelve. I owe to my Uncle George, now residing in Australia, and whom I met but a few years since, much of the detail of this voyage

51

to Cook Inlet, which might otherwise have been lost. He said it was the greatest experience of his life.

The Pacific is an ocean of great distances, for anywhere you want to go it is thousands of miles. Making allowances for sailing deflections caused by wind or current, it is nearly 7000 miles from San Francisco to Sydney, and 6000 from Sydney to the Kasilof River at Cook Inlet, Alaska. The track of the *Washington* was unusual, nearly north over both of the Pacifics, the first part being through coral seas and among dangerous reefs; sighting the headland of Bauro Island of the Solomon Group, and sighting Nauru and passing Joliut atoll in the Marshall Group. South of the equator the seas are simply filled with coral atolls, coral islands formed by a circular fringe of reef, holding a shallow lagoon in the center and with the usual boat entrance on the lee side. They are nearly level with the sea and they are sometimes swept clean by the tropical hurricane.

In the North Pacific, beyond the fortieth degree of latitude, the atmosphere changes entirely in character. Chill winds from the Bering Sea, impinging on the warm Japanese Current, causes at times dense fog. Birds unknown to the tropics gradually make their appearance as others vanish. The new birds are more like fish than anything with feathers. Herds of fur seal float by—sleepers, so called because they lie on their backs with flippers over nose, fast asleep and easy victims of the pelagic hunter with spear or shotgun.

On the way to Alaska, the crew made preparations for the salmon run, and as many as were skillful with axe or saw, turned to on the gill-net punts which were built as long and wide as space on deck would permit.

With the bold Karluk headlands and the Aleutian volcanoes on either hand, the *Washington* sailed through Shelikof Strait and arrived off Kasilof River after a passage of 49 days from

Sydney. Cook Inlet is practically a glacial fjord, forming an indentation of 200 miles, and in 1871 it was yet imperfectly known to the mariner who had to depend mainly on very sketchy Russian charts and to proceed with great caution when navigating its waters. In times of doubt it was always safer to anchor, and to send out a boat to sound and explore in advance of the ship, for the ground was foul, and no precaution was too great. Tidal conditions were the worst trouble.

At the head of the inlet the rise and fall of the tide is greater than anywhere else in the world except in the Bay of Fundy. It is forty feet during the springs, making a five or six knot ebb which carries with it huge blocks of ice, tree trunks and every kind of fluvial debris that could be emptied out of the headwaters. This terrific ebb is reacted upon by a bore which tumbles in with equal violence on its course back. Vancouver relates that while anchored on the west side of the inlet in the *Discovery*, the downcoming ice on the ebb dragged his ship, after parting the cable, back to the sea. It was certainly not a safe place to anchor under any circumstances. This dangerous anchorage was used by the Russians who were first lured by the giant king salmon, known to run in the Kenai rivers, and it could not now be avoided by the *Washington*, which was the first American vessel to arrive there since Russia sold Alaska four years before. The entire nature of the region was, therefore, for the want of more exact information, unknown to strangers. The bones of the *Washington*, bleaching in the sands, are still a warning.

To secure sufficient depth of water, the *Washington* had to be anchored about two miles out on an extensive flat which filled the bight between Cape Kasilof and the mouth of the river where the fishing was done. The shoals and flats were strewn with huge glacial boulders, many of sufficient size to show above water at depths of thirty feet. In this precarious berth the vessel was protected as much as possible from the tidal currents which at this point had an ordinary velocity of four knots; also she derived additional protection from the shelter of Karluk Reef, a shoal just outside the five fathom line.

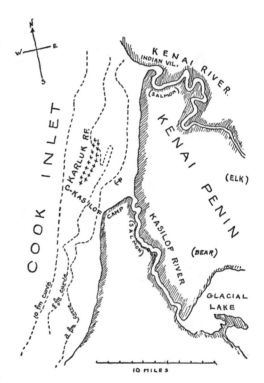

A *diagram map of Cook Inlet*

The *Washington* was then snugged down, by striking the t'-gallantmasts, against the williwaws that swept down from the mountains with great force and made her snap at her cables, which were veered out to the bitter end. But these heavy gusts were not so trying as the northwest gales that were prevalent in this early part of the summer. On the landing of the fishing

54

gear and the erecting of the fishing headquarters on the beach, a considerable number of Indians gathered, first to watch out of curiosity, and later to take a hand in the gill-net punts. There was a small proportion of half-breeds in their number, the descendants of Russian convicts who were formerly brought to work these same streams for placer gold, but who had escaped to live with the natives. They were used to fishing in their own weirs in the desultory manner of the savage, but soon learned the way of the white man. They were an unexpected and valuable help, but dangerous when under the spell of the white man's liquor.

In camp there nearly happened a tragedy which would have been worse for all hands than the loss of the vessel. The Captain came very near to being shot. He had to make a trip to Kenai, the Indian village that was a short distance away, which he thought would take him until the next day. He was on foot and alone. My mother was nervous about being left by herself where there were apt to be ugly-visaged half-breeds prowling about, so instead of turning in she sat up to be on watch until dawn. It was shortly after midnight when she heard footsteps coming directly to her tent and without the customary "haloo" of a friend, and then a hand began to unlatch the flap. With her heart in her mouth she raised her rifle and called, "Sing out or I'll shoot." The intruder distinctly heard the double click of the hammer as it was cocked and returned, and, with an uneasy laugh, "Why, what's the matter, Jinny?" identified himself. On being allowed to enter all he said was, "Well, that was the time you nearly became an orphan." But for all his narrow escape he learned to have a new admiration for his wife's self-reliance and for her primal capacity for defending herself against nocturnal enemies. Next time he would sing out first.

My mother never recovered from her admiration and wonder

for this Alaskan region. When the weather was clear, across the inlet towered two lofty volcanoes of the Aleutian Range, Mount Redout and Mount Iliamna. Beyond the low eastern shores, covered with clumps of timber rose the high Kenai Range, containing large glaciers.

The waters teemed with animal, bird, and even human life, for the sea-going Aleut in his sealskin bidarka seemed akin to both beluga and screaming gull. She accompanied a party up the Kasilof which has its source in a glacial lake in the very heart of a big game country. Above the stream, fish-eating eagles by the hundred were wheeling and swooping down on salmon in the shallows as they leaped up over the rocks in the rapids. Here she became practiced at shooting an eagle on the wing with a small-bore Henry which she always carried about. Bruin, too, was there for his dinner of fish which he dexterously hooked out on his long claws. One of these huge Kodiak bears persisted in ambling toward the party but whether from motives of curiosity or malice will never be known. The Captain stood his ground with a large bore rifle until the bear came well within the 100 yard range, and showed no sign of stopping. He had once been clawed and bitten by a bear while in British Columbia and knew bear nature better than to take another chance. The pelt of this particular bear was one of the largest ever taken from Kenai, and it was long afterwards stretched out on the floor of a bungalow in Sydney, to the astonishment of the natives.

While all hands but the anchor watch were in camp, the *Washington* dragged her anchors during a gale and stranded. Being in ballast and flying light, she was driven high upon the beach; the sand afterwards banked up outside her, and it became impossible, without a dredger, to get the doomed vessel off.

I have heard my father say, in speaking of this disaster, that it was reported to him next year that the sand dunes were piled up so high on the seaward side of the vessel that it seemed inconceivable she had ever been afloat.

The loss of the vessel, important as it was, did not dampen the morale of the expedition. The thing had to be carried through. A landing party was formed and everything taken ashore that could be converted into living quarters. For this there was an abundance of material in the way of spars and heavy sails.

The fishing was carried out successfully, except for the loss of the vessel, which caused an awkward problem in the transportation of the catch to San Francisco. Kodiak, the nearest port, was 200 miles away, and it was finally planned to reach this point in the ship's two boats and a 35-foot whaleboat which had, in view of the coming emergency, been built in the camp. The little matter of building a boat in time of need never bothered the Captain. As the carpenter had three mates on the job, besides the constant supervision of the Captain, the boat progressed fast enough to be finished by the time the party was ready to leave the beach.

When it was nearly time to break camp, a Revenue Cutter appeared on the scene to offer assistance. The Captain would accept no other help except to have his wife taken to Kodiak, and in that way she was enabled to make the trip in comfort and safety instead of enduring the hardship of the ship's boats. The Captain remained at Kasilof until everything was finished and the catch made ready for shipping. He figured that if a vessel could not be found at Kodiak, he could, at least, return for the catch next year. It was practicable to take the crew back in the ship's boats, now that they had been supplemented by the large whaleboat.

To keep off Indians and bears, Thompson, one of the crew,

who was known as the "Rocky Mountain Hunter," volunteered
to stay behind and watch the catch. As he had plenty of ammunition at his disposal and plenty of game roamed the wilderness
inland from the camp, he no doubt thought he could make good
use of his time and make a good collection of furs.

The small boat voyage out of Cook Inlet was largely a matter
of tide work, and it was necessary to land on the beach between
stages. The start was postponed until the spring tides had
diminished, and then, on a high water slack, the boats were
shoved off the beach and a start made for Kachemak Bay,
which by the aid of a northerly breeze, was reached before the
flood set in. That was more than quarter of the distance to be
travelled.

The party, according to George, "lived on smoked salmon
and hard-tack," which he considered to be a hardship, until
they reached the end of the voyage. The Captain had charge
of the big whaleboat while the Mate and the Second Mate had
charge of the other two.

Another stage took them to the cove under the lee of Cape
Elizabeth. By this time the sailing conditions had become normal. From there they made the run across the mouth of the Inlet to a cove at Afognak, near Marmot Island. Camp was made
overnight, and then came the final run to Kodiak. Here two
sealers with empty holds were found, and these schooners were
at once chartered to go to Kasilof for the *Washington's* catch of
salmon, while all hands left for home soon after in the bark
Czarevitch, which had come to Alaska for a cargo of natural
ice.

CHAPTER 5

The *Constitution:*

Mexico and Easter Island

T HE voyage of the *Washington* having been settled up, the satisfied owners next gave the Captain the barquentine *Constitution,* built at the edge of the forest in Puget Sound and named after the famous frigate of the War of 1812. The *Constitution,* though only 362 tons, was running as a packet between San Francisco and Honolulu but was soon after replaced by a larger vessel.

Before the *Constitution* sailed for Honolulu, a Japanese Embassy delegation was expected to arrive on its way to Washington, consisting of Prince Mori and his imposing suite. The Prince's expected landing excited great interest in San Francisco. It was the sort of interest that they would show towards a circus parade, the mood being festive and not at all hostile. There was a large gathering at the head of the dock, with eyes glued at the entrance to the Golden Gate, waiting for the appearance of the steamer. Signals from the observatory indicated a delay of an hour and the crowd became restive. Something ought to be done, and in the spirit of the occasion the Captain, who was near the stringpiece, gave them a little exhibition of fancy revolver marksmanship. His was a hair-trigger Smith & Wesson of which he was very proud. Everybody in San Francisco then carried a gun, principally against hoodlums, and it was a good thing for the respectable owner to be known as a "dead shot," as they termed it. A loon swimming and diving near, was the target. It was well known that these divers were hard to hit. When you pressed the trigger they were under the water before the shot arrived; in fact, it was regarded as a waste of time to try to shoot one. The loon that attracted the attention of the crowd came up near the pierhead and right away took another dive. As it came up a moment later there was a report and off came the loon's head, clean. It was a perfect shot, the crowd applauded, but such casual taking of life did not appeal to the Captain later in life.

Of the *Constitution* I have a less distinct idea than I have of any other of my father's vessels. While I know that I must have been aboard with the rest of my family, there is no picture before my eyes as there is of all his later ships. I have consciously seen the *Constitution* only once, although I was born aboard her. It was in the Okhotsk Sea (I was about six) when we had the *Pato* there. The *Constitution* was out at that time from San Francisco to catch and stow down a cargo of salted cod. Her end came when, together with a number of American and German men o'war, she was wrecked in the great hurricane of Samoa in 1889. Only one ship escaped and that was the British ship *Calliope,* by virtue of her superior engine power to face the wind.

On one of the Captain's runs in the *Constitution* between Honolulu and San Francisco, his chronometer broke down. But as it had always been rated by lunars, the mishap made no difference so far as navigation of the vessel was concerned. In fact, upon arriving in San Francisco, it was found that the passage had been unusually short. Mr. Bichard, the owner, who was waiting on the dock, was amazed, and without saying a word about the circumstances of the voyage, turned on his heel, and returned with the best chronometer watch, an E. Howard, that money could buy. This he presented to his Captain, both as a mark of appreciation and a guarantee that he would thereafter be protected against accidents by having a second timepiece about.

The chronometer breakdown episode throws a light on the navigation of the *Spray* which has never been very well understood, owing perhaps to the Captain's purposeful vagueness on this point. Even professional navigators have taken his tin clock joke seriously. The Captain meant that he employed the same methods in navigating the *Spray* that he had on all of his former vessels. In the hands of skillful observers and patient computers the Lunar Method is reliable within a quarter of a degree longitude, which would be the distance of a high landfall. I have before me the log of the ship *Clive* which in 1859 made a six months' passage, without seeing land, from the English Channel to Madras, and sighted the landfall within an hour of the expected time. That could not be beaten at this day. Captain Shaw reported that he checked his chronometers, which had altered their rates considerably, by lunars. He said he could by this means keep to the sea four years, the period of time that Lunar Tables in the Nautical Almanacs were published in advance.

The *Constitution* was next operated between San Francisco and Mexican ports. There was excitement along the Mexican coast at that time. A pack of outlaws, who would have done credit to more modern times, started some trouble, so great care had to be exercised as to just what port in Mexico a ship was consigned. Most of the disturbance was in Mazatlan, opposite La Paz, at the entrance to the Gulf of California. A gang of Mexicans had seized the British steamer *Forward* which had been left in a rather unprotected berth up the river from Mazatlan. This vessel they armed as a pirate and proceeded to rob ships in port, one of them being the Panama packet under the American flag. Their business for a time was good. Posing as patriots for the "liberating" of their country, they went over to La Paz and some lesser settlements along the coast and extorted funds in the interest of a revolution, which up to that time no one had ever heard of. The Mexican authorities, having no means at hand to cope with highway robbery afloat, appealed to the commander of the U.S.S. *Mohican* and asked him to capture the *Forward*, then in concealment up the same river where the outlaws first took her over. As the *Forward* was not a pirate operating beyond the confines of Mexican waters, the *Mohican* could not have acted without the request made by the authorities. That made, the *Mohican* dispatched a boat party under cover of darkness to capture the *Forward*. There was a sharp exchange of fire. The officer commanding the party was killed and two of the seamen were wounded in what came to be known as the Forward Affair. The *Mohican* turned the *Forward* and the band of outlaws over to the Mexican Government and for a time there was no more disturbance of that kind.

About a year later there was a "revolution" further down the coast. At Acapulco the Captain became a public benefactor, quite by accident, being unaware of the fighting going on up in the hills there at the time. Deep-laden as she was with coal, the *Constitution* took on a war-like profile. As she came around the point and made her appearance in the harbor, the rebels in the hills, who were about to descend and make a raid on the town, took her for a gunboat and vamoosed for cover.

"Captain, you have broken up a revolution," was the boarding officer's first salute. For the garrison was thus given more time to throw up defenses, and the Commandante came on board, attended by one of his staff, to tender his official thanks, and the *Constitution* was made very welcome during her stay in Acapulco.

One of the *Constitution's* round voyages was varied by a trip between Valparaiso and Nukahiva, on which a stop was made at Cook's Bay, Easter Island, for fresh water. This island is known to have a good rainfall that is stored in small lakes in its volcanic craters. The visit was of unusual interest, for on Easter Island are the huge stone images which have long been considered to be one of the mysteries of the Pacific. These are traces of an ancient maritime people of the Pacific, who probably migrated from southern Asia, voyaging in sea canoes as the Polynesians were once known to do, and traveling distances that ranged to a thousand miles between islands. My father and mother, together with the rest of the landing party, returned to the ship with a strong impression of the ancient character of this part of the world, and they could also easily imagine the seaworthy and well-appointed Phoenician ships of thirty centuries before, making Easter Island a depot on voyages to and from the American continent. As the images weigh from five to thirty tons, the *Constitution* could not carry even the smallest of them off, having neither the gear nor the time. In 1886, however, the U.S.S. *Mohican* succeeded in securing some of them for The Smithsonian Institution in Washington, D. C., where they can now be seen.

CHAPTER 6

The *B. Aymar*:

A Tale of Bully Hayes

IN RELATING this story of a life upon the sea, we now come to a point where my father and I first became conscious of being shipmates. That was on the deck of the sailing packet *B. Aymar* bound from Sydney to Amoy.

In Sydney some six months before I had become acquainted with my Aunt Jessie and with my Grandmother Walker, but my parents seemed to have been in the background. We lived ashore in Sydney, probably because my brother Ben was about to be signed on the articles of the ship, *B. Aymar,* for which he was named. The *B. Aymar* (1874) sailed from Sydney to Amoy with freight and some passengers. My father was captain of the ship, which, for the times, was considered fairly large and comfortable. I was too small to know much about commands and ownerships of vessels but I soon formed a very clear idea that my father was a very important man on board. For exercise, my mother would pace the calm evening hours with him on the weather side of the quarter deck, the mate shifting over to the lee side, pretending to be interested in the trim of the sails.

In harkening back to these early events of our family life at sea, I have no intention of boring the reader with droll legends of my infancy but to recall historic events which happened to register.

I was surprisingly young and small for a sailor. In fact I was not more than two and a half. I had never known any other place to play or live but on the deck of a ship and at two and a half I had already a pair of sea legs and I had learned some of the ropes.

The *B. Aymar,* the first home that I remember, was a large sailing ship that went all over the world. There were many sailors besides myself on board, so I did not have to climb the ratlines up into the maze of masts, yards and rigging or to haul on the ropes or to set and take in sail. Good weather meant that I could interest myself at large on deck; high seas and rough weather drove me below but did not fill me with fear. The *B. Aymar* was my second ship. All that I know about the first one was what I was afterward told, but the knocking around on the seas I had sailed had made my muscles hard and my spirit tough for a two and a half year old. My mother was on board, of course, but as yet she didn't count, and although I had been introduced to my father before the present time mentioned, I had never taken him very seriously until this particular voyage between Sydney and Amoy. By this time I had acquired both the faculties of observation and memory. I soon began to remember things because there was always so much going on worth remembering. Events sharpened my wits and made me alert for a youngster. And a distinctly definite event on the ship caused me never to forget the *B. Aymar.*

It was an altercation I had with a fellow passenger, another little boy slightly older, slightly bigger than I, and, as I thought, possessed of a mean disposition. While he wanted to play, everything had to be his way, or no way at all. He was even abusive. That made me sore. I could not fight him for he was much stronger and pugnacious.

The weather was good and the sailors busy at jobs in the rigging and on the masts. One of the jobs going on was slushing down the mainmast. This was done by a sailor getting himself into what was called a "bosun's chair," which was just like a swing board and hoisted up and lowered down the mast to suit the convenience of the slusher. Slush, I soon found, was the grease skimmed off by the cook when he boiled "salt horse," the sailor's term for salt beef. Every day the cook added his skimming to the slush barrel lashed to the side of his galley. The slush was free and available for the purpose of greasing or "slushing down" a mast or anything like that. It took two sailors to slush down a mast, and it was "down," for at the start one sailor was hoisted away on a gantline until he was at the top. He was let down or "lowered away" by another sailor who tended the gantline at the fife rail.

On this particular occasion the sailors slushing down the mainmast had left their bosun's chair dangling near the deck. As soon as my tormentor spied it, he immediately wanted to have me hoist him up to play "bosun's chair." When I got him well up in the air, I let go the gantline, and scampered to the other end of the ship. Down he came by the run. He did not like the way that I tended gantline, but he did not torment me any more.

There is another episode in connection with the *B. Aymar* that is most clear in my mind till this day. My parents were promenading the deck in the second dog watch, as they usually did before going below for the night, when I stopped them to ask "Are there any little boys in Amoy like me?" They both looked at me as if they had never seen me before and regarded my query with surprise and amusement. I was serious, and had they responded seriously, I might have been comforted. But by their smile I knew I was a being separate from the oldsters and that I was living in a world by myself. A new entity was demanding recognition on personal grounds.

When we got to Amoy I found that there were indeed very many "little boys in Amoy like me," and I enjoyed their play with bright and fanciful kites and their toy paper roosters. I was photographed in a Chinese suit, tasseled cap, turned up shoes and all. Mother must have had a lot of fun with me then.

The Chinese toys bring to mind that Santa Claus used to come on board on his appointed eve, with the greatest variety of things to go in our stockings, expectantly hung up around the mizzenmast in the cabin. He never missed, no matter what the sea or the country.

In after life, when I heard more about the *B. Aymar* and our voyages in the China Seas, I came to learn about my father's early life in these very seas in a similar vessel. The trade was the same, and the dangers the same. Typhoons were not more numerous in the early days, but there were more pirates, both Chinese and Malay. They were very bad but usually would not attack a foreign devil merchant ship in a brisk breeze. They would lie and wait for a vessel grounded on a sand bar, like those in Chinese rivers. Or, in a high Malay island, pirates with oars as well as sails might wait for a becalmed and helpless merchantman to come within his range. They would pull out, swarm aboard, murder the ship's people and tow the whole thing inshore for plunder. As the sailing ship was never aided by an engine of any kind to help it get away, it was easy prey for the Malays. The greatest safety was in the open seas.

At the time when we had the *B. Aymar*, the cannibals of the Solomons and the New Hebrides were kept in mind. In Sydney they were greatly feared, for they were too near to be regarded as a joke. The tragedies of Williams and Goodenough were yet household stories on the gruesome side and in sailing by these islands, even when out of sight, their horror could be felt.

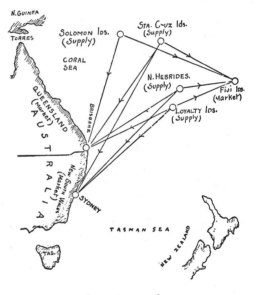

Diagram map of the blackbirding routes as they flourished in the days of Bully Hayes and the Queensland Labor Act of 1865

In addition to this, the sailing track as far as the equator was through seas frequented by the blackbirder. "Blackbirding" was a fancy name given by the South Sea slavers to their particular trade. Between 1865 and 1875 they operated among the New Hebrides and the Loyalties, selling their prey to the not much less particular planters in Brisbane. These kidnappers were never a menace to merchant vessels making legal voyages through their waters but they were occasionally to be met with.

It was while on the *B. Aymar* that the Captain fell in with the celebrated Bully Hayes.

South Sea man-stealing, to furnish plantations with inexpensive native labor, flourished in all of its gruesome glory in the days of the Queensland Labor Act of 1865. By applying the methods of the African slavers under cover of suitable legislation, the Australian planters reduced the cost of their labor to just one-half. During the ten years thereafter there was a traffic in humans that smells to this day as you cruise in the seas where it was practiced. The field where it was practiced was not very extensive, never more than twenty days sail from either Sydney or Brisbane. Natives were decoyed, usually, from the New Hebrides or the Loyalty Islands.

There was a large fleet of vessels in the trade and in the Loyalty Islands, alone, there were fifteen hailing from Sydney, according to the report made by the H.M.S. *Rosario* which was sent out to see how the Colonials worked it. Unable to act, Captain Palmer, R.N., Commander, wrote a book about it after he got back.

And about Bully Hayes? Well, I think we will let the Captain tell his own story about meeting him since he was the one who did. Here is his account:

The dashing trade of piracy was at its peak in the days of the gold-laden galleons, when the successful cutthroat of the seas was rewarded with vast plunder and noble rank as well. In later and degenerate times, the calling became fraught with great risk and inconvenience, as was discovered by Captain Kidd. Then business went from bad to worse, from cargoes of gold and church plate to single chests of specie, and even merchandise. The day came when the pirate must whistle in vain even for a "piece of eight."

After the pirate came the buccaneer, who was never knighted and, when caught, was usually decorated with a halter. In my early days at sea, the Pacific was well-nigh rid of the lawless pests who had robbed, burned, and murdered through several generations; but the last of these and king of them all, Bully Hayes, hove across my course in such a strange fashion that the memory burns vivid to this day. My first meeting with this resourceful ruffian, whose name and deeds fill the Pacific even now, was in 1873. At that time he was posing as a missionary to save his oft condemned neck.

It was early morning when I backed my main-topsail off the Island of Oulau in the South Seas. We were needing fresh provisions such as this island yielded in abundance: cocoanuts, bananas, pineapples, yams, chickens and pigs. In answer to our signal, a six-oared yawl shot out from a leeward harbor and pulled towards us with a fine display of speed and skill.

"Way enough," roared a tall figure in the stern as the boat rounded alongside, and he leaped on board with his crew of beachcombers at his heels, a crowd most amazingly tattooed and fairly belted with knives.

They were incongruous company for their leader, a massively built man well past middle age, standing six feet three inches and wearing an air of great dignity and authority. His speech was slow and sprinkled with godly phrases.

"Stand by," whispered my old mate. "It's Bully Hayes."

I felt a shock of surprise at this first sight of the most notorious scoundrel in the islands, but greeted him with the respect due his magnificent "*bluff*." And what should he want for a boatload of bananas but a *Bible!*

"My own copy of the Holy Scriptures has been worn out by much use," he explained, "and my natives are sitting in darkness waiting for the reading of The Word."

71

His crew of less godly spirits were doing a thriving business with the foremast hands, trading fruit for pipes, tobacco and other worldly commodities which the sailors had on stock. The old buccaneer found, on second thought, that he could use a few stores in addition to his spiritual replenishment. My vessel had a cargo of coal.

My old Scottish mate, whom Hayes carefully ignored because these two had met before under other skies, cruelly suggested to the "missionary" that he had no need for coal for any future warmth.

"You wait a few years," added the mate, "and you'll have more red-hot coals than you can handle, and the Devil will be the stoker. I know ye, you old rip!"

As I remember it, Bully Hayes retorted with a sigh: "My brother, we will all save fuel in the hereafter if we mend our ways in this life. Judge not that ye be not judged."

It was about this time that certain missionary publications were sounding the good news that one of the wonderful works wrought in heathen lands was the conversion of Bully Hayes. I was inclined to give him the benefit of the doubt when he said grace at breakfast on board my vessel. I have heard many clergymen do worse.

When we resumed trading, Hayes put us under obligation to him by giving us more provisions than we asked for, and sending ashore for a litter of pigs and a mother sow to care for them. Then, as a climax of his generosity, he ordered from ashore a canoe load of Marshall Islands mats. One of these, worth more than all the stores he had obtained from us, he courteously presented to my wife.

Meanwhile our ship had drifted in the strong current to leeward until she opened out entrance to a small harbor.

"Yonder lie the bones of my ship, the *Leonora*," said Hayes, with a flourish of his arm towards the inner beach. "She was once the *John Williams II.*"

"The mission ship?" I asked.

"Exactly so," returned Bully Hayes. "Lost in a gale of wind, total loss. But the crew were saved, thank the Lord!"

He doffed his broad-brimmed hat and fairly swept the deck with it as he bowed himself out of our gangway and dropped nimbly into his boat, shouting to his crew, "Push off." And to us, "God bless you all."

"Fill away the main-topsail and board the main tack," I ordered. Round flew the yards and our ship was again striding across the trade winds for Shanghai.

While we were discussing the strange character we were leaving astern, one of my officers said:

"While he was on board this morning, Bully Hayes got a note from our old missionary, Reverend Mr. Snow, who has been in the islands for years and years, begging the old pirate to come to his village in a hurry and settle a row between a white beach-comber and his native wife. I saw the note. It said that the beggar had cut off one of his wife's ears, and she had paid him off by spearing the beast in the leg and taking a slice off his shoulder with a blow of her ax.

" 'Come quickly, dear brother,' wrote the parson, 'or there will be nothing left of either of them.' Here is that old sundowner, Bully Hayes, a pal and a brother to this missionary. He pulls the wool over the eyes of the best of them."

While we bowled along with a good breeze in the evening, my mate, Mr. Shure, entertained me by telling me what he knew about this versatile buccaneer. Mr. Shure knew every celebrity from Kamchatka to New Zealand and he took off his hat to Bully Hayes. As a trader who laughed at law, the man had a record as long as your arm.

He had done many a kindly act and hundreds of natives were indebted to him for a helping hand in time of stress. But woe betide the white man, whether trader or beachcomber, who got in his way! With grim humor he once shanghaied a rival trader by first loading him with squareface gin and then throwing him into a departing ship's forecastle, stripped of everything but what he stood in.

Hayes was no coward, for once upon a time the methods of a German trading company aroused his ire, whereupon, lonehanded, he declared war upon the German Empire. He opened hostilities by turning the German Consulate upside down. He went through the place with an ax and made hash of the office furniture. He then brought his crew ashore and their axes chopped the legation flagpole to the ground, Imperial flag and all.

This cyclonic stroke of diplomacy won for him the profound respect of the natives who could see for themselves that Bully Hayes was a greater man than the Emperor of Germany, himself.

The tidings of his prowess swept through the islands. His trade increased and his fame grew until his schooner was too small to carry his goods.

Now, the missionary bark, *John Williams II*, had been cast away on a coral reef, salved, refitted, and given a new name. As a merchantman she bore the name of *Leonora* and Bully Hayes came into possession of her. For some time he did not realize what a prize he had found. One day on the high seas when the *Leonora* was becalmed, Hayes grew tired of whistling for wind and was rummaging in her old lockers when he found her burgee of other days, the L.M.S. (London Missionary Society) flag, with the palm branch emblem of peace and good will to all. The flag gave him an inspiration which turned his energy into a new channel.

He hoisted the pious emblem to the main, and squared away for the islands for his first cargo of "blackbirds," or kidnapped native labor to be sold to the highest bidder. The islanders were familiar with the vessel and the old flag under which they had formerly gathered for song and worship. They flocked on board with shouts of welcome. This time Bully Hayes led them into the hold for prayers and, as a benediction, clapped on the hatches and headed away for the sugar and cotton plantations, where he sold the congregation.

This heartless business flourished until both English and American warships went in pursuit of Bully Hayes. Admiral James Bruce, R.N., whom I met long after in Gibraltar, pursued Hayes in vain; and Admiral Miller, U.S.N., was on the same trail with fruitless results. The difficulty was that he was never betrayed by the natives. They feared and liked him and stood by him in fair weather and foul.

When "blackbirding" became too hazardous, Hayes entered the trade of carrying Chinese passengers from Hong Kong to Sydney. How was the man to save his neck in Sydney where he was known, and where Admiral Bruce was waiting to hang him from the yardarm? Hayes had no notion of meeting Bruce, or even the collector of customs. He collected at sea all the head money due the Australian Government from his Chinese immigrant passengers. This was a matter of routine business, perfectly plausible because the ship landing these folk at their destination would be held responsible for their tax and their safe delivery.

It was easy for Hayes to work out a plan. His ship arrived off Sydney beach, flying signals of distress: "Ship sinking," "Passengers in mutiny," "Want immediate assistance." The ocean tugs raced for the prize.

"Take off my passengers," cried Bully Hayes to the first tug alongside. "Get these poor suffering, mutinous heathen ashore and come back to the ship. With the pigtails once out of her the crew can keep the vessel afloat until you can land them and return. We've sprung a leak, and the heathen are scared to death of water. They'll murder us all if we don't get rid of them."

The Chinese were genuinely frightened out of their wits. They expected to be drowned. Never did rats leave a sinking ship faster than those wild-eyed Mongolians scrambled out of the *Leonora* and into the tugs, bag and baggage. A little later, the hurrying tugs made fast to Circular Quay in Sydney Harbor and five hundred cackling Chinese started to flee ashore.

"Tax money," demanded the Deputy Collector at the pier. "Taxes before landing."

It was the law, and the tugboat owners had to pay before they could dump their cargo ashore.

Where was Captain Hayes? As soon as the tugs had passed out of range he plugged the auger holes he had bored in the bottom of the *Leonora,* set his pumps a-going, and squared away before a strong west wind.

"That was a tough spell at the pumps," Hayes commented to his mate, while he was counting the tax money. "We bored them holes too damned plentiful; but the old packet needed a washing out after those coolies."

The Chinese were building a big fleet of wooden ships of war and were paying fancy prices for timber. Hayes appeared among the timber brokers with forests to sell. His yarn was that on the island of Ponape he had millions of feet of the finest stock, on the stump. He lacked only a sawmill to turn it into dollars. One of the oldest firms in Shanghai, Glover, Dow & Co., was persuaded to enlist in the enterprise. Mr. Glover said afterward that while Hayes was talking of his timber island he (Glover) could fairly see the branches growing from the walls of his office.

This firm fitted Hayes out with a steam sawmill, cash and carabao to haul the logs to the mill. Hayes first packed the sawmill aboard his ship, and took it, not to Ponape, but to New Zealand where real timber grew, worth the sawing. While he was busy with the task of running away bodily with a steam sawmill, he left his mate "Lanky" Pease in charge at Ponape to take care of the rapidly accumulating property forwarded from Shanghai. The buccaneer intended to pack up those spoils for a second trip, but Lanky set to work with such alacrity that he had the plunder ready for transporting before his captain returned. Then Lanky found a ship of his own and proceeded to load her. The king of the island was a tattooed savage, but he had a shrewd idea of what was going on under his nose. He held a sort of court and was for stopping Lanky in his project. The mate shook the old ship's register in the royal countenance and told the king it was a power of attorney from Glover & Co. to clean up their business on the island of Ponape. Then Lanky went ahead and stripped the island clean and sailed away, the king finally expressing his pleasure of being rid of the whole pirate crew.

When Hayes returned he became fairly apoplectic. His rage knew no bounds, but he could do nothing. The Shanghai merchants chartered a bark, the *Tuck Sing*, to go to Ponape and there load their first cargo of lumber from their new mill. The *Tuck Sing* was too late. Not even a buffalo was left behind.

When the empty bark returned to Shanghai and the merchants heard the story, the entire experience with Bully Hayes seemed like a dream.

Hayes told me of his mate's rascality when it was fresh in his memory, and forgetting his missionary manners, exclaimed:

"I wouldn't have been so put out about it if he had been content with a fair cargo of buffalo, but, God damn him, he took so many that he had to cut holes in the deck to let their horns stick up through. By the Great Shark, when I meet him, he dies!"

It was shortly after this adventure that Hayes was stranded on the island of Oulau, where I first met him. He was casting about for a new ship and was studying ways and means of getting to Samoa where he hoped to find another vessel. His final plan was to borrow the "King's Ship," a dugout of ten or fifteen tons, and in this escape from Oulau.

I heard no more of him for two years. One day in Manila I received a note from U. S. Consul Griswold Herron saying that, 'A countryman of ours, one Captain Hayes, has been brought as a prisoner from Guam, on a charge laid by the Spanish officials of stealing political prisoners.'

I called upon Mr. Herron, who said:

"Hayes insists that he knows you, what do you know about Hayes?"

Of my own knowledge I could tell him nothing very damaging. My information had been picked up piecemeal. I smiled to myself as I remembered our first meeting, which was all in Hayes' favor. I recalled him as a "convert," asking grace at my table, receiving messages from esteemed missionaries who called him "Dear Brother." The outline of his latest escapade as outlined by the consul was as follows:

He had rigged up the king's dugout at Oulau as a schooner,

and with two of his old *Leonora* hands sailed for Ponape, where they took in provisions of cocoanuts and pigs en route for Guam. According to Hayes' story he knew there were Spanish convicts at Guam, "But he did not dream they were so loosely guarded that they could get on his schooner." His log narrated that he had anchored under the lee of the island and landed on the sandy beach abreast his vessel to have a dip in the surf. Before he knew it, a dozen or so convicts had piled aboard his vessel, evidently with the intention of seizing her. "I couldn't help that," he wrote.

The account given by the guards was somewhat different. They swore that Hayes had stolen one batch of convicts and come ashore for more when they pounced upon him from their mangrove ambush, and made him prisoner. When the convicts on board saw that Hayes was nabbed, they cut cable and made off before the wind.

They managed to fetch up somewhere on the coast of Borneo, wrecked the schooner, and made good their escape.

When I called upon Hayes in the Manila jail, I found him in the midst of the governor's family on the veranda discussing religious matters. He was reading very devoutly from the copy of the Bible I had sold him at Oulau. The officers of the gunboat that brought him from Guam had written opposite his name in the logbook, *Cristiano.*

Hayes became a chum of the governor of the prison, and also struck up a friendship with the priest who baptized him in the Roman Catholic faith while he was locked up. Now that he was converted to the true faith, Hayes found an all-powerful friend in the Bishop of Manila.

The buccaneer was a penitent and he made an impressive and moving figure. Fever had twisted and shrunken him until I recognized him only by his long beard and his unusual height and breadth. The light free spring of his gait was gone, and he was the picture of a shuffling monk. To behold the old freebooter, penniless, reduced by sickness, tall, gaunt, with flowing white beard half a fathom long, marching barefooted at the head of a religious procession, and carrying the tallest candle of them all, softened the hearts of his enemies, if he had any in Manila.

So much, then, for the Captain's account of Bully Hayes.

In the days of the *B. Aymar,* Manila Bay was of natural interest for the present artificial harbor was not yet built. The walled city was more Spanish than was Spain. The anchorage for great ships was two miles off from the city. To go ashore, we pulled in our own boat to the landing in the Pasig River. The entrance to the Pasig River is between two moles, and up to the first bridge there is thirteen feet of water. At the right hand on entering, we were frowned upon by a battery of ancient cannon, poking their muzzles through the embrasures. The fortification, built by Chinese labor, was of stone and it ranked as a masterpiece of the XVIth century. It was a safeguard for the Spaniards against the frequent threats of the Mindanao and Sulu pirates who ventured into the Bay of Manila as late as 1899. The inhabitants were subject also to hostilities from the Dutch and Portuguese as early as 1643.

When we landed from the ship's boat it was on the north side of the river, adjacent to warehouses and places of commercial transaction. To the walled city on the opposite bank we seldom went, largely for its want of attractiveness. A boat excursion up the river was more interesting. There were huge snakes in the Pasig as I remember it. The river was navigable by steam launches and especially constructed steamers with flat bottoms of light draught, which went up the whole distance into the Laguna de Bay. The river was crossed at Manila and its suburbs by three bridges. There was a pontoon bridge across the Pasig from 1632 until 1863, when it was destroyed by the great earthquake of that year. A new stone bridge was opened to traffic in 1875, while we were there.

The Walled City was built (cir. 1590) solely with a view to self-defense against the Portuguese and then the Dutch. When in its prime there were eight drawbridges over the moat. They were raised and the city was closed and under sentinels during certain hours of the night. The Walled City was dull, with narrow streets bearing a heavy, sombre, monastic appearance. It was in constant danger of destruction from earthquakes. There was no place of recreation. Only the numerous religious processions relieved the monotony of walled city life.

Within the Citadel were colleges, convents, a cathedral, eleven churches and a weather bureau. The Catholic clergy (Jesuits) operated the weather bureau, originated during the Spanish regime. It is still of great importance to mariners in the China Sea. It has broadcast typhoon warnings which have saved the lives of thousands of river-dwelling Chinese in the area of Canton, giving them a chance to flee before the terror overtook them. As the China Sea typhoons start in the Pacific just to the eastward of Manila, the weather station is in the right spot. A weather observer there is in a position similar to that of the lightning observer in the top of the Empire State Building, New York. The Manila weather bureau also is provided with a seismograph, not for the purpose of prognostication but as a contribution to the science of Volcanology, of which there is plenty in the islands.

The *B. Aymar*, our home for two years, changed hands in Manila, and in connection with her sale to a Shanghai company of merchants, my father met Edward Jackson, an Englishman of personality who had come to live in the Philippines. Besides being a substantial businessman, Mr. Jackson was an accomplished amateur naval architect, having just won a medal for a ship design at an industrial exposition in London. He was now interested in inter-island transportation and he wanted a new 150-ton steamer built from his own plans.

After agreeing on terms, my father decided to build it for him at Olongapo, on Subig Bay, about sixty miles from Manila. It was a natural shipyard site, long before used by Chinese shipbuilders for the construction of Spanish galleons employed between Acapulco and Manila. The galleon traffic was crippled by Anson in 1740 but it continued in a small way until some time later. Now the site was occasionally used by the native Filipinos to make their coasting craft and cascoes. On the inland mountain slopes timber was in abundance and there was a launching beach with good water towards the sea.

Shipbuilding conditions at Olongapo were as primitive as they well could be. As far as plant facilities went, it was as though this was the first vessel ever to be built. Monkeys screeched and scampered from the trees as they fell to the woodsmen's axes. Tagal sawyers ripped the timber into scantling and plank by hand, using a single frame saw. A power frame saw would have been an unspeakable joy, but in the East manpower must be used wherever it can be. The log to be sawed was horsed up high enough for a man to stand under it; the sawyers worked in pairs, the leading man on top, the other to guide the saw, underneath, on its downward stroke.

The contrast between the tropical conditions on Subig Bay and the temperate conditions in Puget Sound was striking; dank exuberance of vegetation took the place of healthful fir balsam; instead of safety on the forest floor, there was peril

82

from poisonous creeping things. When cruising for timber through the forest trails, a sharp lookout was always kept aloft for the boa constrictor which might dangle from a tree branch, ready to drop on passing prey. In such a situation they are dangerous and not timid as when crawling on the ground. Boas are usually ten or twelve feet long, but I have a picture of one thirty feet long which was killed near Olongapo. It can be seen that this specimen has a body as thick as a man's and one of this size is of unbelievable strength.

The sawing of the logs into plank was hard, slow work, paid for by the foot, according to custom. The frames were hewn to shape by narrow bitted axes with straight helves. Our broad axe would have been more efficient, but it was not to be thought of. The timber felled in the mountains was hewn into square logs before it was dragged out, and, considering that some of the wood was nearly as hard as the native's primitive axes, that alone was an awful job. The log was hewn skid shaped on the front end into a sort of nose with a diagonal hole in each top corner to hook the carabao to.

The carabao is the most useful animal in the Philippines; it is a species of water-buffalo and amphibious. When grazing near flooded land it will roam into the water up to its neck and immerse its head for two minutes at a time, searching for vegetable food below the surface. It serves for carting, ploughing and carrying loads upon its back, and for almost all labor where great strength is required for a short time. A native farmer possessed of a patch of ground, a carabao, a bolo-knife, and good health, is like the turtle who "with his head pulled within his shell, told the world to go to hell." When the carabao is well tamed it is docile with its native masters but it certainly does not like the smell of a white man, which it can detect at some distance. At home, the children may do anything with it,

83

play around its heels or use its tail as a means of climbing upon its back. After being worked out of the water for a certain number of hours, carabaos are wisely turned back to wallow in a mud-hole or a creek to recuperate lost energy. If left there for a week or so, they may revert to their wild state and again become dangerous. Only a mounted driver then dares to go in to round them up. When working near a river or a beach they are usually allowed, in the heat of the day, to go in and soak their hides. Though apparently clumsy, carabaos can be very quick and sure with their horns; a cow, to protect her calf, was once known to hook a shark out of the water and to rip it open.

Chinese shipwrights were imported from Manila to do the building. The Tagals did not like these Chinamen and watched them with suspicion. Though peculiar and slow in their methods, they are excellent mechanics, as anyone may see by examining one of their native craft. In the European-controlled shipyards they grow to be more efficient, and there a gang of Chinese boatbuilders will do a better job on a copper fastened teak lapstrake boat than is done anywhere in the United States.

These particular Chinese were from the southern coast, and a savage lot. They were under the control of a patrone who resented the Jackson contract being given to anyone else, and he planned either to seize or destroy the vessel. So great was the patrone's enmity that his son, six years afterwards, attempted to stab the Captain while ashore in Manila. To get hold of the vessel would have been motive enough, for piracy at that time was common in the seas adjacent to China. Even at the present the maritime Chinese easily revert to piracy as an industry, if opportunity offers.

It was between the forest life and the sea that the village of Olongapo stood, and a primitive place it was indeed. The first thing my father did was to build a nipa house for his family, for he always kept the family with him in all of his enterprises. Building a nipa house may seem to be an easy job, but it was not so simple as it looked, for any native would much rather go to a cockfight than work.

These native houses are built with long molave corner posts which are sunk into the ground. Molave is an ant-proof and damp-resisting wood and in the ground it will last a hundred years. The posts are the only part of the house that endures very long. The sills are kept six or seven feet above the ground for safety and health as well as to supply accommodation for the pigs and chickens. The corners are secured by wooden pins, but otherwise the whole bamboo structure is lashed together at the joints with rattan and twisted fibre in the most ingenious fashion. The floor and sides, as well as the window shutters, are made of split bamboo, which affords interstices for ventilation.

Having due regard for the typhoon that flattened houses and even swept away whole villages, this house, when completed, was stayed fore and aft as well as athwartships by stout ropes of twisted rattan secured to stakes driven into the ground. This was something that had never been done in the *barrio*; even the governor of the province heard of it and came to pay a friendly and approving visit.

The roof frame of bamboo is thatched with nipa as is also the wall. Nipa is a narrow palm leaf, made up into convenient units ready to lash in overlapping layers, like shingles. It was this nipa that made all the trouble. The contract for supplying it was claimed by the *Teniente de Barrio,* who had a monopoly on nipa as one of his perquisites of office.

The *teniente* was a functionary who disappeared from the Islands upon the extinction of the Spanish regime. He was both hated and feared by the inhabitants of the *barrio* of which he was the Supervisor, Chief of Police and Marshal, all in one. In an extra-*barrio* capacity he was the representative of the Provincial Government. Insolence, graft and extortion were all his. Over the small and insignificant lives of the natives he almost had power of life and death, for a false and trumped up charge against a poor wretch was always backed up by the court. He could levy a fine of 30 pesos even without authority of the court. Such fine could be expiated in jail at the rate of half a peso a day. The *teniente's* uniform, patterned after some Malay ritual, was to him a serious business. Trousers were not imperative, even upon parade, but he never appeared in public without that abbreviated black jacket which did not quite cover his stern shirt tail. That was his trademark.

To intrench himself in authority, the *teniente* did not deign to a cudgel, but carried a weapon of greater power—a slender black wand which one might have taken for a swagger stick. So long as he had that under his arm, no one dared as much as lay a finger on him, and to do him insult or injury at such a time was to invite a fine or the dungeon.

Whenever my father approached the *teniente* on the subject of the nipa, which he had paid for in advance, there was always a *"Manana."* This did not surprise the natives who were used to the *teniente's* ways and who also knew that complaint to a higher-up would be worse than useless. But the Captain decided that this high-handed official might cross his bow once too often and that he went before a fall. Nothing could be done to the *teniente,* however, so long as he had his stick. But one day a faithful scout came running in with the news that the *teniente* was near at hand, and officially unprotected.

"Where?" demanded the Captain, reaching for his jungle-proof Brier Island cowhides.

"There, there, there," exclaimed the excited scout, pointing into the green shade behind the shipyard. On went the hard-toed cowhides in the interest of the delinquent nipa. It was soon forthcoming, for one judicious application of leather proved enough for the *teniente*. He knew he was licked in more ways than one but gave no sign of hard feelings. Had the news been broadcast he never could have lived it down.

My mother, with her three children, made the best of jungle life during the construction of the steamer. The air was heavy and damp and there was the poison of vegetation as well as the peril of venomous creeping things. Up through the cracks in the split bamboo flooring could crawl centipedes, scorpions, and even a small boa if it took a notion to come in at night and hang down from the rafters, tail first. We found that both centipedes and scorpions had a habit of crawling into our clothes and getting into our shoes while they were not in use, so it was routine to shake and search everything while dressing in the morning.

The most profound impression made upon my childish sensibilities was the effect of the forest noises at nightfall. Nearby was a swamp filled with crocodiles, and their barkings were added to the singing of the locusts. Only in forests like those in the Philippines can one hear such a nocturnal roar. It affects the superstitious tendencies of the natives. It will get a white man if he is alone too long in such a jungle. The native may believe that the bark of the croc is the devil calling to him and to answer the call would be to perish. Long listening to the call sometimes drove a native into hysteria, and the victim was fatalistically impelled to the edge of the forest to call back. By auto-suggestion he was then doomed. My father took me with him when he went to see one of the Tagals, thus sick with fear. The Tagal explained that the Evil One had told him he was about to die, and die he did.

The crocodile in the swamp ran a close second to the boa constrictor as a danger to the logging crew. It was usually found submerged, nose to shore, in muddy water, with only the nostrils, like small craters, above the surface. Its respiration could be heard only at a short distance like a faint whistling snore and so completely was its coloring and texture adjusted to natural surroundings that were it not for the breathing it could not be detected by the eye. Lying thus, it was ready to grab any creature approaching to drink. The crocodile never releases its prey because those front teeth fit tightly into grooves in the opposite jaw.

Life in Olongapo was like being in the primitive jungle itself, and no more was thought of a big snake invading the chicken yard than any other common marauder. They were fond of small pigs as well, but the little pigs were very shy and fled at discovery.

While living there I was badly scared by a boa in the back yard, and as it squirmed off with a swish through the high grass it looked big enough to have swallowed me whole. I was about five at the time and am sure I made the more noise of the two as I put for the house.

Though I was so young, the events in Olongapo were so extraordinary that my growing powers of perception were sharpened to a like degree. That is the reason I now recollect the major events in connection with the building of the steamer on the edge of the wilderness. The rest of the data I fill in from the recounting of the adventure long afterwards. For instance, I distinctly remember the sternpost as it was fashioned to line, and I understood the reason for the bossing at the propeller shaft as well as did the grown men who made it. I was developing an appreciation, of the pictures at least, of Peake's little book on naval architecture, which was used both by Mr. Jackson and my father in working out knotty problems. When I grew old enough, it became one of my first text books.

As the frame of the steamer went up, it soon became evident that treachery was afoot. One night, while my father was away on one of his periodic trips to Manila, my mother was alarmed by the shouts of the Tagals who were surrounding the house. She could see by the light of their torches that they were all armed with axes. They lighted fires and placed a guard over the house for the night. The reason for this warlike assemblage was later understood, though never fully explained; the faithful Tagals had scented a plot by the Chinese, who resented the contract being given to a foreigner, to murder the family during the Captain's absence. It became clear as well, who were our friends, and no overt act by the Chinese was again feared.

A still more insidious plot was laid, however, and that was to block the launching or capsize the vessel on the ways. The Captain kept a sharp watch on the Chinese but, as it afterwards proved, not quite sharp enough. When the final preparations were made for the launching and the dog shores were knocked down, the vessel came to a stop after moving only a short distance down the way. Investigation showed that the ways had been shifted out of line. There was no hydraulic jack nearer than Hong Kong with which to meet the emergency.

Then a remarkable thing happened. The Tagals took the situation into their own hands and, as though a tocsin had been sounded, there began a muster of carabao; carabao came from everywhere and were gathered at the sides of the ways and preparations were made at once to hitch them to a hawser from each bow. It was not an uncommon thing for the Tagals to drag their own small vessels into the water thus, so why not do the same thing with this larger vessel if there were carabao enough to be had?

There was a tumult among the drivers as they mounted their animals and got them in line for one mighty, concerted pull. When all was ready they started a rhythmic chant which welled and ended in a shout that might have shattered the walls of Jericho. The carabao fell in with the idea, stretched out, dug into the sand, surged ahead on the hawsers and away they went into the sea, buffalo, drivers, ship and all.

There was a tumult again, above which the Captain shouted, "Que nombre?", for the vessel had never been named. "*Tagadito, Tagadito,*" they yelled back as the newborn vessel successfully took her bearings on the water. Translated from the Tagalog dialect of Luzon, this was said to denote "Of this place," meaning that she was their ship, for had they not saved the day.

The new steamer was towed to Manila and finished in the Pasig, where she received her boiler and engine. After the trial trip, the Captain took over the 90-ton schooner *Pato* which, in accordance with the contract made with Mr. Jackson, he was to receive in part payment for the building of the steamer. He at once prepared the *Pato* for sea.

CHAPTER 7

The *Pato:*

From Petropavlovsk to Portland, Ore.

Wrth the exception of the *Spray,* the *Pato,* at this time lying at the quay in the Pasig River, was the most inspiring of my father's ventures. It appealed the most to his sense of adventure and was to lead him to his first remarkable voyage. Though she was built in the Spanish Philippines by the Chinese and designed by an English naval architect, the *Pato* was, in model, closely related to the American schooner yacht *Sappho* which defeated the British challenger *Livonia* in the America Cup races off New York. Mr. Jackson did not believe in the "lead mine" yacht and he had just entered a competition in London with a model that would stand upright without a ballast. It was rejected. Admiring the *Sappho,* he had designed the *Pato* on her modified lines as a commercial experiment, retaining the high flat floor of the famous racer. In no part of the world was the *Sappho's* beauty and sailing qualities more talked about than by Englishmen in Chinese waters.

Just what to do with the newly acquired *Pato* was a problem but we were all agreed that it was better to live afloat in however small a craft than on the reptile-infested beach of Olongapo. Our little after-guard had gained a recruit since the *B. Aymar* sailed into Manila to be sold. That was my sister Jessie, who by this time was becoming quite used to her surroundings. Her baby attention was largely occupied with Flagstaff, the ship's cat. Flagstaff got her name because her tail was straight up in the air no matter how the wind blew. She remained with us as long as we had the *Pato*.

After making some inter-island trips, the *Pato* was chartered by the underwriters of a British bark which had just been wrecked on North Danger Reef, lying in the China Sea about 420 miles from Manila. She was laden with the usual valuable cargo carried from China to England, consisting of teas, silks and camphor.

The *Pato*, with the bark's captain aboard, found her hanging by the forefoot to the edge of the coral, ready at any time to slip off and plunge down into the deep water under her heel. There was not a soul on board. After cutting away both fore and mainmasts, the crew had been taken off by a passing vessel and carried to Manila. Luckily they were out of the range of Chinese pirates or they might never have been heard from.

The weather held off and remained moderate while the *Pato* was ranged alongside and filled her hold, cabin and decks. In two weeks, the *Pato* made three round trips between the wreck and Manila, where the salved cargo was safely stored; but at the fourth, the wind shifted and raised a sea. This soon ground up the wreck which twisted around sideways to the wall of the reef, causing it to unhook the forefoot and sink.

The *Pato's* next venture was a cargo to Hong Kong, where all of my father's plans were changed. While overhauling her gear there, some splitting knives left over from Cook Inlet days were found in a locker. Memories of that glorious adventure were stirred and it was then settled that the *Pato* was to become an Okhotsk Sea fisherman.

The Sea of Okhotsk, or the "Okot Sea" as we called it after we got used to it, is an indentation behind the Kamchatkan peninsula. The Kurile Islands are stretched across the entrance

The Pato *arrives to salve the cargo of a British bark wrecked on North Danger Reef in the China Sea, 420 miles from Manila. The bark was hanging to the edge of the coral by her forefoot*

and the port of entry is on the eastern side of the peninsula. The peninsula itself is interesting, well wooded and the home of fur bearing animals. Its rivers ran with salmon, while the banks along its edge, from Cape Lopatka to the Amur, over eighteen hundred miles, teemed with bottom fish, principally cod. Even bowhead whales were taken in this inland sea. When the early American whalers in the Pacific cleaned out the Equatorial Grounds of sperm, they next turned their attention

93

to the bowheads (whalebone whales) of the Okhotsk. One of the Americans first to enter this sea to take whales was Captain Eben Pierce of New Bedford. He it was, many years after, who gave the sloop *Spray* to my father, in Fairhaven.

In Hong Kong the Okhotsk fisheries were well known. The attention of Americans had been called to cod on these extensive grounds as early as 1857 when Captain Turner of the brig *Timandra* made the discovery off the mouth of the Amur River in the Gulf of Tartary. It was not until seven years later that he was able to interest capital in a salt fishing trip which put down a hundred-ton fare in the vicinity of Sakhalin Island. In 1865, six vessels sailed out of San Francisco for these fisheries, and soon after the industry became well established, for all the Okhotsk fleet salted down full fares which loaded their decks nearly to the water's edge. There was even a twenty-tonner in the fleet. When in 1874 the schooner *Flying Mist* was sent to hunt sea otter off Sakhalin, she found it more profitable to change over from furs to codfish. In 1876, the year before the *Pato* went to the Okhotsk, business increased so much that even three-stickers were sent from San Francisco to fish over the side with hand lines.

Hong Kong proved to be a convenient place to fit out. Dories of the Cape Ann model were built by Chinese boatbuilders, and fishing gear was easily procured. Enough seal poachers, sea otter hunters and other flotsam of the North Pacific were found on the beach to make a fishing crew willing to go on shares. These were of the type that the Captain had come to know on the Northwest Coast and they got on well together. And then too, they felt it might give them a chance to prospect again in the North.

With two nests of dories lashed to the deck, the *Pato* sailed for Petropavlovsk, the Russian port of entry for Kamchatka. It is on the eastern side of the peninsula, and the run from Hong Kong was 2900 miles. I have noted before that the Pacific is an ocean of long distances. The *Pato* sailed through the Formosa Strait where she met the great fleet of trading and fishing junks crossing back over to Swatow, Amoy, and other innumerable rocky havens on the southern coast of China. A strong no'easter was blowing down channel. We were on the starboard tack, bucking into it, and the junks were scudding with a free sheet across our bows. They held to windward and did not need to use lee boards. Starboard tack and the rule of the road meant nothing to these Chinamen, who have rules of their own. Several times we were obliged to luff up sharp to pass close under the sterns of some of the junks, giving us a chance to see these craft in heavy weather, passing close aboard to windward. We could answer their friendly gestures and even hear their shouts. The windward work of the *Pato* evidently excited them. These south coast junks looked very wide and able. Their sails were of closely woven brown matting and seemed well adapted to their purpose, reefing and handing with flexibility. The entire quarterdeck over the cabin is used by the helmsman who steers with a very long tiller and a purchase. As each thrashed by, their gear showed admirable tautness and their hulls a wonderful buoyancy, taking not a feather of spray over the weather rail while the *Pato* was sinking her bowsprit into it.

Tsu Shima, in the strait between Japan and Korea was left on the port hand, and next we sighted the Oki Islands, where some fishermen, out in their big sampans, good-naturedly hove some cod aboard of the *Pato*, which we took to be a good omen. Then we put in at Wakanai, at the Strait of La Perouse, for water and fresh provisions. This was the northernmost point of Japan and we had been 25 days at sea and covered about 2000 miles. Rounding Cape Soya, which is the actual termination of Yezo, the *Pato* entered the Okhotsk for the first time and steered westward for Yatrup, the nearest of the volcanic Kuriles. Here, a landing party at Shama brought back with them a miniature Buddhist temple which they had found on the shore and which I afterwards learned to prize highly. Parties of Japanese fishermen carry portable shrines about with them for good luck and this one might have been abandoned in a hurried

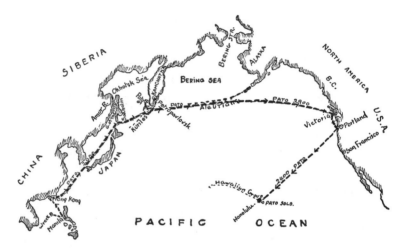

The schooner Pato's *Okhotsk Sea fishing voyage which covered 8200 miles in the North Pacific*

departure. Three days of sailing under the lee of these islands brought the *Pato* into Amphitrite Strait where she entered the Pacific and encountered chill winds and heavy fogs.

The next morning, my mother, all aglow with excitement, called me on deck to see the high, conical peak of Mount Villuchinski, white and glistening in the morning sunlight, high above the fog drifting upon the sea. It was 7000 feet in elevation and 20 miles away. It was one of the sights never to be forgotten in one's lifetime. When the fog lifted we made out a

The B. Aymar, one of the early commands of Captain Slocum, and after whom he named one of his sons.

(Above) The Amethyst, on which Captain Slocum traded for timber in the South Seas in 1882. Illustrated by Charles Rosner.

(Below) Captain Slocum with the Gilbert Island missionaries rescued by him.

Bully Hayes, as a bearded, candle-carrying Franciscan monk, in the midst of his career which included roles as blackbirder, highjacker, Protestant mis-sionary and South Seas racketeer. From an illustration by Walter Appleton Clark.

The Northern Light, from a portrait by Charles Robert Patterson. The Northern Light was considered the finest American ship afloat in its time and was a favorite command of Captain Slocum.

high and bold coast with a line of rugged cliffs hundreds of feet above the sea. The pinnacles of the rocks were literally hidden by the clouds of sea birds that make their homes among them, while at the base were herds of basking and barking sea lions. It certainly looked like the right place to come for any sort of sea life.

If the coast outside was forbidding, the aspect of Avacha Bay, on rounding the heads, was exactly the opposite. Here was one of the perfect harbors of the world, comparable with Rio, Sydney, or Halifax; a fine sheet of water twenty miles in extent. In the summer it is closed in with green slopes to delight the eye of the mariner, wind and sea worn.

Petropavlovsk was beyond the jutting end of a sand spit which formed a bottle-like entrance to a landlocked pool on the north side of the bay. Here the *Pato* rounded to and came to anchor to receive the official visit of the Captain of the Port in order to establish her identity and to show valid reason for invading that distant outpost in the domains of the Czar. This official, as all other Russian officials we ever met in the East, was very affable and spoke excellent English. The formalities over, the family was invited to his headquarters and to a ramble over historic ground. He was not surprised, he said, at the entrance of fishing vessels from San Francisco, for the cod fleet had found it an advantage to quit the Shumagins for the Okhotsk grounds. Several had just come over, he said. Moreover, the *Pato*, being from Hong Kong, was a welcome courier of home news for they had but one mail a year which came overland from Moscow.

The setting of Petropavlovsk is very striking. There is nothing like it in any other port in the world that I know of. Right back of the beach we found a scattered village of log houses with red roofs which stood out from the rich green of the background of hills rising to a considerable height. Back of a valley was the snow-capped Mount Avacha, its 11,000 feet of altitude dwarfing the adjacent mountain ranges. When the *Pato* was there the population was 300, natives and all, who, both directly and indirectly, lived by salmon and furs. Salmon was the principal food. Even the horses and cows learned to subsist and thrive on dried salmon when their natural fodder was wanting. The bears, which were numerous enough to enter the village after an unusually hard winter, lived in the salmon streams to such an extent as to impart a fishy flavor to their meat. Salmon and bear are all very well separately but the combination we found confusing to the palate.

Petropavlovsk, before the Crimean War, had a population of 1000, but it was nearly destroyed by the Allies, who shamelessly attacked this isolated settlement and brought only misery upon a few Kamachadales. At first they were gallantly repulsed by the fleet and a Cossack guard, but after the Russian Government removed its establishment to Nikolaevsk, the Allied forces returned to raze the earth batteries and to burn most of the houses. The settlement after that was left to get on the best way it could.

On the beach, opposite the village, were the bones of a vessel long wrecked. There were a number of wolf-like dogs sneaking about, but they knew what a stick looked like. The house of the main official, into which we were shown with true Russian hospitality, was both high and commodious. My father, on hearing that the harbor was frozen over from November to May, was interested to know how they managed to keep the house comfortably warm in the winter. It was explained to him that the heating was effectively done by the *peechka*, a large chimney which nearly filled the center of the house. It was a combination of oven and fireplace, presenting a heating surface to every apartment. The *peechka* was a development and expansion of the *chual* used by the more northern Siberian Yakuts in their yourts. The primitive Yakuts, not yet having learned to make bricks, made their fireplaces of a cluster of small poles covered by many successive coatings of clay, so that they resisted fire and radiated heat and light to all parts of the room, and were massive enough to retain warmth for many hours. The Russians caught on to the idea, but with the use of brick were able to build a more efficient heater. The Russian *peechka* is much like an ordinary bake oven, but before escaping up the chimney, the heat and smoke are conducted through many flues winding about through the mass of masonry in such a manner as to get it thoroughly heated. When the fire dies out, the chimney is closed and the greater part of the heat retained for radiation. After being fed with fuel all day the *peechka* would supply heat for all night.

Our host told us some of the history of the place. He said it was from here that Bering sailed under orders personally issued by Peter the Great to explore Alaska. At that time, in 1740, they still thought that Alaska was an island, but Bering discovered that it was part of the American continent. Bering, who was a Dane in the employ of the Czar, arrived at Okhotsk with a caravan containing equipment, stores and personnel for two ships to be built for the expedition at that point. The transit across Russia and Siberia took many months. With the two ships built at Okhotsk and which were named the St. Peter and the St. Paul, he put into Avacha Bay to establish a base on the east coast of Kamchatka. That is how Petropavlovsk happened to be founded and so named.

Some of the *Pato's* people explored the ruined earth works on the heights of the small birch-wooded peninsula. These were the remains of the old Russian batteries along the crest of the ridge which divides the inner from the outer bay. They once commanded the approaches to the settlement. As we rambled among the birch, one of the men showed me how to make a whistle from a twig cut from one of the trees. We looked over the very cliff over which an enemy storming party was hurled to destruction on the rocky beach a hundred feet below. The Cossack bayonets, ambushed in this same copse of birch, were a complete surprise. On the beach in front, we found three old cannon balls which were no doubt relics of the engagement between the ships. These were added to the ballast of the *Pato*.

On leaving for the fishing grounds we had as passenger an old native sea otter hunter. He was almost like a sea otter himself, wrinkled and weather-beaten from exposure. Everything was tied on him, even his long and ancient looking gun had the lock tied on with seal gut, and a fork of resting sticks was tied to the fore part of the arm. But no doubt he could shoot straight for all of his looks. The *Pato* came up into the wind off Shumshir Island, in the Kurile Strait, and landed him in a dory.

When the *Pato* explored the banks she found good ground not far from Cape Lopatka. In searching for cod banks the fisherman generally follows the trend of the land, or runs in lines parallel with it. The *Pato* was cruising along that way, my father at the wheel, making a trial cast with a hand line at frequent intervals. It was here that the writer took an active part in the prospective fishing. There was no one on deck but my father who read my mind in an instant as I came on deck and spied the wet line coiled up under the lee rail close to his side. "Don't you touch that!" he admonished. The minute he looked the other way, overboard went the line, hooks and sinker.

"Didn't I tell you not to touch that? Now, haul it in," he commanded. With my little six-year-old arms, I might as well have tried to pull up Kamchatka. Jumping from the wheel he

100

took hold of the line himself, with the remark, "Guess you've got something on it." There were two cod; one of them proving to be the largest taken on the whole voyage. Entirely forgetting my disobedience to orders, he sang out for the crew to come on deck. In came the jibs and down went the anchor in twenty fathoms. The *Pato* had arrived on the Okhotsk Grounds.

Ours were two-man dories that laid out trawls radially from the schooner. A trawl consists of a warp two hundred fathoms long with hooks fastened to it, at intervals of two fathoms. It is anchored at each end, and is under-run by the dory crew who pick off the fish and re-bait the hooks as they go along. This method is efficient and covers the most ground.

When the *Pato* was taking in supplies in Hong Kong, the amount of salt was limited to the requirements of a small catch of fish for the Manila market, but when she started to pull them in, it began to look as if the catch would be large enough to carry to the West Coast profitably. But what about salt?

Luck was with the *Pato* again, for along came the *Constitution* of the Frisco fleet, just loaded, and about to shovel overboard enough unused salt to make up the *Pato's* quota. This waste was belayed, and the salt shoveled into the *Pato's* hold.

While the dories were spread out working the trawls, there were always hand lines at the rail of the vessel. The cook and the extra man on board had theirs, as did the Captain and my mother. Each kept a tally of his catch. Everybody on board, big and little, fished, for it was exciting. The sinker no sooner touched bottom than you had one. The youngest member of the crew, little Jessie, proved to be a high liner by hauling in a fish that was more than a million years old. It made quite a sensation.

While mother was in Alaska she collected some fossil fish which the natives brought to her as curios, and one of these,

101

with the fish knives perhaps, followed us into the *Pato*. When Jessie saw the others pulling in their share of fish, she tied a string to the fossil, furtively lowered it over the side, and then cried out with a great to do, "See what Jessie caught, see what Jessie caught!" It pleased her father hugely, who, after that, regarded her as one of his sailors. He was fond of a joke himself.

In two weeks the schooner was loaded to her marks with 25,000 cod salted down and as the West Coast quotations were expected to continue high it was easy to decide which way to take the fare.

When the fishing was over, hundreds of sea birds still swam about the vessel, cocking an eye in vain for more dinner. The waste from the splitting tables had been a feast for them, mostly gulls and divers. These last astonished us by their ability and speed under water, using their thin narrow wings and propelling flippers, making it difficult to determine just where the bird ended and the fish began.

The voyage to Victoria, B. C., was another 2900 mile run, and followed the general curve of the Aleutian Islands. This afforded interesting sailing and a great circle track at the same time. A landing party on one of the Aleutians brought back some geese. One of the men, who had the only rifle among them, thought he would stay ashore and follow up a bear track which was fresh and led up over the cliffs. In an hour he hailed from the beach and when he tumbled over the rail he was covered with mud and badly shocked from fright. His rifle was filled with mud as well, but no one could get anything out of him further than that he had found the bear. It was clear, however, that he must have plunged headlong down the soft clay on the side of the cliff, with the bear stopping at the top.

On arriving at Victoria, B. C., my father decided to register the vessel at that port. The name and hailing port were painted on the stern to make it regular. After *"Pato"* and *"Victoria"* they carefully put "B. C.," all in bold and well-cut white letters.

Some time afterwards, in Oregon, I overheard a couple of bystanders speculating on just what "B. C." meant and they seriously concluded that it was "Before Christ." They were very probably Missourians who were then moving into Oregon in considerable numbers, the covered wagon then being a familiar sight. It was not likely that these two had ever heard of British Columbia.

I never knew where the *Pato* originally hailed from. As Mr. Jackson, who built and owned her first, was a Britisher, he naturally flew his own flag. As Hong Kong was the nearest British port it was more than likely that the *Pato* was made to hail from there rather than Manila. My father continued to hoist the British flag instead of applying to his own consulate for colors, because no flag was so safe as the British for protection against the cupidity and arrogant insolence of the Spaniards who then ruled the Philippines. The British knew how to handle them while an American was simply out of luck. Among the Spaniards, an alleged minor infraction of the Customs regulations meant confiscation of a vessel, as happened to the *Masonic*. The real trouble lay in Washington where they had not yet quite found out there was any such place as the Philippine Islands. As long as my father owned the *Pato* she flew the British flag.

Only a short stop was made at Victoria before reaching the final decision to take the fare to Portland. The schooner was towed up the Columbia by a stern wheeler. On the way up to Portland our towboat, to effect some minor repairs, beached by running full speed up on the river's bank.

"That looks all right," exclaimed my father to the steamboat man, "but how are you going to get her off?"

"You'll see how we'll get 'er off."

And we did. When they were ready it proved to be simply a matter of churning up a backwash with the wheel, until it made a canal to float off in. Those stern wheelers knew their river.

This was the first cargo of salt cod to be brought into Portland, and I have since heard that as a matter of record it was the last as well. But not because it was unprofitable. Here the Captain obtained a credit which enabled him to settle with the crew on the basis of the San Francisco market quotations. The family came in for its share as well, and my mother was as enthusiastic as any of them. Her share from hand lining over the rail came to sixty dollars, just enough to buy a Singer sewing machine.

My father's trading instincts led him to decide to ignore the middle-man and market the fare himself. For this purpose the *Pato* was taken to East Portland where a suitable place was found for the curing and packing.

The few months that the *Pato* was in East Portland was the writer's first experience, really, in living on land. Life at Olongapo of course was ashore, but that was different.

Our means for reaching Portland, across the Willamette, was by the Stark Street Ferry, a punt which was operated by a winch and chain. The winch was in the punt and the chain ran over a wildcat cranked by the ferry crew. This primitive cross-river transportation could never be imagined by anyone viewing the intricate mass of bridgework now in the same location.

While the cargo was being marketed we all lived in the upper part of a Mr. Newall's house, very near to where the vessel was docked. Mrs. Newall bred canaries, one of which she presented to my mother. His name was Peter and Peter was to live longer than his mistress. It was our united chore to care for Peter, and he was a beautiful singer. The Newalls had a son, Rufus, who was slightly older than I, so he did not show any interest in me other than to oblige my mother by showing me the way to school. The few months in East Portland were my first and practically my only taste of a regular school. To be sure that I was correctly registered, mother wrote my full name on a piece of paper. I knew that my name was Victor but I was not so sure about the other one. It was a graded school and my end of the curriculum was the ABC chart, which became more comprehensible during the month that I was there. I enjoyed mixing with boys my own size and kind, in studies, at lunch and at recess, when we played fort in the wood shed. I enjoyed the smell of the Oregon wood, so much more agreeable to the nostrils than the noxious tropical timber I had lately been associated with.

As the packing crew sealed up the cured fish in tin boxes for distribution, my father, now turned travelling salesman, went on the road carrying as a sample an honest unbleached Okhotsk cod by the tail. That was his style. (Much later, after he came home in the *Spray,* I saw him do the same thing in New York, when he carried a Cape Cod turkey by the tail, unwrapped, from Fulton market along Broadway to 12th Street.) At first he found that on account of their rather dark color, his fish were not popular and that the buyers were inclined toward the alum-bleached cod which were already on the market. On seeing this obstruction ahead he skillfully put his wheel down and came about on the tack of a pure food advocate. Thereafter he carried two cod by their tails, one bleached and the other unbleached, to prove the difference. He believed in his own product, made others feel it, and successfully sold the whole cargo at a handsome profit.

Though the Okhotsk experience was interesting and profitable, it was decided not to repeat it. Distance to the Okhotsk

105

Sea was too great for so small a vessel. Besides, the *Pato* was really part of a Philippine project which the Captain had in mind at the time of the sale of the *B. Aymar* in Manila. That was to engage in the timber business with China. There were good prospects in that direction, for the secretary of the Celestial Navy, or his equivalent in office, had decided to supplant his gorgeous and picturesque mandarin war junks with wooden war vessels of a more modern kind. In other words, a new Chinese navy was being built and the prices for Philippine timber were good.

With a view to selling the *Pato* in the Hawaiian Islands, we sailed to Honolulu, and there the family was again settled ashore. During this time the *Pato* made several trips, inter-island, and the chance to sell her came about in an unexpected way. The crack mail schooner, *Hilo*, had just left the dock, and was well out of the narrow coral entrance to Honolulu, when a belated sack of mail was rushed down. But the vessel was gone. There was consternation, of course. As the *Pato* was casting off her lines, my father joined in the spirit of the occasion by calling out, "Heave aboard here, I'll take it out to her." Beat the *Hilo?* Nothing like that was ever heard among the Islands, but the messenger, who thought he saw a joke, handed the sack over.

The *Pato* cast off and made sail amid cheers from the dock. Then a piece of sailing took place which could not be appreciated by the onlookers. The wind was blowing in gusts from the mountain slopes. One such gust had just passed the *Hilo* and she lay rolling with flapping sails. As the *Pato* cleared the reef, she picked up the beginning of the succeeding gust, which heeled her over and drove her with great speed toward the motionless *Hilo*. The throng on the wharf saw the *Pato* bearing down upon their champion like a train of cars. Then she blanketed the *Hilo* and the sack of mail was tossed aboard. The *Pato* was more than a match for the *Hilo* anyway, for the *Sappho* stuff was there, but it took the turn of a spectacular race to make her reputation.

A victory such as this could not be kept out of the papers, and the fame of the *Pato* was spread abroad. Finally my father received an offer in gold which met his approval, and he at once engaged passage to San Francisco in the German bark *Christine,* about to sail. We were all on board on sailing day when a hitch developed in the proceedings. The planter who was buying the *Pato* attempted at the very last to substitute silver, which was low in exchange, for the gold agreed upon. For this adjustment the sailing was held up an hour while negotiations were being concluded. At last the Captain was seen striding down the dock with the bag. It was gold. My mother was sitting on the after deck in a wide rattan chair when the bag was tossed into her lap with—"Virginia, there's the schooner."

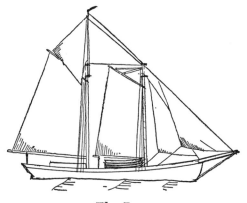

The Pato

CHAPTER 8

The *Amethyst:*

Timber Trading in the Pacific

The trip back to San Francisco from Honolulu, in the *Christine,* was across a fine weather belt, and without unusual incident. Captain Schulze, a well disposed man, made his passengers feel at home, or as nearly at home as sea-going passengers could be made to feel. To make it more enjoyable for my mother, Mrs. Schulze was aboard and they became lifelong friends. The isolated life which my mother lived deprived her of the companionship of other women which she should have had. We became interested in the German crew and officers, the latter using good English. Mr. Felike, the second mate, had been a hussar in the Franco-Prussian War. He had a sabre with which he had killed a Frenchman. He had never wiped it off, and he was proud of the blood stains of seven years' standing, on the point of the blade. He, as well as all the other Germans, regarded this consecrated weapon as a symbol of patriotism. Though a good sailor and a reliable officer, he had a great fondness for terrifying Mrs. Schulze by relating to her tales of shipwrecks and of his own escapes from death and disaster. We heard long afterwards, through the chief mate, that Captain Schulze got rid of Felike in a Mexican port, for that very reason.

The German way of living was new to us. On our ships we had never carried any other live stock than chickens. When about half way over, the Germans slaughtered and dressed a pig, and that meant a great feast, fore and aft. About all that was wasted of that pig was the squeal. When the steward set the tureen before Captain Schulze, he got ready for it with an expression of satisfaction.

"This is blood soup, don't you like it?," was his interrogatory explanation to my father, who had unconsciously registered repulsion. The German was both surprised and disappointed and could not understand why an American could not appreciate such a delicacy.

On the *Christine* I saw the chip-log used for the first and only time, for my father regarded it as a relic of the Ark.

In San Francisco, my father at once negotiated for a vessel which would be suitable for the China-Philippine Island timber trade, and hit upon the *Amethyst*. She was my father's fifth vessel and for three years he employed her in the China trade exclusively. With the exception of the sloop *Spray*, in which he later sailed single-handed around the world, this was the most interesting vessel he ever had.

The best thing about the *Amethyst* was that she was built by Thatcher Magoun of Medford, Massachusetts. Because of the fact she was the product of that particular builder's yard, her fifty-six years, when my father bought her in San Francisco, did not mean a thing. In accordance with the practices of that era of solid ship construction, she was framed with seasoned live oak, copper fastened, and planked with native white oak, cut not far from the spot she was built. She was good for an-other fifty-six years if kept clear of rocks and ice floes.

Both ship and builder had interesting backgrounds. Magoun was the first to establish a regular shipyard on the Mystic River. He laid down eighty-four vessels between 1802 and 1836. His family came originally from Scotland; the ancestor, John, settling in Hingham, Massachusetts, about 1665. Thatcher learned his trade in Brigg's yard in Salem, later came to Boston and worked with Humphreys, laying down the lines of the *Constitution*. After the launch of the famous frigate, he went to work in Barker's yard in Charlestown, which afterwards be-came the Boston Navy Yard.

At Barker's, Magoun spent much of his time in the mold loft and assisted at the modelling. While there he made the model of the first vessel which he was going to build in the great shipyard he was to found in 1802. That vessel was the *Mount Aetna* of Medford. Magoun's ship shed was one hundred feet high and contained stocks for two vessels, which could be built at once. Besides this, his plant contained a joiner and a blacksmith shop. The live oak for the frames was pro-cured from the South; the other timber for the construction was found in the immediate vicinity and was cut down where towns stand now.

Ships of that time were very thoroughly kneed and through bolted, making for the homogenous fabric which could be "rolled down hill without hurting," as the saying then was. On going down into the hold you would find shining copper bolt heads in knees, breasthooks, crutches and deadwoods. There are very few remaining examples of this form of construction, which made for a solid ship. The only one I know of in this country is our frigate *Constitution*, in which Magoun had a

111

hand in the building, in 1797. An inspection of the *Constitution's* hanging horizontal and diagonal system of kneeing off, will, on a large scale, give one some idea of how Thatcher Magoun's vessels were built.

The ship *Amethyst* was built in 1822 for the Jewell Line of Boston. She was 100 feet long, 28 feet beam and 18 feet depth of hold and registered 400 tons, which was not considered small for a ship in her day. Her owners at that period were operating a fleet of three other full rigged ships; the *Topaz*, *Emerald* and the *Sapphire*. The *Amethyst* was built as a regular transatlantic packet carrying cargo and passengers, and was regarded as tops in New England shipbuilding of the time. Her cabins were below deck and were handsomely fitted up in mahogany and horsehair, then stylish. In common with all packet ships she had bluff bows adapted for such voyages and she made some very fast passages, one being seventeen days from Liverpool to Boston. This round voyage was so unusually short it was said in Boston that on hearing his vessel was coming in, one of the owners hurried down to the wharf to find out why the captain had turned around and come back. It was only when he showed the owner some recent Liverpool papers that he could be convinced a round trip had been made. This record was held by the *Amethyst* for thirty years when it was finally beaten by a ship three or four times her tonnage. The early 400-ton packets were all forced out of the traffic by the preponderance in both tonnage and sail area of the famous clippers.

The *Amethyst,* sold in New Bedford, became a whaler and made some successful cruises around the world. Entering the Pacific, she engaged in equatorial sperm whaling and made summer voyages to the Bering Straits hunting bowhead. Then, less romantic days fell upon the old vessel when she was turned into a collier to ply between Puget Sound and San Francisco.

When my father, as the new owner, took over, work was at once started fitting her for the timber business. After coppering, a new deck was laid to replace the old one badly chewed up by wear. Then her bluff bow was pierced for the loading port. Complete new running gear was rove off and a new suit of sails ordered, for it was customary to carry at least three suits of sails on foreign voyages: one, the best, for heavy weather; the second best for light breezes; and the old rags for slamming about in a calm. This last treatment was very bad for new sails. The everlasting bending on of different sails and the replacement of chafed gear makes the major part of a sailor's labor at sea. Sending down and bending on a course or a topsail takes all hands.

As soon as we had debarked from the *Christine* in San Francisco and bid good-bye to our German friends, we took up quarters at the Clipper Hotel and for three or four months lived a town life. The hotel was at the foot of Market Street and not far from the water front where the unforgettable Sacramento steamer docked. For a half hour before sailing each day she played the Prison Song from 'Il Trovatore' on a lusty and full-lunged 'calyope.' That was how the San Franciscans got their grand opera. The small steam organ which used to play at the tail of a circus parade could be harsh and strident enough, but the one on the Sacramento boat had the full pressure of a marine boiler for inspiration.

"The Chinese Must Go" slogan of the Denis Kearney faction made things lively while we were in San Francisco. Chinese had been imported in large numbers by the builders of the Union Pacific Railroad and when that work was done the "Heathen Chinee" immortalized by Bret Harte, was ruthlessly turned loose to compete with West Coast labor.

Repatriation might have been the answer to the problem but forcible expulsion and violence were the only remedies advocated by the hoodlum terrorists of San Francisco. Kearney harangued his followers in a remote section of the city called "the sand lots" (Sand Lot Riots), and on the night when the grand slam was supposed to be pulled off, Kearney headed a torchlight demonstration which halted under our windows at the Clipper Hotel. The mob had unhitched the horses from Kearney's open barouche, and with much cheering dragged it along by hand. My father, who had no sympathy for Kearney or his methods, had an overmature egg ready for him as an expression of his opinion, but my mother dragged father away from the window by the coat tails and told him that if he threw it and hit Kearney (as no doubt he would as the distance was short and the projector's aim pretty good), the mob would burn down the hotel. Mother was very likely right. The situation looked very serious for the peace of the city and an attack on the Chinese that night was only averted by the appearance of the Militia upon the scene. Then Kearney tried to crash the gate on General Grant at the Palace Hotel, where he was very pointedly snubbed. After that, Kearney lost his following and there was no more anti-Chinese trouble in San Francisco.

During the period of waiting for the reconditioning of the *Amethyst,* my father left his family in San Francisco and went to visit his old home in Nova Scotia. He did not see his father that time, he having re-married and removed from Brier Island to the Ovens near Lunenburg. On returning, my father brought with him his youngest brother and sister, Ingram and Ella, who were to sail with us to the Far East. Uncle Ingram was to spend the rest of his life on the Pacific, first becoming purser in a Japanese company and then under the British flag, in the White Star Line, with headquarters in San Francisco.

The railroad journey across the Continent at that time was in the nature of an adventure and the Captain took a keen interest in everything he saw during his travels overland. On the way East, at Altoona, Pa., he resented an annoyance to a lady who was travelling alone. When the train pulled into the station, he settled with the fellow as soon as he confronted him on the platform. It was a biting, frosty morning and he said he felt extra athletic. He knocked the intruder cold. It was soon generally understood what the fracas was all about, and along came the head waiter to conduct the Captain to the hotel for refreshments at the railroad's expense.

"Colonel," he said, "you'se the man to travel on 'dis here railroad!"

He later received a polite note from the lady's brother in acknowledgment of the courtesy.

While travelling, he acted as correspondent for the San Francisco *Bee*, for he was taking an interest in public affairs and was always writing. We find an account in the *Bee* of his visit in Washington to President Hayes, whom he found at the "helm of the Ship of State."

"How does she steer?" asked the Captain.

"She gripes," returned the President.

Gradually we changed our quarters from the hotel to the vessel and began to feel ready for sea again, for we were becoming a seagoing family all around. Uncle Ingram was shipped as cook. He was a slim six foot two and the caboose galley on the *Amethyst* was about five foot two but there was a scuttle in the roof right over the standing place before the range. Chief mate was Mr. Golder of Bath, Maine, and we are to hear of his remarkable adventures later on. He was a natural rover who seemed to know no fear, especially of cannibals. He was a full bearded man of medium height, heavily built and

115

with a punch like a pile driver, rather slow of speech like most determined men of action. He took time to think, and then did it.

My Aunt Ella, at that time a young woman of eighteen, had all she could do helping mother with her growing family. Before seeing the East again, Aunt Ella was to become a world traveller.

On the voyage across the Pacific to Manila, a stop was made at Honolulu to discharge a cargo of badly stowed railroad iron, and also to land a party of planters who were emigrating to the Hawaiian Islands. This transaction more than paid for the entire trip across, but the way the *Amethyst* rolled was a matter of comment for some time after. In the effort to stow the cargo in such a way as not to make the vessel too stiff, so much was placed in the 'tween decks that she became crank, but not enough to make her unsafe. Railroad iron is considered to be a bad cargo no matter how you take it.

In Honolulu Mr. Golder, our mate, left us, very much to our regret, for he was a good sailor and a valuable man. On the way to Honolulu he made me a small model of a schooner, hollowed out, decked, and with a main hatch that would come off so you could see below. It was carefully rigged and looked very smart and I cherished it for a very long time afterwards.

In Honolulu there was a schooner anchored near us which looked as though she was built from the model, a smart fishing vessel from Gloucester, out from round the Horn to become a Bering Sea seal poacher. The owners in Honolulu were in the market for a skipper who would care to take over that kind of job, and Golder thought he would fit into it. Anyway it suited his temperament. My father did all he could to get it for him. I ran across Golder some ten years afterwards in Montevideo, when he was mate of the fine bark *Harvard* and I was "flag captain" of the *Aquidneck*. He told me all about the poacher.

"After I left the *Amethyst*," he related, "I took the schooner to Hakodate, where we got ready for the Russian Islands" (Commander Islands). "There were three white men aboard, the rest were Japanese used to seal poaching, which is a branch of sealing all in itself.

"We worked an island that was leased by the Russians to a syndicate and they protected the syndicate's interests by maintaining a guard schooner to keep watch and cruise about the islands. I watched the schooner and when I thought it was well out of the way, I'd dive for the rookery and clean up. The island had a high peak and I put a man up there with a spyglass when I landed the crew on the beach, to look out for that guard schooner. I knew that I could outsail him when it came to a chase but the point was not to let him see me at all and get reported at Petropavlovsk. Once the guard schooner nearly caught me on the beach, and I think he must have seen the end of my boom as I was swinging around the island, for I saw the end of his bowsprit coming around the other side. But there were no carcasses on the beach for him to see. What we had, we hove into the boats and skinned them down in the hold. We made some good hauls and it paid. The skins were turned over to a bank in Hong Kong, which sent them to London. Seal was ten dollars a skin, and sea otter seventy-five dollars.

"In the winter we didn't lose any time but traded with the Gilbert Islanders for copra. We put in a regular trade room and rigged a boarding net as soon as we came to an island. That is the way schooners do because they have such low rails. If the natives start to rush up the net, you can get them through the meshes. At the gangway there was a hole in the netting and a man with a revolver on each side. We let just one come through at a time.

"One day there I had trouble. It was on account of the king's prime minister. He was a bad one. Even the king was afraid of him, for he had great control over the people. A little while before I came to the island, a Chinese junk had drifted onto the beach and the natives murdered the whole of them. The prime minister was the leader in that.

"Well, as soon as I anchored, I sent a square face of Dutch gin ashore to the king as an opening gift, but the prime minister got hold of it first. He came off with the king, primed and ugly. When we got down into the cabin he wanted more gin. I refused, and he began to flourish his knife and set up a war yell. The others started to get excited. I knew that had to be stopped, so I slipped up alongside and socked him right behind the ear. He dropped in a heap, and the king jumped up and cried, 'Kill him damn him, kill him damn him!' The king had learned some English from the missionaries and he wanted me to polish off his minister right then and there. He could have done it himself and I wouldn't have stopped him, but he was scared of the power the fellow had over the people. I sang out for the Japs and they threw him, still unconscious, into his canoe, and the whole lot of them skedaddled. It was seeing their champion go down before the bare fist of a white man that queered the business, for they didn't come near us again and I laid there for two days.

"We were doing well with the sealing next summer, but the end had to come, for the guard schooner spotted us. Next thing we knew there was the smoke of a steamer over the edge of the horizon, and we knew it was a Russian man o' war from the Petropavlovsk station. He didn't have far to come and there was not much time to get ready for him. If they found as much as a hair in the hold it would have meant the Siberian salt mines for all the white men. There were a thousand seal and twenty-five sea otter down in the hold. They all went over the side, and the hold swept and hatches on again.

"When the Russian officer came aboard he looked over the deck and at the numerous Jap crew but didn't take the trouble to look into the hold. He knew better. I tried to make things easier by showing him my false log, but he merely observed, 'I take it that you are a pretty good pilot in these waters and you will be taken in tow.'

"He towed us to Vladivostok where the authorities seized the schooner but discharged the crew and all hands. They were very decent though, didn't touch any of our personal things and they even allowed me to keep my sextant and gold chronometer watch."

That was Golder's yarn.

To come back to the *Amethyst:* The second leg of the voyage across the Pacific was to Guam, where fresh water and supplies were taken aboard. Rounding the reefs to the northward of Apra, the *Amethyst* was met outside by a whaleboat manned by the Spanish pilot and his crew of natives. On filling away the main topsail the boat was taken in tow but it pulled apart before we came to an anchor off the landing. We could see the bottom under us and all about was green and luxuriant vegetation in profusion. Our decks were soon loaded with bananas, yams, papayas, breadfruit, and many other of the good things that grow on this bountiful island.

My father put ashore in his own boat and took the pilot with him. Together they started to ride by bull cart to Agana, the capital and the port of entry at the same time. They wound painfully around the five miles of coral road along the shore and through some native villages. The road was hot and the high wheels of the bull cart grew harder and noisier. The wheels turned slower as the craft began to take the steeper grade near the end of the road. "That Yahoo bit the carabao's tail whenever he got tired of twisting it," declared the Captain when he gave his reasons for becoming disgusted and getting out to walk. He found the natives very like the Malays of the Philippines, indolent by nature and cruel to their animals. He had been reading Swift and "Yahoo" had become an epithet for certain occasions.

Guam is the southermost of the Ladrones, a fine tropical island of moderate height, about thirty miles long and with some good anchorages. It was well known to the early navigators as a good place to seek in order to recuperate from scurvy, ever since Magellan discovered and named the group in 1521. The town of Agana with its heavy masonry buildings and red tiled roofs is one of the oldest of the Spanish seats in that part of the world. The Spaniards forgot Guam for a century after they discovered it and then it became a stopping place for the Manila-Acapulco galleons. Agana was then taken seriously. The last galleon passed in 1815, and due to the lack of contact with the outside world, which followed, the once promising settlement fell asleep. It grew to be more typically Spanish and to remain so longer than any other place in the Spanish colonies. Communications were so infrequent that even as late as 1898 the Governor of Guam did not know anything about the war with America, until the U.S.S. *Charleston* came to capture his island. He thought the gun fired by the warship on entering Apra was a salute, and the punctilious Spaniard actually apologized to Captain Glass for being unable to return the courtesy. It was like comic opera, and that was Guam in a nutshell.

Instead of using the Strait of San Bernardino, the *Amethyst* made the passage from Guam to Manila around the north end of Luzon; the open navigation and favorable winds more than compensated for the difference of an extra two hundred miles of sailing in a square-rigger. In Manila the Captain renewed some personal and business friendships and found no trouble in establishing credit with the banking house of Peele, Hubble and Company for a cargo which was to be supplied by Mr. Henry Brown, the timber merchant of Lagumanoc in the Province of Tayabas.

Lagumanoc is on the north side of Tayabas Bay, and at the mountainous isthmus which joins the southern end of Luzon with the Camarines Peninsula. The high volcanic ridge, extending for many miles between Luzon and its peninsula, sustains a forest of valuable hard woods which is probably the finest in the world. In it are tropical woods of nearly every description: Ebony, Camagon, Narra, and Tindalo, for fine cabinet work; and at least fifty varieties of timber for building purposes. Of these last were a few that were in special demand for ship timber. At the head of these was Molave, equal to our live oak in many ways, and in addition it was proof against the sea worm and the white ant as well. It came in logs 35 feet long by 24 inches square, often crooked, which made it all the more suitable for ship frames. There was Betis, another anti-seaworm wood, straight and long, for keels; Antipolo, still another anti-seaworm wood, for under water planking; Dugan, the iron wood, which sinks like a stone, and while not anti-seaworm was very strong, durable and good for keelsons; Batitinan, for the outside planking of ships; together with Luan, which was used to plank the Manila galleons because the Spaniards discovered that it did not splinter with shot; the tall Mangachapuy, springy and durable for masts and decks. The other woods were Ipil, Bansalangue, and Banaba, all useful in their places.

We learned from Mr. Brown that he had to maintain a very large force of native woodsmen as tree fellers and cutters to ensure a reliable supply of timber to meet the market. After

121

the manner of their kind they expected to work only when paid a month in advance. Besides obliging him to follow them up to see that they worked at all, this arrangement took considerable ready cash. He had a sense of humor, however, and did not let it worry him. His genial and easy disposition made him very popular with his native crews, both in the forest and on the beach.

Lagumanoc has a very good little harbor and the village of nipa-thatched houses is set upon a well drained promontory above the beach, making a very desirable place to live. Here Mr. Brown had the most pretentious house, presided over by his native wife, the Senora, and her retinue of servants and relatives. On account of our racial and linguistic differences, this lady was rather shy of her husband's customers and preferred to receive us at her house rather than to come off aboard the *Amethyst*. In her own home it was easy to see who held the wheel, for Europeans find native wives perfect housekeepers and thrifty managers.

Mr. Brown was an amateur artist. His sketch book was full of clever drawings made during his timber cruising, and naturally the subjects related to wild life, some tragic, some amusing, for he often saw the funny side of things. In it were adventures of banca men on the rivers, with the crocodile and the boa; travelling carabao carts deep in the mud in the rainy season; cockfights; fiestas; bits showing the extreme luxuriance of the forest growth in the Atimonan region where he spent most of his time; trees, great and majestic, loaded with a profusion of hanging plants.

Mr. Brown was aboard nearly every day while we were loading and he seemed to enjoy the contact with our European home life on the vessel. Incidentally, it was from this gentleman that I received my first lessons in drawing. Pencil and paper were imported from Hong Kong. My mother, who was quite an artist herself, encouraged the idea.

One of my father's favorite stunts, in which we all joined, was the Sunday picnic. It was usually projected to some predetermined point, so the picnic was a sort of small exploring expedition. We used the ship's boat, manned by native oarsmen engaged for the day, my father being very careful not to interfere with the Sunday holiday of any of the crew who might have their own ideas of an outing. At Lagumanoc there was a small river bordered by large trees which gave a faint indication of what the great forest beyond was like. At a suitable open space on the bank of the river we would land for the picnic. It is by occasions such as these that I remember the Philippines the best.

The methods used by the natives in felling trees were as primitive as those used at Olongapo, and the native fellers used the same type of Malay axe with the extremely narrow bit and the same straight helve. Once felled, the logs were laboriously hewn square with these same narrow-bitted axes, preparatory to being dragged by carabao over many miles of mountain trails to the beach for shipment. Because the logs would sink, they had to be floated out to the ship on a raft called a *balsa*, the Spanish word for raft. The *balsa* consisted of two huge bundles of bamboo with poles lashed crosswise underneath on which to carry the logs. This floating gridiron was hauled from the beach to the ship by a long warp.

Occasionally, the logs would be sent down a river, and then the means of transportation would be a large *banca* (dugout canoe), with a pair of logs lashed under the outriggers on each side. This method was more uncertain, however, because a slop of water in the bay would easily sink the whole thing and then it would be a job to raise it again. An object on the bottom like

123

that, or an anchor, was easily seen against the white coral bottom in depths of ten or twelve fathoms.

When the *balsa* was hauled off it was taken under the vessel's bow with a line to the end of the jib boom, and the loading was done by two tackles, and all the heaving was done by hand; the heaviest purchase lifted the inboard end out of the water and landed it upon the bow port and then the tail purchase boosted it all the way into the hold. As it was wet and slippery it went into the hold by the run, without the need of rollers. Once in, it was taken in charge by the hold gang and properly stowed. This did not take as long as the heaving up, so there was a chance for a sit down in between. It was here that I got my first ideas of stowing cargo and a centipede bite on my bare foot as well, which was very painful for months to come. The bite swelled up every full moon for several moons.

The port bow once let in a boa for a rest from a long swim across the bay. These huge serpents travelled long distances by water and were quite common. They were also timid when not in the trees and at the cry of "cobra" the natives chased this one out of the hold and into the bay again with long bamboo poles.

There were several other points at which we gathered timber through the beautiful inland seas among the islands and one of these was Bantigui. While loading there the Captain, who always did a bit of timber cruising on his own, discovered a very large rosewood tree that grew on the slope of a hill, and he decided to cut it down. Authority to do so was contained in a permit issued to him by the Bureau of Forestry in Manila, so he landed a chopping gang. The tree was of great height and the roots were buttressed to such an extent that the chopping stage was high from the ground. After three days' work they cut it through, and we all went ashore to see it crash among the surrounding smaller trees when it fell. The labor was a bad speculation, however, for after again cutting the log in two it was still too unwieldy for the beach crew to launch in the water, and it had to be abandoned. It was estimated that it would have brought five thousand dollars in San Francisco, for bar tops.

It was at Bantigui that two natives brought off a large boa for sale in a *banca*. It was a small *banca* with the crew at each end and the boa, lashed head and tail and coiled around the outriggers, occupied the middle. The boa was lively and strained first at one lashing and then at the next, as long as it was alongside. It was a fearful thing and the sight of it threw my little brother, Ben, into a fit of hysterics. The natives had captured the serpent by a safe and ingenious method, using a live and vociferous pig for bait. The pig got away, though, leaving the would-be seeker of his bacon secure in a sort of elongated eel trap. Inside of the trap the boa was tied up with twisted rattan rope and handled by about as many men as could get around it. There must have been quite a crowd to coil the thing around the outriggers of the *banca* the way we saw it. Failing to sell it to the *Amethyst,* they probably made snake hide of it and ate the rest.

The lower end of Luzon, where we found most of the timber, is a field of active volcanoes, and earthquakes are frequent. The one which we experienced was at Atimonan, just across the isthmus from Lagumanoc. In plain view from the vessel was a large church with a tower which served as a useful landmark on entering the bay. It was a Sunday morning and nearly all the people in the town were at mass. The first sign of disturbance that we noticed was the rattling of the chains in the hawse pipes and then the vessel began to vibrate. On looking over the side we discovered the trouble. The water was boiling all over the bay. Then we heard a great and concerted cry as the worshippers swarmed out of the portals of the church, running, all with their arms in the air as if imploring Heaven for protection. And then we saw the tower sway from side to side several times. But in a few moments the tremor ceased, leaving the tower with a decided list to one side. The sight and sound were dreadful but no life was lost.

The Captain suspended a plumb bob in the rigging to demonstrate the list of the tower to the padres when they came aboard to lunch the next day, and then we were invited ashore to view the cracks made through the six foot walls. It is only by employing massive masonry that the Spaniards were able to keep any buildings up in these islands. If the old church had not been built like a fort, which it really was, it would have crumpled in a heap on top of the people gathered within its walls.

After two years of brisk trading, the timber market for ship stock declined. The Chinese began to consider iron construction and placed some orders for gunboats in London. This was certainly the more progressive policy and what they should have done in the first place, but from mandarin junks to iron in a single leap was too much to be expected.

The timber voyages consequently became less frequent and were varied by freight charters. The typical charters were coal from Nagasaki to Shanghai, and from Nagasaki to Vladivostok. The first time the Captain anchored in Nagasaki he was quite disturbed by his new sampan man, for it was customary, and even obligatory in some places, to hire a native boat for the go-ashore work which was quite constant. As soon as the Captain was ready to go ashore he shoved off in dignity, first casting an approving eye over the perfectly squared yards and harbor stowed bunts of his vessel, and gave the last orders to the mate.

126

He could find more work for the mate in a minute than the mate could do in a day. His eye, first on the vessel, then fell upon his sampan man who was artlessly puffing at the sculling oar. The Captain's puritanical sensibilities were outraged.

"God damn you, put on some clothes!" he roared.

The sculler stopped and looked in wonder and amazement at his glaring passenger. He did not know English and could not understand what was wrong. After another sampan had shouted something to him that made him get into his kimono, he took up sculling again, as hampered as though he was in irons.

Our freighting charters took us a number of times between Shanghai and Nagasaki. Nagasaki was clean and interesting. My father no longer swore at the sampan man for not having enough clothes on. He began to get used to the Orient. There was lots to see when entering the harbor of Nagasaki and we were always excited over the savory smell of fresh beefsteak smothered in onions that was in the galley very soon after the compradore's sampan met us outside when the pilot came aboard. We had a regular compradore in Nagasaki and he seemed to know what was wanted on a ship just in from Shanghai.

The entrance to Nagasaki is all rocks and on the right side, going in, is a rather steep cliff hung on the face with twisted and crooked stunted pine trees, clinging to the rocks with prehensile roots. My father said that cliff would have been a good one for the

> "old man of Comer
> Who stood on one leg to read Homer,
> When he felt it grow stiff,
> He jumped over the cliff,
> And that ended the Old Man of Comer"

He was very much amused by my book of Edward Lear's limericks, with its absurdly drawn pictures and particularly the one of the "Old Man of Comer."

My mother bought my books in Hong Kong. One was a German funny book of pictures that the German pilot who took us into Shanghai never got through with. As soon as he came over the rail, he would head for me, with a "Vere ees dot book?" I would get it for him and he would start laughing. The strip of pictures he liked best was the "Rhinoceros Hunt." The synopsis of that remarkable hunt was that the hunter appeared in the forest, not with a gun but with a huge monkey wrench and a screw nut. Having attracted the attention of a rhino, it put for him at full speed. The hunter headed for a certain tree, and so did the rhino. The hunter dodged behind the tree but not so the rhino, who ran his horn through the tree; on went the screw nut over the protruding point and a few turns of the wrench made the rhino captive. The other subjects were of the same type of humor and no doubt the descriptive lines in German made him think of his homeland.

Leaving off rhinoceros hunting and getting back to Nagasaki, I am reminded of something which I saw on going in, which causes me to remember my Uncle Ing's six-foot-two cooking in the five-foot headroom caboose galley. He was intrigued by the beauty of the cliff scenery that we were passing, but had no time to leave the savory steak on the fire. Not missing a trick, he stood like a human periscope, with head and shoulder up though the scuttle in the roof, taking in all the sights as we sailed to the anchorage.

While Japan was at peace with China, there was always a whole lot of apprehension among the foreigners in Nagasaki of an attack on the port by the Chinese. Warships of several nations were there to protect their nationals in case the Chinese came in. Our own American man o' war was the U.S.S. *Ticon-deroga,* a wooden corvette armed with smooth-bores, obsolete since the Civil War. While she was still there, a Japanese "iron-clad" just built by Armstrong in London came in, and anchored in the fleet. That, in 1880, was the first modern ship of the Japanese Navy. The Jap was armed with Armstrong breech-loading rifles which their gunners were soon to learn how to use.

While ashore one evening we were witness to something that was good. Some Britishers were in port, and on shore we met a typical British man o' war tar, wide straw hat with turned up brim, whiskers, and with a pretty good load of *samshu* in his upper 'tween decks. He was reeling drunk and tacking from one side of the street to the other when he spied a Nagasaki policeman. The policeman was no joke but the European tar thought he was, for the minion of the law was rigged out in the. medieval manner. He was as much out of date as the Japanese ironclad anchored out in the harbor was up to the minute. The Nagasaki policeman had on a kimono, and for his night duties he was equipped with a staff about like a broom-stick, and a paper lantern. Jack boarded him and took possession of the staff and the paper lantern, staggering off with them with the remark that if the Jap wanted to fight, he would give him "ten fights." The disarmed policeman stood by, nonplussed, but swift revenge came his way. Our reeling tar, still with the staff and the paper lantern, then tried to upset a rickshaw containing two persons. Those two persons turned out to be officers belonging to his own ship!

The *Ticonderoga* got up some boat races, which was the usual thing when men o' war of various nations gathered in a foreign port. Part of it was some sailing cutter races in which the merchant vessels were invited to compete. Now the *Ame-*

thyst never would have been taken for a speedy vessel, with her bluff bow and square box-like stern, and her launch, carried across the main hatch, was of a similar model. She was painted black and was very much battered by hard usage. She was rigged with a split-lug sail. But the mates turned her bottom up on deck, smoothed her down like glass, and gave her an underwater coating of pot-lead as the others were doing. The split-lug was overhauled and made to set perfectly, and with a racing crew to hold down the weather gunwale, our launch appeared at the line to wait for the gun. There was a smile at first at the rather uncouth appearance of the Yankee competitor, but it wore off soon after the race started. The Yankee just sailed away from the whole of them, as much to the surprise of her own crew as to the others.

While in Chinese and Japanese ports the *Amethyst* always had a lot of joiner work done about her topsides and down below by native mechanics who were very good. It was not only a good thing for the property but also a first class advertisement for ornamental Philippine woods. But that type of advertisement came near not working once, in Hong Kong, when my father called a Chinese timber buyer's attention to a set of beautiful rosewood bits recently installed in the main fiferail, with the suggestion that the wood would do for their ornate and elaborately carved coffins.

"You wanchee coffin, me no wanchee coffin," snapped back the Chinaman, who thought at first it was his own possible funeral that was alluded to. The same merchant, however, became one of our best customers. The Orientals were sometimes very slow in arriving at what the Occidental meant. In Nagasaki we had a Japanese joiner and cabinet maker do some work in our cabin. My father thought it was his chance to get a spread eagle carved for the *Amethyst's* stern, but the

Japanese always looked puzzled whenever the subject of the bird came up. The idea was not gotten across to him at all. Finally he was taken in the sampan to view the spread eagle across the stern of the *Ticonderoga*. "Ah, you want fowlo," he exclaimed, and the misunderstanding was cleared up.

At Vladivostok, most of the coal from the vessel was discharged directly into the bunkers of a Russian man o' war. It was transferred in sacks carried on the backs of convicts, who were driven like animals by the overseers.

During the same winter we made a trip to Hakodate for a cargo of natural ice for Hong Kong. At that season of the year we found Hakodate the natural place to procure such a cargo, for on beating against a strong and freezing wind in Tsugaru Strait, the *Amethyst* became the very picture of an Arctic exploration ship. Fore shrouds and head gear were a solid mass of ice. It was a taste of the sub-Arctic which was to be found only a little further along to the Kurile Islands.

From Hong Kong the *Amethyst* proceeded in ballast to Shanghai for a consignment of gunpowder destined to blow up some rebels in Formosa. On entering the waters of the wide and muddy Yangtze, a pirate, who had boarded us in the guise of a pilot, attempted the grounding and possible seizure of the vessel. The first thing that excited suspicion was the presence of a well-armed junk hovering altogether too close to our weather quarter. Seagoing junks could always lay up a point higher to the wind than a square-rigger, and under ordinary circumstances this would not have attracted undue attention. At that time all junks carried a tier of guns on deck as a protection against the other pirates, so there was no telling which was which. The Captain knew that there was shoal water under his lee and he suddenly demanded of the pilot, who had his own lead boy, "How muchee water you catchee?"

"Me catchee plenty water," came the sullen reply.

The Captain then grabbed the lead himself. On learning the truth he put the helm alee, and at once came about, clearing the danger, much to the surprise of the pilot who meanwhile had been dumped into his sampan towing alongside. The armed junk, which also went about, picked him up and stood off. They probably chopped off his head for fumbling the job. Pirates in these waters seldom attack a ship under command, but prefer to board one that is disabled in some way. This is true even at the present day when such piracy along the south coast is of frequent occurrence.

The gunpowder was for the Chinese Government, and it was taken to Tainan where the vessel was met outside by some agents who came off in a tub lashed to the top of a long catamaran. These were followed by small junks which took the dangerous cargo off.

This was the last business the Captain did with the *Amethyst*. Soon after, while lying in Hong Kong, he sold out his interest in that historic vessel and took over some shares (Captain Kinney's) in the *Northern Light,* a large full-rigged ship which was in port at the time.

CHAPTER 9

The *Northern Light:*

Liverpool and New York

The *Northern Light* was launched
in 1871 at the shipbuilding plant of George Thomas, Quincy
Point, Massachusetts. She was built to the order of William
Weld and Son of Boston, who in 1880 sold the ship to Messrs.
Benner and Pinckney, Burling Slip, New York. She was a three
deck ship of 2000 tons, with a length of 233 feet, a breadth
of 44 feet, and a depth of hold of 28 feet; her loaded draft
was also 28 feet. She was named for an old clipper ship, built
in 1851 at South Boston, which had established several records
for quick passages to the Pacific Coast.

The later-built *Northern Light* represented a type of medium clipper brought out to supersede the out-and-out clippers
which could not carry half as much cargo. The older *Northern
Light* carried only 2000 against 4000 tons on the later vessel,
and with the same size crew.

No one of the present generation can form any sort of an idea of the majestic grandeur of a ship of the *Northern Light* class, not only as a picture, tearing along under a cloud of canvas, but even when lying quietly at anchor with the forest of yards correctly squared and harbor stows on the sails. It was a sight to compel a feeling of awe merely to look aloft to trace out the massive hempen shrouds and backstays, to say nothing of tracing out the leads of the running gear. To know that was in itself an education, and to be master of all was a big job. There were many such masters, and many such ships.

The *Northern Light* was the largest of twenty wooden ships from the same ways at Deacon Thomas' yard, near the present location of the Fore River Works. It is remarkable how a ship-building tradition sticks to one place. The exact spot where this ship was built was visited later by the Captain, just after he launched a much smaller ship, the little *Spray*. In her day the *Northern Light* was considered in New York, her hailing port, as the "finest American vessel afloat."

There was a big difference in the way of room on the deck of the *Amethyst* and that on the *Northern Light,* for her quarter deck alone was nearly the entire length of the *Amethyst*. My first wonder, which provoked a smile from the mates, was the enormous size of the new vessel's topmast backstays, which looked to me like tarred hempen hawsers, neatly turned over huge deadeyes, with polished brass caps covering the tops of the bends.

The Captain's transfer of interests from the *Amethyst* to the *Northern Light* came under the official supervision of a remarkable man who happened at that time to be U. S. Consul in Hong Kong. This was none other than Colonel John Singleton Mosby, late of the Virginia Light Cavalry, better known north of the Mason and Dixon line as "Mosby's Guerillas." He was appointed by President Grant who thought it time that a man of his unusual stamp was sent out to guard the interests of that orphan, the American Ship, in the Far East.

Colonel Mosby was, in manner and in speech, an American all through; he had none of the cosmopolitan touch and might have been taken for a typical Yankee rather than a Southerner.

The formula for the concoction of his favorite breakfast dish leaked out in the American colony. This was a highly spiced Spanish omelette which was always ready for him wherever he went. It is a wonder he never grew suspicious that it was served to him so often. It became a custom to invite the Colonel out to the ships to breakfast, and while thus out to the *Northern Light* he discussed a ship tax, to which he was opposed, and passed the remark that "it was illegal taxation that fired the 'shot around the world!' " This was the first I ever heard of the Battle of Concord.

Colonel Mosby was tall and angular and was said to have so many sabre cuts received in battle that he couldn't walk straight. A strong profile, high forehead and serious expression indicated the character of the man, and anyone could see that he was yet a fighter. His predecessor, who had been in Africa, left a Zulu assegai hanging on the wall behind the desk and this the Colonel took down to run an objectionable skipper out of his office soon after he first got there. To the other consul the assegai was merely a curio, but to Mosby the savage weapon was of practical use.

While we were yet in Hong Kong, Colonel Mosby named and registered my youngest brother. On discovering that a name had not yet been chosen, he volunteered, "Since this is In-auguration Day (March 4, 1881), let's call him Garfield," thus naming the youngster for a man he might rather have scalped twenty years before.

While on the subject of vital statistics I may as well make

135

note of the rest of our family. All of us were born either on a ship or abroad. I "gave orders for the first time," so I was told, on the packet *Constitution* in San Francisco. Benjamin was registered at the U. S. Consulate in Sydney, N.S.W., and named for the bark *B. Aymar.* Jessie was born in Olongapo and registered at the U. S. Consulate in Manila. Garfield we have just referred to.

The loading of the *Northern Light* in Manila took about a month. The anchorage for such a deep-drafted ship, at that time, was about two and a half miles from the city. Since the American control of the Philippine Islands, docks protected by breakwaters have been built with thirty feet of water alongside, the deepest docks in all the Far East except Shanghai. In loading "sugar and hemp," the sugar was naturally stowed in the lower holds while the hemp was screwed into the upper 'tween decks. The stowing was all by native labor which came off to the ship in the early morning, paddling their own canoes, 50-foot dugouts, each filled to capacity, looking more like cannibals coming than anything else; that sinuous winding of the paddles dipping in the water looked so wild and savage. But it was only in appearance.

There was a native crew and cox'n in the ship's boat, which made the long pull morning and evening to the landing at the Pasig. While on this trip to and from the shore, we as often passed the dismal hulk of the American ship *Masonic,* lately seized by the Spanish authorities for an alleged infraction of the customs regulations. The captain was murdered at sea and the mate put in at Manila in distress without having the manifests ready. Carabineros were at once put aboard and the ship dismantled.

From Manila to Liverpool our route was by way of Banka Strait, on the coast of Sumatra, and through the Straits of

Sunda to the Indian Ocean and the Cape of Good Hope. Perhaps there would be a stop at St. Helena in the South Atlantic. The usual stop was made at Anjer Point, Java, for fresh supplies as this was the last call. Boats came off before the anchor was down, to swarm aboard with their wares to trade. Here there was no "everything got, monkey no got," for we had monkeys galore as well as musk deer and a civet, called a musk cat, good to keep the rats off. The deck was piled with yams, sweet potatoes, baskets of eggs and crates of chickens. These last were berthed in a large coop built on the main hatch. The job was to keep the otherwise useful musk cats from making raids on the chickens at night. Chicken, before we reached the Cape, cloyed the appetite of the crew and a growl was heard for "good old salt hoss what yer can feel all night in yer stomik a-nurishin' of yer."

We had a typical English crew which had originally shipped on the vessel at Cardiff when bound out to Hong Kong; it had the usual cosmopolitan sprinkling that was to be found on all American ships. On mastheading the topsail yards at Hong Kong they turned out to be a regular chantey crew with good voices and a will. "Tail out men and give us Boney," sang out the mate as soon as the upper topsails were sheeted home. There were thirty men from the tail end to the leading block at the deck and "Boney was a warrior" made the ship shake with the rhythm of the chorus. "Ranzo," "Blow the man down," and "Hanging Johnny" were in their repertory, with "Johnny Bowker" on the boarding of the main tack. Some chanteys have lyric beauty, but they are all work songs to make the hauling twice as easy, and they all have a story.

The *Northern Light* entered the Mersey on Christmas Eve, carrying into Liverpool the largest single shipment of sugar to date. The city was hidden by a fog as we came to an anchor in the river to await next morning's tide in order to enter the docks. We had been six months at sea and had seen nothing of any land during that time except passing glimpses of Table Mountain and St. Helena, and that only for the purpose of rating the chronometers. What say ye present time navigators who never think to pass from one day to another without the time signal radio cups glued to your ears?

As the Christmas bells began to sound on Christmas morning, the overhanging mist just unveiled the spires of the city to lend magic to the happy peals. A long sea voyage, with its isolation from all land sounds and smells, tunes the perceptions to a high pitch which can only be known to those of us who have had the experience.

Half of the crew did not wait for the formality of docking, but as soon as the sails were stowed and bunted to the tune of "We'll pay Paddy Doyle for his boots," they slid over the side into boats sent for them by some latter day, but less notorious, "Paddy Doyle." All the sailors did not fall as victims to these harpies of the shore, and those who did were not to be blamed; it was their country and they had for many months journeyed far and wide, and with an accrued payday which they were not long to keep.

At the top of high water we were towed into the West Waterloo Docks, a part of the locked-in dock system of the Mersey, for with the thirty-foot tide that runs in this river there is no such a thing as a ship lying at an open wharf. What they did in Liverpool before the docks came into being would be interesting history.

Having discharged our sugar we followed the course of some of it through the great refinery; a transition from the crude and sandy product of the Philippines to crystal lumps ready to drop into the teacup. We did the same with the hemp, which we followed to the rope walks and saw our baled fibre of the abaca plant twisted into stout cordage.

At the Langdon Graving Docks the ship was re-coppered and her prodigious accumulation of barnacles, due to so many months in tropic seas, was incidentally removed. This marine growth was a curiosity even in a seaport of the importance of Liverpool and clearly explained the 160 day passage from Manila; it also got into the papers and visitors came far from the country to collect specimens of *lepas anatifera.*

While in the West Waterloo Docks the *Northern Light* replaced her bowsprit with a new one which was to have been shipped by a rigger who contracted to do the job at a certain time. He was not on hand when he said he would be, so the Captain told the mate that he had better scrape together a gang from the dock and ship it; and this was done. It was no sooner in than the rigger came on board in a truculent mood. An altercation ensued on the main deck near the fiferail, and the Captain was cited to appear in court next morning. The contrast between the plaintiff and the accused seemed to amuse the magistrate. The rigger appeared very much bandaged and attended by both a doctor and a nurse. When the magistrate had heard the complaint and the evidence, he turned to the accused. "You are coming back to Liverpool, Captain?"

"Yes, your Honor, I shall always come back to Liverpool."

"The case is adjourned until you return to Liverpool."

On leaving the Mersey we had a typical Western Ocean hard case crew, with a bucko mate to match. He knew his men perfectly and they knew him as "Black Taylor." Mr. Taylor, whom my father ever after regarded with the greatest respect, was a swarthy down-easter, a loyal, powerful and fearless officer. He had the open and free manner with his subordinates of a born leader, which made him popular with the majority of

139

decent hands, but a thorn in the flesh to the soldiers and larrikins. Of these two latter classes there was a fair proportion, whose only object was to get to New York and who took no interest in the ship which had to be put in "apple-pie" order before entering her home port.

For the purpose of better carrying on the work, the southern passage before the northeast trades was selected, making an easy and leisurely voyage of forty days. In choosing this route the *Northern Light* gained time, for the American ship *Triumphant,* which left Liverpool at the same time we did, took the northern passage for it and came into New York battered by northwest gales and but a day ahead of us. We sailed in looking like a yacht. Our masts were scraped down, yards painted, standing rigging all tarred down, deck houses and bulwarks painted, and decks holy-stoned.

The mate is the manager of the crew. For the first week or so out of Liverpool the weather was bad, particularly off the Bay of Biscay where the sea was very high. Sailors like bad weather for it is then they get the most rest. At the very worst all the mate can find for them to do is plaiting sennit and making thrum mats in a snug corner under the forecastle head where they may keep the furtive dudeen agoing. The mate knows this; he has been there himself and doesn't bother them because he, too, is taking a rest.

As we entered the trades and the weather got fine, Mr. Taylor encountered difficulty in getting things started and remarked at dinner one day: "Captain, I can't get anything done out there," motioning with his head toward the main deck.

"Mr. Taylor, you know what to do. And if you have any trouble with those soldiers and sea lawyers, I will pay the expense in New York."

It must not be inferred that the Captain favored "belaying

pin soup" or any other form of brutality; only he would tolerate no "soldiering." Taylor knew just what to do and he had a sense of humor as well.

That came out in his good treatment of a poor stowaway who came on in Liverpool with only a tin whistle for baggage. On this he was an artist and he had also another accomplishment, ventriloquism. With this he would "throw his voice" up on the foreyard and make an unseen hand up there throw back guff to the deck, much to the mate's amusement. A king could enjoy a jester, why not a chief mate? Everybody liked the tin whistle ventriloquist, who had unbounded confidence in himself and great buoyancy of spirits, and invited respect. Taking it by and large the voyage across was satisfactory and happy.

It was an early spring day (1882) when we first made out the coast of New Jersey at Navesink, the light off-shore breeze wafting to us the sound of train whistles along the beach. Towards evening the tug *Joseph Bertram*, spied the big sail half drifting toward her port, and without much preliminary bargaining, ranged ahead to take our line.

Down came the jibs by the run; up went the mainsail, then the foresail. In came skysails, royals, t'gallantsails, and lastly the huge topsails. All had done their work and no fancy stows were made, for the light sails were already coming off the yards and the heavier lower sails would be unbent and stowed away by the shore rigger gang boarding the ship at the dock when the crew had gone.

The passing out of the hawser to the towboat was always the real end of the voyage. Then "channel fever" was at its height with every man in the crew on the jump with a will; there was a thrill and a satisfaction totally unknown in these steamboat days.

The *Northern Light* came to an anchor off Red Hook, to

141

dock the next morning at Pier 17, East River, just under the great Brooklyn Bridge, about to be opened, and of which we had heard the fame on the opposite side of the world.

As soon as we were discharged at Pier 17, we moved to the northward of the Brooklyn Bridge. When I first sighted the bridge from the anchorage down in the harbor, I was greatly disappointed; it was such a tiny line against the sky. In my mind I had pictured something enormous to look at as soon as I got up in the morning for my first sight of New York. At that time I had not yet learned to make allowances for the imagination. But when we towed to a berth right to the south of the New York tower, I began to be amazed by the bulk of the structure, reaching one hundred and thirty-two feet above the water and extending clear over the River. I was not ignorant of the Bridge for we had on board *Harper's Magazine* containing an article about its engineering and building features, from the sinking of the tower caissons to Mr. Farrington's bosun's chair trip across on the first wire. Mr. Farrington was the master mechanic. He did it to encourage his men and he was greatly surprised and abashed by all the blowing of steamboat whistles and fuss that was made over it.

When we moved up river our rig was so high that we had to strike the topgallant masts to the topmast caps. A gang of shore riggers did that. We had hemp standing rigging which made it very hard work for them to trice it up and make it shipshape for the moving. In passing under the bridge I received a complete impression of its great magnitude. As we came directly under, a painter, suspended underneath in a bosun's chair, reached down and gave our main truck a dab with his brush when our pilot shouted up to ask him how near we were. It was near enough.

142

New York waters at that time swarmed with small paddle boats darting hither and thither up and down the rivers, and with small, primitive paddle ferryboats plying between Brooklyn and New York.

Our ferry was the Fulton Street Ferry and sometimes we went on the Wall Street Ferry. The ferries had a funny squeal to their whistles which were going all the time as they twisted their way among other craft.

On our first Sunday in New York we went to Manhattan Beach with a party consisting of several other sea captains with their wives and families. The ride to the beach, after we got over to the Brooklyn side, was on a steam train with open cars. We enjoyed the train and thought it was a jolly outing. But there were two things about Manhattan Beach which did not please my father. The first was the alleged clam chowder served at the Pavilion. Who ever saw any clam chowder that did not have milk in it? He would have liked to go right in there and show them how it was made down east. The other thing was Gilmore's Band which played classical numbers. He would rather have heard "Blow the man down" and some tuneful melodies done on the cornet. He was fond of the simple and soulful tunes. But Patsy Gilmore got a hand for all that, for my mother enjoyed him.

Soon after we arrived in New York, a reporter from the *Tribune* came aboard the vessel. His account of the visit appeared in the *Tribune's* "Local Miscellany" column on June 26, 1882. It read:

"At Pier 23, East River, lies a typical American ship, commanded by a typical American sailor who has a typical American wife to accompany him on his long voyages, and to make his cabin as acceptable a home as he could have on shore. No one, to look at the graceful lines of this vessel, her Yankee rigging and sails, her bold cutwater and her noble stern, could mistake her for any other than an American ship.

"This vessel is the clipper ship *Northern Light,* owned by Benner and Pinckney of this city. A visit to her deck suggests two sad and striking thoughts, one that American sailing ships are becoming obsolete and the other that so few American sailors can be found. She is commanded by Captain Joshua Slocum who is one of the most popular commanders sailing out of this port, both on account of his general capability and his kindness to his crew. The tautness, trimness, and cleanliness of this vessel, from keelson to truck and from stem to stern are features not common on merchant ships. The neat canvas cover over the steering-wheel bearing the vessel's name and hailing port, worked with silk, is the handiwork of the captain's wife. Descending to the main cabin, one wonders whether or not he is in some comfortable apartment ashore.

"When a *Tribune* reporter visited the ship, Mrs. Slocum sat busily engaged with her little girl at needlework. Her baby boy was fast asleep in his Chinese cradle. An older son was putting his room in order and a second son was sketching. The captain's stateroom is a commodious apartment, furnished with a double berth which one might mistake for a black walnut bedstead; a transom upholstered like a lounge, a library, chairs, carpets, wardrobe and the chronometers. This room is abaft the main cabin which is furnished like a parlor. In this latter apartment are the square piano, center table, sofa, easy chairs and carpets, while on the walls hang several oil paintings.

"In front of the parlor is the dining room, which, together with the other rooms, exhibit a neatness of which only a woman's hand is capable.

"Going on deck, the captain showed with great pride, the cleanly kept steam engine in the after end of the forward house. It was used for handling cargo, condensing water, extinguishing fire, pumping the bilges or for other emergencies. The carpenter shop was next visited. In this was a long bench with vise, a lathe, saws and other tools for new work or repairing.

"The captain's baby bears an honored name. He was born in Hong Kong on board the *Amethyst*, the oldest American ship afloat. The birth of this child was on March 3rd, 1881, and the following day he was chistened and registered by the United States Consul as James Garfield Slocum. General Garfield acknowledged the compliment by a letter to the child. The *Amethyst* was commanded by Captain Slocum. She was better known in Chinese waters as 'Old Hickory' or 'Old Eighteen Twenty Two,' the year in which she was built. The burgee never displayed the vessel's name but simply the Roman numerals of the year in which she was built, MDCCCXXII. This burgee and an ensign with the stars arranged in a circle was made, also, by Mrs. Slocum. It was in this vessel that Captain Slocum feared he would end his sea-faring career in a typhoon in the China Sea, eighty miles eastward of Great Loochoo.

"The *Amethyst* was also a fast ship and a few years ago was as much talked about as the *Alaska* and other fast steamships of the present day. When the *Amethyst* returned home, Captain Slocum was given the *Northern Light*."

It is true that our family life on board ship was rather unusual. My mother reflected the culture of her home in Sydney. She was both artist and musician. Every day from 9 to 12, school was conducted in a consistent manner. Spelling, reading and arithmetic, suited to our different ages. In New York at that time, I was the eldest at 11, Ben was 9, and Jessie about 7. Little Garfield was not yet on the school list. Discipline was maintained by a switch stuck over a picture in the cabin and the culprit had to fetch it himself when it was needed, but that, I must say, was not often.

As a pupil I was greatly interested in the reading which at times broke away from the formal school book to the memorizing of classic verse. My mother got that idea from her father who was, as we have seen, an amateur actor with a Shakespearean repertory. In our life on the ship, Saturday was field day, devoted to the cleaning and tidying of our rooms and mending of our clothes. On the Sabbath we had Sunday School. We memorized the Anglican catechism and learned collects. My task was to memorize, at each lesson, a verse of a certain chapter of the Bible. By this method in the course of time, I came to know the whole chapter by heart, which was excellent practice in King James' English. The man at the wheel once told me that he heard me reading about the three holy men who walked unscathed through Nebuchadnezzar's fiery furnace. He was greatly impressed and he would have liked to hear more. The Scriptures have great weight with people both in the wilderness of the land and the wilderness of the sea.

During the years that my father had been sailing the seas he had been not only a student of the sea itself but also of general subjects, particularly the histories of the early navigators and their voyages. One of the cabins of the *Northern Light* contained a library of at least five hundred volumes representing the standard works of the great writers. Such company at sea made an ideal atmosphere. His reading was not altogether devoted to technical subjects, but was very wide from a literary point of view, gleaned from the works of the essayists like Lamb, Addison, Irving and Macaulay, to whom he was always looking as models of style in his own writing. His favorite historians were Gibbon, Hume, Bancroft and Prescott. Of the

146

poets he liked Tennyson the best, and of course Coleridge's "Rhyme of the Ancient Mariner," the albatross part of which he knew by heart. All the people in "Don Quixote" were to him living characters, as were also those in "David Copperfield" and "Pickwick Papers." He simply revelled in the tales of Sinbad the Sailor. On the other hand, he was familiar with the works of Darwin, Huxley, Spencer and Simon Newcomb. The cabin, with its orderly and well fitted bookcases looked very much like the study of a literary worker or a college professor.

I remember his reading Irving's "Life of Columbus," and the table discussions of the great navigator's triumphs and misfortunes as well as the shameful treatment of the Indians by the gang of cruel adventurers at their heels.

CHAPTER 10

The *Northern Light:*

Two Mutinies, a Boatload
of Ex-cannibals and *Krakatoa*

Ⓘт was in August, 1882, that the
Northern Light was loaded with case oil at Hunter's Point,
Long Island, for Yokohama, Japan. The petroleum trade with
the Orient was then just opening and the refined product was
shipped in wooden cases, each containing two five-gallon cans
of oil, which were stowed in the hold by stevedores, just as gas-
oline is now carried in steamers to Australia, New Zealand,
China, Africa or elsewhere, in the track of the world-spreading
auto car. The usual loading place at Hunter's Point was New-
town Creek, and here at all times could be seen a line of large
sailing ships waiting in turn to receive cargo. These ships were
obliged to strike their t'gallantmasts before passing up under
Brooklyn Bridge, which has only about 132 feet of clearance.
It was customary completely to re-rig while loading, and to

pass out to sea by way of Long Island Sound instead of back by the way of Sandy Hook. It saved time.

The crew of twenty-five seamen who tumbled over the rail of the *Northern Light* as all was ready to cast off was no better and no worse than the usual crew and was typical of the time. In addition to the foremast hands, a ship of the *Northern Light's* size and importance carried three mates, a bosun, carpenter, cook and steward. The last three were rated as "idlers" because they slept in all night, but they had important deck duties just the same. Of the foremast hands who tumbled over the rail, not one man in three knew where he was going, nor did he care. They were recruited according to Port Law, and by means of a tug boat were delivered at the ship by a functionary then known as the "shipping master," an office long since passed into oblivion, and very properly so. That was in the days when East River, below the Brooklyn Bridge, was still a forest of spars from all the seas and when figurehead and jib-boom were often thrust over South Street to meet the upper windows of the houses. All this seems but yesterday to those of us who have seen it.

The business of finding crews was peculiar to the times and may deserve a word of explanation. It was a system controlled by a ring. From top to bottom they were parasites and their methods were the methods of thugs. The game was made up of four factors, and the chief factor was Jack himself, a creature of certain very fixed vocational and social habits. The second factor was the "crimp" who acted as runner (and blackjacker) for his boss; the third was the sailor's boarding-house keeper, who in turn was in league with number four, the shipping master himself, whose trick it was to turn the human product over to the consumer of his energies. It all worked out very smoothly so long as there was a demand for crews for sailing ships. The system was so well managed by the ring in control of the crew-shipping business in the most important American sea ports that it was well nigh impossible for a ship master to obtain a crew, or for a man to ship as a sailor before the mast, except through the channel of the ring.

To take a typical case: Jack, in the port of New York, who like as not has been "stung" before, is met on an inbound ship with a fair payday to his credit. The "crimp" gets aboard from a Whitehall rowboat; his painter is attached to his boathook and this he very expertly hooks into the channels of the ship as she is yet towing up the Narrows, the crew furling sail for the last time and coiling down the lines for docking.

Anyone who has been at sea and away from land for six months knows the meaning of "channel fever" when entering port. Jack, and all on board, are in a state which is far from normal; some may, indeed, be in a state of semi-delirium. The suave "crimp" well knows the psychology of this state of mind, which makes Jack an easy mark for the fakirs who swarm aboard. He is first plied with vile rum. Then his usual tale of woe is sympathetically listened to, with the ready assurance of a better ship if he but comes along. Jack's payday might not bring him more than a hundred dollars, but that is enough to interest the crimp's boss, for there are quite a number of "Jacks."

Jack is not altogether a fool and sometimes has a shrewd suspicion of the sailors' boarding house, but from lack of acquaintance he has a strong distrust of all things pertaining to the land, and most of all, the brick sidewalk. There is no break in the atmosphere of brine between the fo'castle and the inviting door of the land refuge and it is this which gives him a vocational security, so to speak. So, with his "donkey" obligingly handed to the wagon waiting on the dock, he is driven with his mates to the web, where in congenial company

151

he is soon feeling like a king and is almost as soon separated from his payday, representing both the labor and hardship of perhaps more than a year. But this is not all of it. For before a week has passed, he is in alleged debt to the so-called boarding house, and like a victim of ghouls he is ready for the next step. The shipping master on South Street has a call for a deep water crew, with two months' advance to every man.

These advance notes, intended to be a convenience to the seaman as an aid to dependents left ashore, were the cause of much evil, but none of the ring would handle a crew without an advance note, due and payable at a stated time after the ship's departure, say 24 hours. The boarding house keeper has the usual crew to supply. Suggestion, rum or the blackjack, as the case may require, is brought to bear upon Jack, who is produced at the shipping office and signed on the ship's Articles in legal form. The boarding house keeper and the shipping master have a mutual understanding about the advance note, and the settlement is made with Jack on the basis of both what he owes and what he *does not owe*. The score for lodging, drinks, and money supposed to have been advanced, are all in the bill, and it is carefully explained to the bewildered Jack, "Here's five dollars ya got, and here's the five dollars ya *didn't* get." That was no joke, but a regular formula which went unchallenged for reasons made very apparent.

Then the whole bunch, with dunnage and "donkey's breakfasts" convoyed by their former friends, find themselves on a tug and headed out for a ship anchored out in the stream for finishing touches. Under the hand of the rigger, who with his gang is not entirely free from danger of being shanghaied himself, the ship has been made ready for sea, and sits expectantly on the bay, solemn and black, with yards squared, and *all ataunto*.

On striking the deck, the drunks are hauled for'ard and chucked into the fo'castle with the offhand assurance to the mate, "They'll be good men when they come to." The ones that are sober enough keep on going until the familiar roar of the mate puts them again in touch with their natural surroundings.

This iniquitous system of shipping crews was as harmful to the ship and her owners as it was to her crew. If Jack was a "good fellow" he would snap out of it and consider himself lucky, taking it all by and large, as part of his destiny. To the sullen or reflective mind, the treatment would leave a scar when he came to realize that the landsharks had not only trimmed him of the payday of his previous voyage, but had him for two months to come on the present one. By long usage, the latter was called "Working up the Dead Horse." The ceremony of the burial of the "Dead Horse," attended with an appropriate chantey, at the expiration of the two months, is another usage of the sea, but a story all in itself.

Both the seamen before the mast, and the mates, were rough. A mate who showed a weak spot was worse than useless both to ship and crew. On American ships at that time, the best mates were graduates of the fo'castle, having been selected for posts aft on account of their qualities of leadership, not only as seamen but as superior men mentally and physically.

When well out at sea the first business of the mate and the second mate was with the fo'castle "bucko" if there was one, of his own watch. The argument was sharp and decisive, as it had to be determined at the very start who was going to run the watch. In the same manner it had to be made very plain who was running the whole ship with its great responsibility of lives and property, removed, while on the high seas, from the jurisdiction of courts and protection officers of the law. In this connection I wish to have it understood that while the Captain was an inflexible disciplinarian he was by no means in favor of the "bucko," fore or aft, and looked upon them both with disfavor.

In good time, with the Hell Gate pilot on board, the *Northern Light* broke away from her dock, and the long hawser was stretched out ahead by the towboat *Joseph Bertram*, which was to take us 150 miles down Long Island Sound. But misfortune was already afoot, for when the towboat cast off about opposite New London, it was found that the rudder would not work under sail. While following in the wake of the towboat, nothing unusual had been noticed about the steering gear. The tops'ls had been set by steam by the deck officers, assisted by the few men who were as yet able to lay aloft or take a turn around the niggerhead of the donkey engine in the after end of the main deck house. This was an innovation on American ships of the time and was only used in emergencies. But there was no steam for hauling in the hawser when the towboat blew for letting go. Now there was hell to pay on the forecastle head. The chief mate, Mr. Knowles, turned out to be a "bucko" of the real down east bull type that "ate 'em alive." He entered both fo'castles and chased all hands, drunk or sober, out on the deck and lined them up on the hawser, going down the line with a belaying pin to get the slackers into action. It was his job to get that hawser in before the ship ran over it! And in it came. He then set the jibs and the foresail, and an attempt was made to get the ship under control by taking the braces to the niggerheads and bracing the yards. The tug boat made a bee line back to New York, paying no attention to our recall signals. By this time it was apparent we had to be towed into some port for repairs, though there was easy anchorage in the Sound where we were.

By good luck the ship was worked over to within signalling

154

distance of New London, where she was met by a local pilot
and towboat, and proceeded to take up an anchorage off Pequot
Point. In the meantime a full fledged mutiny had started. It
showed itself first in the treachery of the leadsman in the
chains, who called out false soundings. These mystified the
simple-minded Connecticut pilot who declared, "Thar ain't no
such water as that here, Captain."

The latter scented the trouble and said quietly, "That'll do
the lead."

Murin, the leadsman, and afterwards the ringleader of the
mutiny, understood it as well as he sullenly slunk off to join his
shipmates for'ard.

On coming to anchor, the crew, with Murin at their head,
openly refused to make the sails fast after clewing up. They
declared that the voyage was ended and demanded to be put
ashore in the tug. They were down on the mate for his treatment of them on manning the hawser, and they also thought
they saw a chance to beat the advance notes and get the best
of the boarding-house keepers. But this would have done them
no good, for once back in New York they would again have
fallen among thieves, so far as seagoing was concerned. As the
sequel showed, it would have been much better for the ship to
have put all hands on the beach and to have sailed with a clean
set of Articles.

As only the topsails and foresail had been set, the afterguard
managed to pass some gaskets around to canvas, and the signal,
"Mutiny on Board," was hoisted and displayed to the U. S.
Revenue Cutter *Grant*, then stationed at New London.

Their demand to be put ashore having been refused, the crew
attempted to rush the quarter deck. It was a formidable looking
crowd as they came tramping aft in close formation, armed
with handspikes and whatever else they could lay hands on.

155

The Captain intercepted them down on the main deck, on their own level, with a drawn revolver and a cool, clear-cut order to "Stop at the peril of life."

They stopped, and stood in their tracks, and not one man moved out of line until he was called. "Murin, you are the ring leader and you are to go in irons," said the Captain. "Pass up to the quarter deck."

Murin passed while the rest of the crew were held in line. As Mr. Knowles was in the act of putting the irons on him, Murin lunged with a sheath knife. Getting inside of the mate's guard, he forced him back against the cro'jack pin rail at the break of the hook and stabbed him furiously in the abdomen four times. The mate fell to the deck as Murin was thrown down and secured. At this moment assistance from the cutter came alongside in response to the signal. It was Captain Fenger of the *Grant* and an armed boat's crew. He immediately took charge and restored order. The crew was ordered seated on a spare spar on the main deck, searched and ironed in regular style. Half the crew were locked up pending better behavior, in each fo'castle, and it was Captain Fenger's suggestion that the most warlike be kept for a while on bread and water, "without too much bread in it."

The murderer Murin, in double irons, was taken from the ship by the Coast Guard. His victim was removed in a tug to the hospital where death was stayed for two months, as we learned nearly two years afterwards. What became of Murin we never exactly knew, except that he escaped the hangman's noose which he richly deserved.

A diver found that the lower pintle of the *Northern Light's* rudder had been broken off at Hunter's Point. It was replaced without going into drydock. By this time the crew had decided to turn to, at the earnest reasoning of the Captain, who talked to them "man to man." Their main grudge was against Mr. Knowles and he had been superseded by another mate sent from the New York office. This was Mr. Nubagin, a man of entirely different type from his predecessor and with far greater experience. He had seen some Naval service in the Civil War, which had given him fighting enough to last the rest of his days and which gave him poise besides.

The track of a sailing vessel on a long voyage was very different from the track now projected for full-powered steamships. With the sailing vessel the navigator had not only to take the objective and the Great Circle into consideration, but he had to make use of and understand the laws that govern both the atmosphere and the sea. The route was laid to conform with the path of the prevailing winds, with their consequent currents, which, having an average drift of from 15 to 60 miles a day, were a very important factor. So in the course of months of sailing, it made a difference whether the ship made use of the prevailing winds and natural conditions or tried to sail against them. There were exhaustive sailing directions and carefully compiled current charts at hand, so there was no chance about it. I have made a sketch map of this voyage to Yokohama which shows how it was frequently done at that time.

The northeast trades are picked up in longitude 40 W., and latitude 34 N., the track being carried nearly over to the Cape Verde Islands, to make best use of the southeast trades when they are met at the equator, after worrying through the doldrums. On making the southeast trades the course is forced slightly to the westward, the ship steering "full and by," on the port track, and making the best of it until reaching the region of variable winds and calms in latitude 25 S. and about longitude 30 W. The course is then laid for Tristan da Cunha, and here the brave west winds of the "Roaring Forties," as they are

157

almost always called, are first taken up to run the easting down, giving the Cape of Good Hope a wide berth, skirting the southern limit of the South Indian Ocean in a composite great circle, and passing south of Tasmania. Before this everlasting drive of westerly gales the current sets at an unmistakable rate and direction and its advantages were very soon discovered by the early navigators, who were not slow to use them. In a well-found ship there is nothing to fear from being bowled along in the "Roaring Forties." On the track to the eastward of Australia, and up through the Pacific Islands, the southeast trades are carried, and then the monsoons have to be depended on. It was all a regular system.

On the return home from the East, the course is laid west of Borneo and close to the Island of Sumatra. This route is through the narrow Banka Straits, between two bold shores, each covered with a thick tropical forest. It was while beating through this strait that a certain ship was said to have brushed the trees so closely with her yard arms that the monkeys' tails got jammed in the brace blocks. This improbable story is offered as the reason the monkeys in that region are now tailless.

At the Sunda Straits the southeast trades are again taken and carried, with the South Equatorial Current, across the Indian Ocean and north of Mauritius, passing this time close to the Cape of Good Hope to make use of the swift Agulhas Current which has the velocity of our own Gulf Stream at its narrowest point. At the Cape, the interrupted southeast trades are again taken up and, to make the best use of the Guinea Current, the course is laid for St. Helena and Ascension, sighting both islands. This gave the ship her last chance to check chronometers on the voyage, for as I have before remarked, at that time there was no radio tick to go by. From Ascension the course is close to Cape St. Roque to make the best use of the northeast trades.

These are lost in latitude 25 N., to enter the region of the great anti-cyclone. All of the foregoing may sound very technical, but the information was necessary to the equipment of the sailing navigator.

After getting to sea, the New London mutiny, though to all appearances quelled, broke out like a smouldering fire in one form or another, during the remainder of the voyage. There was one faction which had sworn to cut the Captain's throat for taking them to sea; and yet another, of less violent intention, which openly maintained that they had to kill Knowles, saying, "If we hadn't, he'd a-killed us."

The new mate was a man of quiet dignity, who knew his billet, and there was no bluster about him. He was well suited to handle the difficult berth he had tumbled into. The second mate hailed from Baltimore, and his name was Flynn. I remember him very well; tall, red, and raw-boned. He was well disposed, but rather inclined to get rattled about the work on the deck. With a slouch hat pulled down a bit too far in front, his pet phrase was, "Flynn can't see *everything*." I heard a song a little later in Yokohama, of how "Billy Flynn got drinking gin," which leads me to marvel how a catch word or a jingle of a rhyme can illuminate the memory.

The third mate, a young fellow by the name of Mitchell, also from Baltimore, followed the Captain from the *Northern Light* to the *Aquidneck*. Flynn did the same thing. The bosun was a Hollander, a quiet and reliable man of the sea, who figures later in the story of the voyage. The carpenter was a stolid old German who never could understand the Yankeeisms of his mate, Dimmock, and his Connecticut humor. But that did not bother Dimmock, whose presence on board added much to the safety of the ship. Though he had never been to sea before, he came on at New London, taking the place of a man removed ashore as a witness to the stabbing. He was a veteran of the Civil War and had always lived in New London, where he worked as a machinist. His joining the ship resulted from a table conversation the Captain overheard in a New London restaurant. The topic was the mutiny going on in the harbor, and Dimmock, one of the party, remarked, "I believe that ship is all right, and I wouldn't mind going to sea with Captain Slocum, myself."

My father, sizing him up as serious, said quietly, "If you would like to come along, I guess you can. I'm the captain."

"Be you?" cried the astonished Dimmock, "Well by Gosh, I'll go."

As good as his word, he was on board the next day and being a machinist by trade a place was made for him on the articles as carpenter's mate. As the Captain spent a good deal of his time in the shop where they were building a bandsaw, they became very good friends and on equal terms as craftsmen. My father was very informal when it came to work and was a puzzle to his officers who thought he ought to have more "swank."

Before the Line was reached all hands had worked down to a settled routine and showed a good sign by holding singsongs on the main hatch during the second dog watch when it was fine weather. This was a near approach to a contented ship, for only such could muster up spirit enough for such a festive gesture. The traditions of crossing the Line were observed when Neptune entered the ship from over the bows to initiate all land-lubbers entering his domain. That was another good sign.

The voyage was without unusual incident from the line to Tristan da Cunha, except that the great Comet of 1882 put in an appearance and grew higher and larger in the sky as we approached the Cape. It looked ominous and was the cause of great fear among the more superstitious on the ship. Here we met with the "Roaring Forties" and began to run our easting down in the short longitudes, from the Cape to the coast of Tasmania.

In this region, bound east, the long, heavy square-rigger showed off to the best advantage, running before a moderate gale and a good-natured following sea. It was weather for low sails as we bowled along under stowed royals, but with tops'l stunsails set out to windward during the first section of the passage. This was my last view of stunsails set on a merchant ship at sea.

Sweeping around Tasmania we started to make our northing to the eastward of Australia, and up through the Pacific Islands. With more than passing interest we noted that the course lay near the Solomons of evil reputation. Even in a big and well appointed ship there was yet a thrill upon sighting the lofty mountains of a cannibal island, for with coral reefs about, one never knew just what was going to happen.

The top adventure of the voyage, though, was to be in these very waters. That was our rescue of some ex-cannibals that we sighted adrift in a whaleboat. It was in an open space of the sea to the south and west of the Gilbert Islands, and at daylight. Two hours earlier and they would have been passed by to their fate, for there were not many ships sailing those waters.

Even today, December 10th never rolls by but that I know it, so deep was the impression made upon me at the time when we sighted this small speck on the lee bow, bobbing like a nautilus on the great grey-blue ocean. It was not even a small trading vessel as we first supposed, but an open boat, with five souls in it. We backed the main yard and drifting down to within heaving distance, gave them a line and hauled them alongside.

One or two of the occupants were barely able to make the line fast to the boat; the rest were stretched out and helpless.

161

A gantline was rove off and they were hoisted on deck, one by one, starved, and more dead than alive. Their boat, too, was taken on board and landed across the main hatch. It proved to be a 21-foot double ended boat in good condition, and strangely enough, built in Rotterdam, according to mark. In the boat was an old man, an old woman and three young men, all native islanders. As they dropped on deck the brandy was broken out at once and this none of them refused except the old man, who said with a shake of his head, "Me missionary," and pointing from himself to the sky, added, "Taboo." This was understood to mean that it was no use and that he was done for. But when he was moved into the pilot house and out of the sight of the others, which he ascertained by carefully looking about, the brandy was proffered again with better results.

After that there was no taboo for him, or any of them for that matter. The old man's next word was "Apamama." That was one of the islands of the Gilbert Group we were then approaching. From our position it was 600 miles to the N.N.E. He became more communicative and looking at the moon, which was then visible during the day, pointed once, and clapped his hands as if making a period. He then looked at the sun, holding up all ten fingers, and by this we knew that they were from Apamama and that they had been adrift upwards of 40 days. By another sign he made us understand that seven had died, and so we learned that there were twelve when they started.

That was enough of their pitiful story for a beginning. The next thing to be done was to make a start towards restoring them to health by careful nursing and feeding.

The second chapter of their story was learned from the boat itself as it was unloaded and cleaned. It smelled of sea slime and of decayed dried fruits. There was also a box of missionary literature, including some small geographies, all in a Polynesian language. The maps in these geographies became useful as a means of communication, for picture talk is universal. Once clean and dry, their boat was fitted with a platform over the thwarts, and a tent was made for them by hauling a tarpaulin over a ridge pole. Here they were comfortably housed. When a better understanding was established, it was learned that they were native missionaries, that the old man was a deacon and the old woman was his wife. They had been sent from Apamama to Nanuti, an island seventy miles to the south'ard, on an expedition. Here they remained twelve days, and on their return trip to Apamama, they were blown out of their track by a storm, to be lost in the sea. That seven of the party had perished (the first was a woman) was enough to show that they suffered from starvation and, had it not been for the rainy season of the changing monsoon, all would certainly have perished from thirst long before their 40 days had passed.

The next day after they were settled, we were surprised by having the youngest of the men come aft and ask in broken English, "Captain, where ship bound?"

"Japan."

"Ship no stop Apamama?"

He was told that if it was a possible thing, and the winds permitted, they would be put off at their own island. Whereupon he said, "Captain, I thank you. King very glad. Give plenty copra."

The Captain speculated on what his chances would be of being made governor of an island, on personally restoring these subjects to his majesty, but luck was against the conjecture for we made Apamama on a squally night and a sea infested with coral reefs was no place at that time for a big ship. There was, however, another island in a better position, 360 miles to the northwest, on which they could be landed without danger to the ship. This was Ebon, one of the Marshall Group and they knew all about it. The inhabitants of Ebon were hostile to their people and they did not want to be landed there at all, showing unmistakable signs of terror when preparations were made to clear away their boat. Two of them even hid under the fo'castle head so as not to be found. The Captain felt that he had no more right to cast them adrift from the ship in that spot than he would any of his own crew, so all was belayed that night. The next day Japan, 2400 miles away, was pointed out to them in their own little geography, at which the deacon nodded intelligently. That he knew about Japan and preferred it to Ebon, was very plain, and so it was decided to continue the voyage without further stopping at cannibalistic islands of the wrong kind.

When we reached Japan the castaways had been 35 days on the ship and had journeyed from a region of coral islands and a warm sea to one of keen winter winds. As it grew colder they were clothed accordingly from the "slop chest" and on a frosty morning they stood at the rail and wondered at the "smoke" when they exhaled. They looked over the rail in amazement at Fuji, mantled in snow and glistening in the sun, the deacon exclaiming, "Big island, big island."

When we brought our castaways into Yokohama, they were turned over to the mission, being missionaries themselves. The Captain had an account of their adventures all written up and ready for the papers as soon as a reporter came over the rail looking for an item. He got a big one, and the publicity was in good time. But in a day or two the deacon sent a call of distress to the ship and the Captain could not avoid responding to inspect their shore quarters. He found them huddled and freezing in a paper house that only Japanese, accustomed to such a habitation, could live in during the winter. These people had never known cold weather and the new climatic conditions were in a fair way to killing them with pneumonia. The Mission was willing enough but had nothing to give except Bibles. Being foreign castaways, the U. S. Consul had no authority to take action for their relief. The Captain saw that his duty towards them was not yet ended, for action was needed at once to get them started towards home. He stirred up some more newspaper publicity and, by circulating a subscription list among the European merchants, secured on the first day pledges to the amount of $750. This subscription was headed handsomely by the *Northern Light's* agents and both the United States and British Ambassadors put their hands to it enthusiastically. At the end an advertisement had to be put in the paper to stop the money from coming in. The plan was to land them in San Francisco with a substantial bank credit in their favor. The Pacific Mail S.S. Company, offering to transport them, boat and all, free of charge, took them on the *City of Tokio* to San Francisco. Thence they were transported to Honolulu, and from there to their own island by a local schooner. They had made a circuit of over 11,000 miles and after seeing a land blanketed with snow and many other strange sights, they were delivered in good health to his majesty, the King of Apamama. Upon hearing all this had been accomplished, the Captain declared, with Sinbad the Sailor, "Allah is great."

While the *Northern Light* had been doing the good work of rescuing and sending home the Gilbert Island missionaries, the old mutinous spirit, hatched in New London, was still smouldering in the hatches. It must not be supposed that the *Northern Light* was a "hell ship" in any sense, for the grub was good and there was no ill treatment on board; but a small ring persistently nursed the original grievance started at the beginning of the voyage. As I said before, it would have been wiser to have beached the whole crew, conceding to their demand at New London and to have started clean.

On long voyages the organization upon which the safety of the ship depended was a much more serious problem in sail than that which now obtains with the cargo steamer. At the time of which I write, a passage at sea often lasted from four to six months, without coming in touch with the land. A modern cargo steamer is seldom out more than 40 days at a time.

At the conclusion of open hostilities in New London, there had been a sheath knife muster and every man had his sheath knife returned to him with the point struck off by the carpenter, on the spot. The point of a sheath knife adds nothing to its proper use, and the best intentioned in the crew saw no injustice in an order which placed every man on an equal footing as far as suspicion went. After that, possession of a pointed knife was regarded as a declaration of war against the government of the ship.

A sailor's sheath knife, on a sailing ship, was part of his proper rig. He carried it in his belt back of the right hip. It was needed constantly on deck and aloft, for splicing a line to cutting a buntline stop. Expertly used it was also an important item of his mess kit, and he considered himself generally helpless without it. In a moment of anger, when the blood is hot, his sheath knife may become his weapon and an ugly one it could be.

Shortly after we picked up the boat with the native missionaries in it, the man at the wheel, one morning, quietly passed word that there was trouble again forward. Zelanski, a morose and apparently inoffensive young Russian, was careless enough to grind a villainous looking knife at mess and to brag that it would "be in the Captain's heart before they made Yokohama."

166

His bunk was searched and a bowie knife, as described, was found under his mattress. He admitted that it was his. In the muster at the mast it became evident that he had uttered murderous language, and that the safest thing to do was to keep him securely in irons until he could be turned over to a consul. But in Yokohama, the U. S. Consul would not consent to his discharge and merely locked him up in the shore calaboose pending the ship's departure from port. This was a mistake on the part of the Consul, for the shore confinement turned the man's morose hatred into a blind fury. He thought he was being held by the ship. Some of this got into the papers, as well as a rather lurid account of the original mutiny in New London, giving both the ship and the crew a hard name. This Captain Slocum refuted in a public letter, in which he stated that the larger part of his crew was a credit to any ship, and that he would not want to have better men under his command. There was a request by some of the crew for copies of the paper to send home to their people, for an open statement of confidence had an ameliorating effect. It looked for once as though the trouble was over. The men started to know their captain. But Mr. Nubagin, the mate, began to fail in health, and so his valuable moral influence on the crew was wanting and after "Billy" Flynn's exhibition of himself in port, he was dead as far as discipline or example went. It was as much as he could do to keep his billet.

Having discharged her case oil, the *Northern Light* was to sail for Manila in ballast to load sugar and hemp for home. When sailing day came there was a final request to have Zelanski paid off, but the Consul still refused, maintaining his original stand that the man must be taken to sea.

"All right," returned the Captain, "but if you must send him, please see that he is secure and unarmed."

167

Then a rumor circulated that the crew would refuse to put to sea. The spirit of revolt was again in the air; things did not look good on sailing day. The topsails were sheeted home and the upper topsails were mastheaded by steam in sullen silence. There was no chantey. On the order to man the windlass, Mr. Nubagin took the forecastle head with all hands to weigh anchor. Even though the ship was homeward bound, the pawls clanked very slowly and there was not the usual heaving around with a will.

As the mate hailed, "Anchor short, Sir," two constables brought the prisoner off in a steam launch and stood with him at the gangway, ready to deliver him to the ship. He was loose and ready to kill, which both the constables must have known. As the Captain came along the deck he was confronted by Zelanski who, unrestrained by the constables, made a run at him with a knife. He missed his mark. Although the Captain did not expect the attack and was unprepared, his natural alertness enabled him to guard off and to fell his assailant who, the next moment, was ironed around the maintopmast back stay for safe keeping for the time being. Looking for another attack by the rest of the Zelanski gang, whoever they were, and taking no chances this time, the Captain went below and reappeared with a repeating carbine that was part of the ship's armory. He first very pointedly ordered the two constables down the gangway to their launch. Then mounting the wheel house aft, he ordered the mate to break out his anchor and hoist the jibs. With the whole deck in range, he literally got the ship under weigh at point of a gun.

Zelanski became a problem again, and at Manila he was permitted to detach himself from the ship in a manner that did not require any consular supervision, but which was quite satisfactory all around. What harm was it if a cargo port was left open with a lighter just outside? After he was gone the ship was much different.

This particular voyage was destined to be one for the viewing of the wonders both of the firmament and the earth. On the way out there was the great comet, and now on the home passage from Manila to New York, we were to participate in what has since been called the most appalling catastrophe since the dawn of human history. This was the eruption of Krakatoa, a volcano in the Straits of Sunda, our gateway from the East to the Cape.

Krakatoa had been in a quiescent mood for over two centuries. Covered all this while by a dense tropical bush, and showing no signs of seismic action whatever, it was regarded as extinct. However, it astonished the scientific world by breaking out into a regular "live one" and with great violence, about two months before our arrival in the Straits, in apparent sympathy with the earthquake shocks which had extended the entire length of Java. For a given area, Java has the greatest nest of volcanoes in the world; in this region earthquakes are of such common occurrence as to attract but passing attention, so we paid no more than the usual amount of interest to the phenomena preliminary to what was to come.

In sailing for Anjer Point, we were followed by two other American ships, both bound as we were, from Manila to New York. They were the *Wm. H. Besse* and the *Jonathan Bourne*. There was a light breeze, and all three ships in a line within easy signal distance of each other, when we observed the *Besse* to come up suddenly, all standing, and stop. She had grounded on a reef which had been cast up by sub-marine volcanic action in the very spot over which we had passed but a quarter of an hour before. The sea was trembling and in bubbles. A lead that was cast came up from the bottom so hot that it melted out the

169

tallow armor, showing that it was of a temperature higher than the boiling point.

The *Northern Light* braced her yards and came up into the wind, but as the *Bourne* came up astern of the *Besse* and hove to, to offer assistance, we kept off again for Anjer, which was by this time but a few miles distant.

A visit to the town showed that it was in a state of military activity, the Dutch authorities being at the time interested in a punitive expedition to put down a small rebellion that was going on in Sumatra. In gaudy trappings and with burnished arms, the native colonial troops filed aboard of a gunboat to convey them across the Strait, and to war. They might have saved themselves the trouble, for Nature was at that very moment marshalling mighty forces which within a month were to wipe them out of existence, friend and foe alike, by the tens of thousands.

Before we left Anjer, the *Bourne* came in and reported that the *Besse* had grounded easily, was in no immediate danger, and that a tug was on the way from Batavia to her assistance. The *Besse* was afterwards floated and towed to Batavia, and did not get away to resume her voyage until some weeks later when the Straits became clear.

As the *Northern Light* passed Krakatoa, the volcano was in the awful majesty of full eruption. It did not have the usual cone form that is seen in volcanoes, this having been blown off in some remote geological period by an explosion far more violent than the one now about to occur. This had left a depression in the center of the island with an elevation of 1200 feet on one end, occupied by the present crater. Here a bright fire burned, throwing up a column of black steam and ashes which reached a culminating altitude of seventeen miles by sextant measurement. The fall of ashes made the sea all about white with pumice stone. For days after passing it was washed upon our deck by the lively sea.

But we were not to know the story of all that happened until we put into the Cape, in distress from storm. There we learned that a fissure had opened at the base of the island, allowing the sea to pour down into the seismic fire below. The ensuing explosion blew off the top of the island, which vanished to dust in the upper atmosphere. Two years later this same dust was to descend to the earth and make the "Yellow Days." The final detonations, which lasted for 36 hours, were unmistakably heard over a thousand miles away. At Batavia, a distance of only a hundred miles, the detonations were described as deafening. These grew in violence until the very last one, which was the most terrifying of all. Then the giant became suddenly quiet.

The *Wm. H. Besse,* passing but two days after, reported that there was nothing unusual to be noticed about Krakatoa, although the altitude of the cone had been reduced 600 feet by the explosions. This observation was not quite accurate, for the profile of the island had been materially changed.

The fall of ash in the final hours of the eruption caused a total darkness which added to the terror and horror of the tidal waves which drove in, wrecking coast towns all about and taking toll of more than 36,000 lives. The Dutch gunboat which we saw going to war was landed in the jungle of Sumatra a mile and a half inland and fifty feet above normal sea level.

Of the fate of Anjer itself we heard different reports and I am not at all sure that the town which now exists is the same one that I saw. It was then one of the most notable of the landmarks of the route between the Far East and the West.

As the *Northern Light* was being swept by the Agulhas Current around the Cape, she was met by heavy gales from the westward which kicked up a mountainous cross rip. Here at the meeting edges of the two great streams, racing in opposite directions, are to be found the mightiest seas of any ocean. The *Northern Light* was hove to, and doing nicely, when the rudder head twisted off, allowing the ship to fall off into the trough of the sea before a jury gear could be rigged to bring her head back into the wind. Gigantic pyramidal seas, regular graybacks, swept over her from rail to rail, and with their sheer weight, caused her to wallow under water, causing a strain which started a heavy leak. The sea would have swept men from the pumps on deck, but the steam gear was rigged and that kept the vessel free.

At daylight, after a night of heavy laboring, a new peril showed itself. That was the danger of capsizing, for the pump was bringing up cargo from the lower hold in the form of "molasses" from the sugar mixing with the incoming sea water. Wind and sea moderated and became calm, but the list to port increased to 30 degrees. Then orders were given to break hemp out of the upper 'tweendecks and hoist it over the side to counterbalance the weight taken out of the bottom of the ship. Boats were cleared and provisioned for the next emergency, but a few hours work on the hemp caused the ship to regain her stability, or enough to put her out of danger. Bales of hemp floated to windward as far as we could see. But land was less than 20 miles distant and in the roadstead of Port Elizabeth we found a haven of refuge. Nothing but the Captain's resource and seamanship saved the *Northern Light* from going to the bottom off the "Cape of Storms" as it was once rightly named by its discoverer.

In Port Elizabeth the ship was entirely overhauled, the job taking two months. In the first place the topsides were entirely recaulked. The principal leaks were found to be in the wood ends, at and above the water line. The foremast was unstepped, rebuilt, and stepped again by the ship's company, assisted by another crew from a British ship in the port. The crew rigged the shears, using for the purpose the fore and main yards. The hemp standing rigging, which had been strained in the gale beyond further use, was condemned and an entire gang of new steel wire put in its place by shore riggers.

The biggest job, however, was the stowing of the cargo which was contracted for by longshore stevedores. The lower hold had been emptied near the pump well when the sugar in that section, mixed with sea water, had been drawn up to be thrown into the ocean. This space was again filled with the same kind of cargo from the lower 'tweendeck. As this was in matting bags, by this time solidified, it was an awful job and went very slowly.

In Port Elizabeth there was a "lame duck" industry along the strand supported by ships entering in distress, just like the *Northern Light,* to be re-fitted for sea. In such transactions it was often considered legitimate to fleece the underwriter, but in this case the contractors discovered a master who was as particular in regard to his prestige with the underwriters as he was with the owning house.

In Port Elizabeth some important changes were made in the ship's personnel also. Mr. Nubagin, who had been confined to his room all the way across the Indian Ocean with an intermittent fever, had to be sent home. He was replaced by a Mr. McLean, an energetic Scotsman who had spent a good deal of time in the diamond fields of South Africa. Being a real sailor he was just the man to finish the rigging. A change also was made in the third mate, the new officer being capable looking and presenting good discharges which afterwards proved to be forgeries, and he himself to be a British ex-convict at the Cape "for his health." Before joining the ship as an officer, he had met some of the malcontents of the crew in a gin mill and there a plot was concocted to seize the ship and take her to some port themselves.

"The trouble with you," he told the crew, "is that you don't know anything. I'll go aboard, and if you stick to me, I'll show you what to do with the Old Man."

The Captain had no reason for suspecting the new third mate until insubordination was shown on the quarterdeck in connection with his sending some gear aloft on a gantline. With studied insolence the mate told the Captain to "mind his own damned business." The mate was then backed up against the sheerpole and after his insolent bluff was taken out of him, he was sent forward to the bosun's quarters. The bosun, who was the same little Hollander who shipped in New York, was made third mate. The disrated man, instead of taking his things to the bosun's quarters in the after end on the deck house, went to the fo'castle and mixed with the crew, thereby showing his colors for the first time. No action was taken on his conduct however until the following day, when all hands were mustered at the mast for an understanding. The Captain appealed to the reason of the crew and said plainly that he considered the man's act to be one of open mutiny and put it up to them to tell him what to do. Several agreed that it was mutiny, to be acted upon accordingly. The Captain's cool and judicial manner disarmed the malcontents among the number before him on the main deck, for they knew they were dealing with a man who did not know fear. The mutineer was called out of line and placed in irons for the safety of the ship during the rest of the voyage home. That was the last flurry of the New London mutiny.

Without further incident, tragic or otherwise, the *Northern Light* arrived in New York, spick and span, and in much better condition than when she towed out through Long Island Sound eighteen months before. Her new gang of steel wire standing rigging made her look particularly trim, and it certainly added greatly to her windward qualities, the yards bracing up another point. A change came in the ownership of this fine ship, however, which resulted in the Captain's selling out his shares and becoming the sole owner of the little bark *Aquidneck,* of Baltimore.

CHAPTER 11

The *Aquidneck:*
Down to Rio

For a time after quitting the deck of the *Northern Light*, the Captain looked to steamboating. But the opportunities offered deck officers were limited. Besides, his independent habits were too deeply ingrained to make him take kindly to a step backward while he saw a chance to hold on. As one of the old school of merchant seamen he could not forbear clinging to the old order of things to which he was peculiarly fitted, but which at this time, in American ships at least, was obviously dying out.

Our proud fleet of clipper ships was an anachronism. It was out of date as early as the fifties, for while American investors in marine securities were sentimentally applauding skysails, stunsails and fast passages around Cape Horn and elsewhere, the handwriting was already on the wall. The only importance of the clipper ship to us was that it was the culminating expression of our own national sea-mindedness before it went into decay. It is true that this was a glorious period of marine supremacy, but that is all the good it did us; and that sweeping of the seas with unrivalled tonnage and of the skies with unmatched clouds of towering canvas was only an idle boast.

Two other elements were already at work in England and other European countries: one of these was steam, and how to use it; the other was the iron hull, and how to build it. To this progress in ocean navigation our own investors were blind in their conservatism.

While there was ready New York and Boston money for investment in fast clipper ships, the offered shares in steam, on this side, went begging. The foundation of world trade is the cargo ship, and the transportation of commodities from one part of the world to another is the chief business of commerce. Understanding this principle, the English and the other sea peoples of Europe, slowly and doggedly, not only developed the large freight-carrying iron steam tramp but with equal foresight developed the trade routes to put them on. In this way our competitors got a fifty year start on us and these are the reasons why the American ship is where it is today. We lost our grip when gripping was good.

When we woke to this fact in the nineties, it was too late; the plums were gone. And except to make a secondary attempt at steamboating, we have nearly faded out of the picture. At the best it furnished employment to but a small percentage of our stranded sailing ship men.

My father was not opposed to steam or to steamships but, for himself, felt impelled to keep on as he had started. So with a shot still in the locker, he bought the *Aquidneck* for the South American trade, hoping to keep his own deck under his feet and determined to make the best of it. She was a Baltimore-Rio clipper and according to his own description later on, this vessel was "a little bark, which of all man's handiwork seemed (to him) the nearest to perfection of beauty, and which in speed, when the wind blew, asked no favor of steamers." He bought the vessel at the settlement of the estate of Captain Cheeseborough, who built and equipped her to suit his own taste and fancy without regard to expense. The result was as close to a yacht as a merchantman could be.

The *Aquidneck* was built in Mystic, Connecticut, in 1865, in the yard of Hill and Williams, for Mr. Cheeseborough of Baltimore, at a cost of $50,000. She was a single decked vessel; 140 feet long, 27 feet beam, and 12 feet depth of hold, being 365 tons register. She was finely modelled with a round stern and sharp bow. The stern was decorated with the usual gilded spread-eagle of the period, while the fiddle head was also a carved and gilded eagle's head. There was a long poop with a half deck underneath for the stowage of gear and a house on the main deck underneath for the accommodation of the crew's quarters, the galley and the carpenter shop as well as quarters for the cook and the carpenter and bosun. She carried eight men before the mast. Though built as late as '65 she was rigged with single topsails, for the handling of which the eight men and bosun were none too many.

As the vessel had been laid up for some time there was much overhauling to be done to put her back into a shipshape condition. In the first place, the well-stretched hemp standing rigging was changed to steel wire and at Woodall's drydock she was caulked and re-coppered; and once ready for sea again she took on a cargo of flour for Pernambuco.

During the transition of our interests from one vessel to another, the family lived in Boston with my father's sisters. My mother found the change from the mutinous turmoil of the last year and a half a very welcome one. Voyaging with cutthroats was to her like voyaging with a volcano under the hatches, and the nervous strain caused by the constant alarms at sea had undermined her health, for she was predisposed to a weak heart.

The voyage to Pernambuco was pleasant, and once the vessel was moored to the reef breakwater which shelters the port, we had some good times ashore. One of these was a picnic in a cocoanut grove, and after that we went several times in our boat to the reef where the surge was always pounding outside. This was an adventure as well as a lesson in natural history. My mother was always cheerful and none of us children suspected the malady that was soon to take her away from us. From Pernambuco we sailed for Buenos Aires, but soon after passing Santa Catharina mother was taken sick and was put to bed. She never saw land again, for soon after anchoring in the roadstead the end came. That was on July 25, 1885. There is no need of my looking at a calendar for the date, which sixty-five years ago was written on my heart, never in this life to be effaced.

We laid her at rest in the English Cemetery at Buenos Aires, under the Southern Cross. Peter, her pet canary, given her by Mrs. Newall in East Portland, knew something was wrong nor uttered a note for a long time after. Peter had made glad music for us for seven years in calm and storm, only to fall victim to a strange cat which came aboard soon after while we were yet in the River Plate.

From the River Plate we sailed, with a freight, for Maceio, and found there a ready cargo for New York. On this passage we made the fast run of nineteen days, which excited press comment. In the northeast trades along the West Indies the *Aquidneck* reeled off 350 miles a day, while it held good.

When we returned home, my sister and two brothers were

sent to live in Boston, while I was kept on the vessel, a decision I have never since regretted, for I would rather be a sailor than anything else. It is a useful field of activity and a most interesting one. Anyway, that is how I became a sailor.

The *Aquidneck's* next voyages were three short ones between Baltimore and Pernambuco, but on the last one home we had not such good luck. On looking aloft one morning, just as we entered the edge of the Gulf Stream, it was discovered that the mainmast head had carried away, and that it was left swaying, with the heel of the topmast, on the trestle trees. The only thing to do was to keep all hands aft, wear ship, and bring the whole thing down by the run. The mainsail was hauled up and all hands mustered on the braces. The helm was then put aweather and, as the head swung off and the yards squared, down came the whole business, crashing in a heap in the waist and over the lee rail. The snapping of the falling mass of spars was terrific. The only thing comparable with it would have been the grounding of the vessel on a hard sand bar in a heavy sea with all standing. The wreckage was all saved and taken on board, leaving us the foresail, foretopsail, fore topmast staysail, jib and spanker under which to work the vessel into port. The mizzen topmast and the fore t'gallantmast went in the partial dismasting.

Then began a real battle with wind and sea. For ten days the gale alternated between sou'west and nor'east or nor'west. When the wind was fair, a gain would be made, only to be lost when it shifted, for there was not canvas enough left on to forereach with into a heavy sea and to hold our own until it became fair again. One night, after reefing the fore topsail, we found one of our number missing. It was Olaf, a young Norwegian who had shipped in Pernambuco. The last seen of him was in the ratlines while we were all coming down on deck and our

181

condition was dismal enough without having a shipmate vanish in the gloom.

On the tenth day of the struggle, and when the wind happened to be fair, a seagoing tug from Delaware Breakwater, out looking for lame ducks after the blow, hove in sight. We must have looked helpless to the tug skipper, for his figure for a tow to New York sounded very much like salvage. The *Aquidneck* shot back with a rather indifferent counter-offer which made the tug skipper give a twirl to his wheel, and an emphatic jingle on his engine room bell. He nearly got out of sight but ranged alongside again and hailed, "Cap, I've got to go into New York anyway, and I'll take you in for about the price of the coal." As this proved equal to splitting the difference, we took his towline aboard and shackled it to the end of our chain cable, leading out through the hawse pipe. There was no sooner a strain on that towline, and our sails stowed, when it screeched again out of the northwest, but the tug was good for it.

It was a happy crew next morning that saw Sandy Hook abeam and by noon the *Aquidneck* was tied up at Pierrepont Stores, in Brooklyn, where we were to discharge. Just after the lines were passed, the second mate, the same "Billy" Flynn who was on the *Northern Light,* and a superstitious man, was alone on deck. He was nearly scared out of his boots. An apparition rose up before him out of the lazarette hatch. It was the long lost Olaf, who had stowed away in the hold in terror on the stormy night when we all thought he had gone over the side. He had been living on sugar for those ten days while we were mourning his supposed fate.

The following spring the *Aquidneck* was ready for sea again with a new mainmast, made and fitted in Brooklyn. We had now owned the vessel for two years and she was in much better shape than when we first took her over. My father had spent the winter in Boston and married Miss Henrietta Elliott of Mount Hanley, Nova Scotia. She came to sea in the *Aquidneck*, bringing with her my little brother Garfield. Ben and Jessie were given homes by my father's sisters in Natick, Massachusetts, where they went to school.

Bound for Montevideo, the *Aquidneck* went to sea on the left semi-circle of a hurricane, which, with its center well out on the Atlantic, was past the danger point. Its position was proved by the northwest gale which was blowing, and under normal conditions could have been used for a first rate fair wind as a start for the voyage. The glass was rising, but the heavy sea was still running as we made our offing and began scudding on our course under nothing but a reefed foresail. With a tight ship all would have been well. But some seams in the decks, which had been merely filled with pitch instead of properly caulked, broke open while the vessel was running before the heavy following sea which flooded the main deck as she bowled along. We were loaded with case oil, not a heavy cargo, and the vessel did not labor.

But the water began to gain on the pumps which were kept constantly going for thirty-six hours. That was a desperate sensation, pumping for all you were worth, and at the same time feeling that the ship was going down under you. It was like pumping the Atlantic Ocean through the vessel. The sounding rod at last showed six feet, meaning that the hold was just half filled with the sea water we were battling against. The long roaring seas that at first only tumbled over the rails, now began to tumble over the stern as well, showing that the vessel was becoming "logey" and losing her buoyancy. Next would come the loss of stability, and then we would have to cut away the masts to prevent capsizing, for being loaded with oil and no ballast, we knew that it would be physically impossible to sink. While we were still pumping, and while the steward was provisioning the boats, ready to abandon ship, the leak was discovered along the break of the poop, where a torrent of water was found pouring down into the hold. Working in the water roaring about our ears, we plugged the gaping seam with strips of sail cloth and strands of rope. Then the pumps began to gain on the water. To make things easier, we rapidly ran out of the hurricane and into normal weather, where all of our troubles were forgotten. That is the way with a sailor; it would never do if he took all the jams to heart that he ever got into.

Having discharged at Montevideo, and salved a cargo of Bordeaux wine from a scuttled Spanish brig further up the river, a cargo of baled hay was next loaded for Rio de Janeiro.

Owing to an epidemic of cholera then prevalent in the Argentine, the charter proved to be subject to fluctuating quarantine restrictions which were to prove disastrous to our interests. On sailing it was found that instead of going to Rio, according to charter, the vessel was ordered by the Brazilian consul to Ilha Grande, the quarantine station of Brazil, there to be disinfected and to discharge her cargo in quarantine.

We arrived at Ilha Grande, our destination, on January 7, 1887, and came to an anchor within musket range of the guardship. She happened to be the armored *Aquidaban,* a turret battleship, commanded by Captain Mello. (This was the same Mello, with the same *Aquidaban,* who headed the Brazilian rebellion some years later when Captain Slocum in the *Destroyer* was after him "with dynamite, that time, instead of hay.") The *Aquidneck* found several other vessels also riding at quarantine. On the next day, January 8, the officers of the port came alongside and ordered us to leave, saying that *the port had been closed that morning.* We had been in port twenty-four hours before the order came through. "But we have made the voyage," protested the Captain.

"That is no matter," returned the guard. "Man the windlass at once or the guardship will put fire into you," emphasizing the order by thrusting a forefinger into the palm of his other hand. He wanted to see the men on the windlass before he left our side.

There was no question what the order meant. If there had been only men on board, the best thing would have been to let them fire away, or to have chucked the hay overboard, but we hove up and took it back to Rosario.

On our arrival there we found things better than they were when we sailed. The cholera had ceased (it was on the wane when we sailed from Rosario), and there was hardly a case of the dread disease in the whole country east of Cordova. That was indeed a comfort, but it left our hardship the same, and led, consequently, to the total loss of the vessel after dragging us through harrowing trials and losses, as will be seen later.

This Ilha Grande decree, really a political move, was merely intended by the Brazilians as retaliation for past offences by their Argentine neighbors; not only for quarantines against Rio fevers, but for a discriminating duty as well on sugar from the empire; a combination of hardships on commerce which was more than the sensitive Brazilians could stand. They decided to teach their republican cousins a wholesome lesson. However, their wish was to retaliate without causing war, and this was done. In fact, closing the ports as they did at the beginning of Argentine's most valuable season for exports to Brazil, and with the plausible excuse of fear of a pain in the stomach, so filled the Argentines with admiration for their equals in strategy, that at the earliest opportunity they proclaimed two public holidays in honor of bright Brazil.

The difference ended to the satisfaction of all except the owner of the *Aquidneck*. We stopped first at Buenos Aires, where the officers of the guardship, at sight of the returned American bark and her cargo, were convulsed with laughter. We naturally could not see the joke.

Back in Rosario we met a merchant who, while he regretted the misfortunes of the vessel, exclaimed, "Carramba, my own losses are great." It required very little reasoning to show us that the least expensive course was the safest one to adopt, and on the merchant offering to pay for the marketing, the Captain found it wisest not to disturb the cargo, but to lay up instead with it in the vessel and await the reopening of the Brazilian ports.

On April 9, 1887, news came that the Brazilian ports were open. Cholera had long since disappeared in Santa Fe and Buenos Aires. The Brazilians had established their own beef drying factories, and could now afford to open their ports to competition. This made a great stir among the ships.

While lying idle, moored to the river bank just below Rosario, our crew, composed mostly of Finns, broke out one Sunday morning in a drunken frenzy after an all night bout. With reinforcements from three other ships, they were subdued without loss of life and lodged in the calaboose to cool off. Their places were taken by a gang much worse, as we learned when it was too late. When the cholera was at its height the jails were opened and the birds released. We shipped at least four of these who were guilty either of murder or of highway robbery. They were all sheep thieves. One of them a burly scoundrel with an ugly sabre cut across his face, was known as "Dangerous Jack"; while "Bloody Tommy" was more of a sneak. He had a cat-like eye that would follow one around. He bragged, rather unwisely for himself, while helping to dress some mutton on board, that "he would just as soon cut a man as a sheep." They were a hard looking set.

The *Aquidneck* sailed down the Parana River at the head of a fleet, and at daylight on the morning of April 29 sailed into Ilha Grande for the second time with the same cargo of hay. We came upon the entrance in a fog, and all day heavy gusts of wind came down through the gulches in the mountains, laden with fog and rain.

Two days later the rest of the hay fleet came in and found us anchored under the highest mountain. There were eight days of sullen gloom and rain in this place. Then the holds were fumigated and we were considered healthy enough to be admitted to pratique in Rio, where we arrived May 11 to discharge.

At the fort entrance to the harbor of Rio we were again challenged and brought to an anchor at the bar. The *Aquidneck*, it would seem, had outsailed a cablegram which should have preceded her. When they challenged a vessel from this fort, they fired one, two or three shots, if necessary, to bring a ship to, at a cost to the ship, if she were not American, of eight mil reis for the first shot, sixteen mil reis for the second and thirty-two mil reis for the third. The *Aquidneck*, being an American vessel, had the thirty-two mil reis shot fired first, to bring her to.

After all the difficulties were cleared away, the tardy cable arrived, and being identified by the officers we weighed for the last time on this voyage and took up our destined berth in Rio. To quote from the *Aquidneck's* log: "The cargo was at last delivered and no one was made ill over it. A change of rats was also made at Rio. Those we brought gave place to others from the Dom Pedro Docks where we moored. Fleas too skipped about in the hay, as happy as larks and almost as big; and all the other live stock we brought from Rosario—goodness knows

187

of what kith or kin—arrived well and sound from over the water, notwithstanding the fumigations and fuss made at the quarantine."

From Rio we sailed for Antonina, in Paranagua Bay, to load a cargo of yerba maté for Montevideo. Here it was thought by some of the cutthroat crew that there must be a considerable sum of money aboard. On a still night near the time of sailing, murder, with robbery as its object, was attempted on the afterguard. There was a savage attack which was met by quick action.

"Dangerous Jack," ploughed by a .56, I took ashore about midnight, still howling and cursing. "Bloody Tommy" was left where he fell for the police to inspect the next morning. Face down on deck, and in the rigor of death, he still clutched the same knife he had used killing sheep. He had already two murders to his credit, but this time he did not get his man, and he mutely told his own story. It was a night of horror.

The Captain was placed on parole by the authorities to stand investigation, though the case was clear. With a Spanish sailing master and a Brazilian crew on board and with myself as flag captain, the *Aquidneck* proceeded to Montevideo. Here the Captain arrived soon after, but left his wife and Garfield in Antonina.

In Montevideo some of the Brazilian crew contracted smallpox while ashore, and in a day or so after leaving port, this scourge broke out, leaving only three souls to work the vessel back to port. We anchored off Flores Island quarantine station and set the yellow jack. The doctor came off, took one look, and ordered us to the port of Montevideo, twelve miles distant. The topsails had been left standing during the period of anchoring, or we could not have moved without more crew. As it was, the three of us not only hove up the anchor, but with it the weight of the submarine cable to Montevideo as well. It came up, hooked to the bill of the anchor, but we cleared it without damage to the cable. With our sick and dying aboard, who should have been taken off at the quarantine station, we anchored in the outer roads of Montevideo, and from here the stricken men

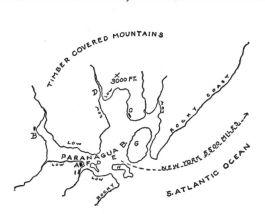

Sketch map of Paranagua Bay

Key: *a* Town of Paranagua *b* Antonina *c* Guarakasava Village *d* Guarakasava River, the source of timber supply *e* Where the *Aquidneck* grounded *f* The anchorage of the *Aquidneck* after grounding *g* Despeças Island *h* Mel Island *i* Paranagua River and shipyard where the *Liberdade* was completed and fitted for sea after the wreck of the *Aquidneck*.

were towed back to Flores in the vessel's longboat. All of this valuable service cost the *Aquidneck* heavily.

Back at Paranagua the vessel was shifted over to an arm of the extensive Paranagua Bay where she was to load.

The timber of this country was very much like that of the Philippines, for most of it would sink and had to be floated off to the vessel, lashed to large dug-out canoes wrought from

189

gigantic trees. Someone indicated that further inland there might be finer timber than that which was offered at tidewater in Guarakasava, so the vessel's longboat was rigged for exploration and was away from the vessel until next morning. The party got back on board again very much fatigued and bedraggled. The trouble was that the longboat was not large enough for comfortable timber cruising. If we were going into the Paranagua timber business, the *Aquidneck* must have a regular tender.

Its construction was immediately decided upon. Native sawyers, who whipsawed by hand, were put to ripping forty-foot Spanish cedar logs for boat plank. Ironwood, that would sink, was in similar fashion ripped into thicker plank for the partially flat bottom, for a dory-like type of hull had been decided upon. Natural crooks of another very hard timber were brought in from the forest by the woodsmen, for frames. By that time we had the bottom cleated together, the stem made and erected, and the transom up. The length of the boat was limited to the space between the break of the *Aquidneck's* poop aft, to the after side of the fore deck house. Besides the native sawyers who ripped the plank, there were four on the job at the start, and progress was rapid.

We spent Christmas of 1887 at Guarakasava. The bark loaded soon after but grounded on a sandbar while beating back to her anchorage at Paranagua. There she remained, broadside to the open sea, to pound until her back was broken. After twenty-five years of good service, the *Aquidneck* was to end her days as a coffee hulk in Santos, where she was finally burned.

The foreign crew found a ship for Montevideo where they had first joined the *Aquidneck* in lieu of the stricken Brazilian sailors. To go to Montevideo ourselves was the last of our thoughts, so we set about to solve the problem of returning home in a vessel of our own. We all decided on completing the Guarakasava boat. The idea, novel at first, took shape in reality and we became enthused over the prospect of an adventure —in the right direction.

The Aquidneck's original sail plan as a Rio coffee clipper. She was later rigged as a bark.

(Above) The crew of the Liberdade. Left to right: Captain and Mrs. Slocum, Garfield and Victor.

(Below) The Liberdade, photographed after her arrival in Cape Fear River, Wilmington, N. C.

The Liberdade *portrait of Captain Slocum taken in Washington in 1888.*

(Below) A cross section of the submarine bow gun of Ericcson's Destroyer, *which was commanded by Capt. Slocum in the Mello rebellion.*

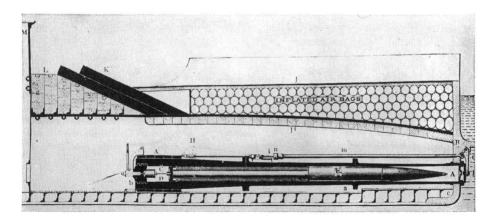

(*Above*) *The* Destroyer *as she lay in Pernambuco Harbor. She was the command of Captain Joshua Slocum before his voyage in the* Spray.

(*Below*) *The crew of the* Destroyer *with Captain Slocum, who is seated at the left.*

CHAPTER 12

The *Liberdade:*

5510 Miles in a 35-Foot Boat

W<small>E HAD</small> no idea when we began to direct our efforts toward the completion of the Guarakasava tender that our family of four was to make one of the most interesting and original voyages ever sailed. The human element was unusual. Women are not usually given to travelling long distances in small boats and it was still more exceptional to have a child of seven along, though he proved a very good sailor. In fact little Garfield's great confidence in the boat, even though she was not, as he said, "big enough to pray in," was an inspiration to the rest of us.

We therefore turned all of our energies toward the fresh project, the difficulties of which were duly considered. Swift ocean currents around capes and coral reefs were taken into account; and above all other dangers we knew would be the fierce tropical storms which surely we must encounter.

But our boat would be built stout and strong, we said, one in which we should not be afraid to trust our lives even in storm. Seaworthiness was the first and most prominent feature of our small ship; next to that she should sail well, at least before free winds. We counted on favorable winds, and so we found them for the greater part of the voyage which soon followed.

Our plan now was to plank the frame of the tiny craft, lower the hull over the side of the *Aquidneck,* and have it towed to a small shipyard we had patronized for some work on the *Aquidneck* awhile before. There, upon the boss' invitation, we completed the fitting for sea. The shipyard owner, a young and sympathetic Brazilian, even tendered us the use of part of his house while we were working on the small vessel.

The most laborious part of the job on the hull was jack-planing the 40-foot handsawed cedar plank. As they were sawed by hand, without gauges, it was easy for the sawyers to leave much unevenness that was equally hard to plane down. For this work a plank bench was rigged near the rail on the quarter-deck of the *Aquidneck* and protected from sun and rain by an awning. It took the writer about a month to jack-plane those plank, a task which he remembers very well. The plank were then put on lapstreak, without doubt the strongest way to build a boat.

Our kit, with which my father and I worked, was meagre and not altogether suited to the building of a boat. In the vessel's carpenter shop there had been two handsaws, an axe and adze, a jack-plane, some augers and bits. The last were not always of the right size, so the holes were enlarged by the expedient of running through a piece of red-hot small jackstay iron. Lapstreak clamps, such as those usually employed by boat builders, were missing, but we made substitutes from the crooked guava trees, and used wedges. In Paranagua we found carriage bolts which could be used in some places and we found copper nails for the lap-rivets, but no burrs. The latter we improvised by hammering out large copper coins, called "dumps," cut them into diamond-shaped pieces and punched holes through them. This solved one metal problem.

Fastenings we gathered up in various places, in the form of old muntz metal sheathing, and brass hinges from doors and skylights. These the natives melted and cast into nails. The cut ends of copper fastenings were also re-cast into nails. A number of small eye-bolts from the spanker boom of the *Aquidneck* were turned to account for lashing bolts in the deck of the new vessel.

The ironwood planks in the bottom were 1¼ by 10 inches. For the sides and top, cedar was used, each plank reaching the whole length of the boat. This arrangement of exceedingly heavy wood in the bottom, and light on the top, contributed much to the stability of the craft. The ironwood was as heavy as stone, while the cedar, being light and elastic, lent buoyancy and suppleness, all that we could wish for.

From this point I shall let my father tell his story of the "Voyage of the *Liberdade*."

The hull being completed, by various other contrivances and makeshifts in which, sometimes, the "wooden blacksmith" was called in to assist, and the mother of invention also lending a hand, fixtures were made which served as well on the voyage as though made in a dockyard and at great cost.

My builders balked at nothing, and on the 13th day of May, the day on which the slaves of Brazil were set free, our craft was launched, and was named *Liberdade* (Liberty).

Her dimensions being—35 feet in length over all, 7½ feet breadth of beam, and 3 feet depth of hold. Who shall say that she was not large enough?

195

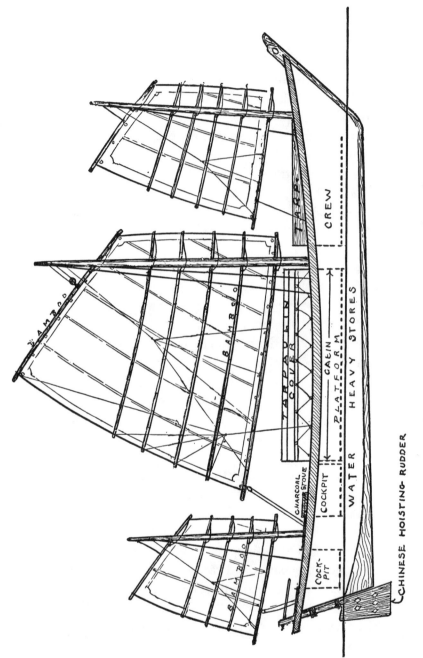

Cabin profile and sail plan of Liberdade as fitted for the voyage from Brazil to New York. Length, 35' 0"; Beam, 7' 6"; Depth of hold 3'; Draft, 2' 6"; Weight, 6 tons.

Her model I got from my recollections of Cape Ann dories and from a photo of a very elegant Japanese *sampan* which I had before me on the spot, so, as it might be expected, when finished, she resembled both types of vessel in some degree.

Her rig was the Chinese *sampan* style, which is, I consider, the most convenient boat rig in the whole world.

This was the boat, or canoe I prefer to call it, in which we purposed to sail for North America and home. Each one had

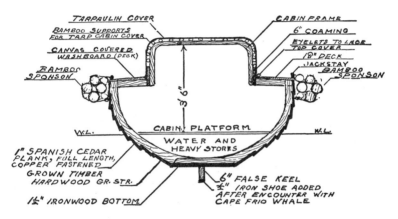

Midship Section of the Liberdade

been busy during the construction and past misfortunes had all been forgotten. Madam had made the sails—and very good sails they were, too!

Victor, the carpenter, ropemaker and general roustabout had performed his part. Our little man, Garfield, too, had found employment in holding the hammer to clinch the nails and giving much advice on the coming voyage. All were busy, I say, and no one had given a thought of what we were about to encounter from the port officials further up the coast; it was pretended by them that a passport could not be granted to so small

197

a craft to go on so long a voyage as the contemplated one to North America.

Then fever returned to the writer, and the constructor of the little craft, and I was forced to go to bed, remaining there three days. Finally, it came to my mind that in part of a medicine chest, which had been saved from the wreck, was stored some *arsenicum*, I think it is called. Of this I took several doses (small ones at first, you may be sure), and the good effect of the deadly poison on the malaria in my system was soon felt trickling through my veins. Increasing the doses somewhat, I could perceive the beneficial effect hour by hour, and in a few days I had quite recovered from the malady. Absurd as it was to have the judgment of sailors set on by pollywog navigators, we had still to submit, the pollywogs being numerous.

About this time—as the astrologers say—a messenger came down from the *Alfandega* (Custom House), asking me to repair thither at midday on the morrow. This filled me with alarm. True, the messenger had delivered his message in the politest possible manner, but that signified nothing, since Brazilians are always polite. This thing, small as it seems now, came near sending me back to the fever.

What had I done?

I went up next day, after having nightmare badly all night, prepared to say that I wouldn't do it again! The kind administrator I found, upon presenting myself at his office, had no fault to charge me with; but had a good word, instead. "The little *Liberdade*," he observed, had attracted the notice of his people and his own curiosity, as being "a handsome and well-built craft." This and many other flattering expressions were vented, at which I affected surprise, but secretly said, "I think you are right, sir, and you have good taste, too, if you are a customs officer."

The drift of this flattery, to make a long story short, was to have me build a boat for the *Alfandega*, or, his government not allowing money to build new—pointing to one which certainly would require new keel, planks, ribs, stem and stern-post —"could I not repair one?"

To this proposition I begged time to consider. Flattering as the officer's words were, and backed by the offer of liberal pay, so long as the boat could be "repaired," I still had no mind to remain in the hot country, and risk getting the fever again.

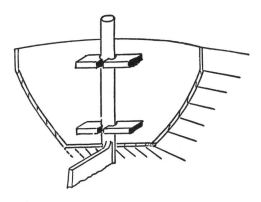

How the Chinese hoisting rudder of the Liberdade *was hung*

But there was the old hitch to be gotten over; namely, the passport, on which, we thought, depended our sailing.

However, to expedite matters, a fishing license was hit upon, and I wondered why I had not thought of that before, having been, once upon a time, a fisherman myself. Heading thence on a new diplomatic course, I commenced to fit ostensibly for a fishing voyage. To this end, a fishing net was made, which would be a good thing to have, any way. Then hooks and lines were rigged and a cable made. This cable, or rope, was formed from vines that grow very long on the sandbanks just above tide water, several of which twisted together make a very serviceable rope, then being light and elastic, it is especially adapted for a boat anchor rope, or for the storm drag. Ninety fathoms of this rope was made for us by the natives for the sum of ten milreis ($5.00).

The anchor came of itself almost. I had made a wooden one from heavy sinking timber, but a stalwart ranchman coming along, one day, brought a boat anchor with him which, he said, had been used by his slaves as a pot-hook. "But now that they are free and away," said he, "I have no further use for the crooked thing." A sewing-machine, which had served to stitch the sails together, was coveted by him, and was of no further use to us; in exchange for this the prized anchor was readily secured, the owner of it leaving us some boot into the bargain. Things working thus in our favor, the wooden anchor was stowed away to be kept as a spare bower.

These arrangements completed, our craft took on the appearance of a fishing smack, and I began to feel somewhat in my old element, with no fear of the lack of ways and means when we should arrive on our own coast, where I knew of fishing banks. And a document which translated read: "A license to catch fish inside and outside of the bar," was readily granted by the port authorities.

"How far outside the bar may this carry us?" I asked.

"*Quien sabe!*" said the officer. (Literally translated, "Who knows?" but in Spanish or Portuguese used for, "Nobody knows, or I don't care.")

"Adios, senor," said the polite official; "we will meet in heaven!"

This meant you can go since you insist upon it, but I must not officially know of it; and you will probably go to the bottom. In this he and many others were mistaken.

Having the necessary document now in our possession, we

commenced to take in stores for the voyage, as follows: Sea-biscuits, 120 lbs.; flour, 25 lbs.; sugar, 30 lbs.; coffee, 9 lbs., which roasted black and pounded fine as wheaten flour, was equal to double the amount as prepared in North America, and afforded us a much more delicious cup.

Of tea we had 3 lbs.; pork, 20 lbs.; dried beef, 100 lbs.; *baccalao secca* (dried codfish) 20 lbs.; 2 bottles of honey, 200 oranges, 6 bunches of bananas, 120 gallons of water; also a small basket of yams, and a dozen sticks of sugar-cane, by way of vegetables.

Our medicine chest contained Brazil nuts, pepper and cinnamon; no other medicines or condiments were required on the voyage, except table salt, which we also had.

One musket and a carbine—which had already stood us in good stead—together with ammunition and three cutlasses, were stowed away for last use, to be used, nevertheless, in case of necessity.

The light goods I stowed in the ends of the canoe, the heavier in the middle and along the bottom, thus economizing space and lending to the stability of the canoe. Over the top of the midship stores a floor was made, which, housed over by a tarpaulin roof reaching three feet above the deck of the canoe, gave us sitting space of four feet from the floor to roof, and twelve feet long amidships, supported by a frame of bamboo, made store-room and cabin. This arrangement of cabin in the centre gave my passengers a berth where the least motion would be felt; even this is saying but little, for best we could do to avoid it we had still to accept much tossing from the waves.

Precautionary measures were taken in everything, so far as our resources and skill could reach. The springy and buoyant bamboo was used wherever stick of any kind was required, such

201

as the frame and braces for the cabin, yards for the sails, and, finally, for guard on her top sides, making the canoe altogether a self-righting one, in case of a capsize. Each joint in the bamboo was an air-chamber of several pounds buoyant capacity, and we had a thousand joints.

The most important of our stores, particularly the flour, bread and coffee, were hermetically sealed, so that if actually turned over at sea, our craft would not only right herself, but would bring her stores right side up, in good order, and it then would be only a question of baling her out, and of setting her again on her course, when we would come on as right as ever. As it turned out, however, no such trial or mishap awaited us.

While the possibility of many and strange occurrences was felt by all of us, the danger which loomed most in little Garfield's mind was that of the sharks.

A fine specimen was captured on the voyage, showing five rows of pearly teeth, as sharp as lances.

Some of these monsters, it is said, have nine rows of teeth; that they are always hungry is admitted by sailors of great experience.

How it is that sailors can go in bathing, as they often do, in the face of a danger so terrible, is past my comprehension. Their business is to face danger, to be sure, but this is a needless exposure, for which the penalty is sometimes a life. The second mate of a bark on the coast of Cuba, not long ago, was bitten in twain, and the portions swallowed whole by a monster shark that he had tempted in this way. The shark was captured soon after, and the poor fellow's remains taken out of the revolting maw.

Leaving the sharks where they are, I gladly return to the voyage of the *Liberdade.*

The efficiency of our canoe was soon discovered: On the

24th of June, after having sailed about the bay some few days to temper our feelings to the new craft, and shake things into place, we crossed the bar and stood out to sea, while six vessels lay inside "bar-bound," that is to say by their pilots it was thought too rough to venture out, and they, the pilots, stood on the point as we put out to sea, crossing themselves in our behalf, and shouting that the bar was *crudo*. But the *Liberdade* stood on her course, the crew never regretting it.

The wind from the sou'west at the time was the moderating side of a *pampeiro* which had brought in a heavy swell from the ocean, that broke and thundered on the bar with deafening roar and grand display of majestic effort.

But our little ship bounded through the breakers like a fish— as natural to the elements, and as free!

Of all the seas that broke furiously about her that day, often standing her on end, not one swept over or even boarded her, and she finally came through the storm of breakers in triumph. Then squaring away before the wind she spread her willing sails, and flew onward like a bird.

It required confidence and some courage to face the first storm in so small a bark, after having been years in large ships; but it would have required more courage than was possessed by any of us to turn back, since thoughts of home had taken hold on our minds.

Then, too, the old boating trick came back fresh to me, the love of the thing itself gaining on me as the little ship stood out; and my crew with one voice said: "Go on." The heavy South Atlantic swell rolling in upon the coast, as we sped along, toppled over when it reached the ten fathom line, and broke into roaring combers, which forbade our nearer approach to the land.

Evidently, our safest course was away from the shore, and

203

out where the swelling seas, though grand, were regular, and raced under our little craft that danced like a mite on the ocean as she drove forward. In twenty-four hours from the time Paranagua bar was crossed we were up with Santos Heads, a run of 150 miles.

A squall of wind burst on us through a gulch, as we swept round the Heads, tearing our sails into shreds, and sending us into Santos under bare poles.

Chancing then upon an old friend, the mail steamship *Finance*, Capt. Baker, about to sail for Rio, the end of a friendly line was extended to us, and we were towed by the stout steamer toward Rio, the next day, as fast as we could wish to go. My wife and youngest sailor took passage on the steamer, while Victor remained in the canoe with me, and stood by, with axe in hand, to cut the towline, if the case should require it— and I steered.

"Look out," said Baker, as the steamer began to move ahead, "look out that I don't snake that canoe out from under you."

"Go on with your mails, Baker," was all I could say, "don't blow up your ship with my wife and son on board, and I will look out for the packet on the other end of the rope."

Baker opened her up to thirteen knots, but the *Liberdade* held on!

The line that we towed with was 1⅛ inches in diameter, by ninety fathoms long. This, at times when the steamer surged over seas, leaving the canoe on the opposite side of a wave astern, would become as taut as a harp-string. At other times it would slacken and sink limp in a bight, under the forefoot, but only for a moment, however, when the steamer's next great plunge ahead would snap it taut again, pulling us along with a heavy, trembling jerk. Under the circumstances, straight steering was imperative, for a sheer to port or starboard would have finished the career of the *Liberdade,* by sending her under the sea. Therefore, the trick of twenty hours fell to me—the oldest and most experienced helmsman. But I was all right and not over-fatigued until Baker cast oil upon the "troubled waters." I soon got tired of that.

Victor was under the canvas covering, with the axe still in hand, ready to cut the line which was so arranged that he could reach it from within, and cut instantly, if by mischance the canoe should take a sheer.

I was afraid that the lad would become sleepy, and putting his head "under his wing" for a nap, would forget his post, but my frequent cry, "Stand by there, Victor," found him always on hand, though complaining some of the dizzy motion.

Heavy sprays dashed over me at the helm, which, however, seeming to wash away the sulphur and brimstone smoke of many a quarantine, brought enjoyment to my mind.

Confused waves rose about us, high and dangerous—often high above the gunwale of the canoe—but her shapely curves balanced her well, and she rode over them all in safety.

This canoe ride was thrilling and satisfactory to us all. It proved beyond a doubt that we had in this little craft a most extraordinary sea-boat, for the tow was a thorough test of her seaworthiness.

The captain of the steamer ordered oil cast over from time to time, relieving us of much spray and sloppy motion, but adding to discomforts of taste to me at the helm, for much of the oil blew over me and in my face. Said the captain to one of his mates (an old whaler by the way, and whalers for some unaccountable reason have never too much regard for a poor merchantman) "Mr. Smith."

"Aye, aye, sir," answered old Smith.

"Mr. Smith, hoist out that oil."

"Aye, aye, sir," said the old "blubberhunter," in high glee, as he went about it with alacrity, and in less than five minutes from the time the order was given, I was smothering in grease and our boat was oiled from keel to truck.

"She's all right now," said Smith.

"That's all right," said Baker, but I thought it all wrong. The wind, meanwhile, was in our teeth and before we crossed Rio Bar I had swallowed enough oil to cure any amount of consumption.

Baker, I have heard, said he wouldn't care much if he should "drown Slocum." But I was all right so long as the canoe didn't sheer, and we arrived at Rio safe and sound after the most exciting boat-ride of my life. I was bound not to cut the line that towed us so well; and I knew that Baker wouldn't let it go, for it was his rope.

I found at Rio that my fishing license could be exchanged for a pass of greater import. This document had to be procured through the office of the Minister of Marine.

Many a smart linguist was ready to use his influence in my behalf with the above-named high official; but I found at the end of a month that I was making headway about as fast as a Dutch galliot in a head sea after the wind had subsided. Our worthy Consul, General H. Clay Armstrong, gave me a hint of what the difficulty was and how to obviate it. I then went about the business myself as I should have done at first, and I found those at the various departments who were willing to help me without the intervention of outside "influence."

Commander Marquis of the Brazilian navy, recommended me to His Excellency, the Minister of Marine, "out of regard," he said, "for American seamen," and when the new document came it was *"Passe Especial,"* and had on it *a seal as big as a soup plate*. A port naval officer then presented me to the good *Administradore*, who also gave me a *passe especial*, with the seal of the *Alfandega*.

I had now only to procure a bill of health, when I should have papers enough for a man o' war. Rio being considered a healthy place, this was readily granted, making our equipment complete.

I met here our minister whose office, with other duties, is to keep a weather eye lifting in the interest of that orphan, the American ship—alas, my poor relation! Said he, "Captain, if your *Liberdade* be as good as your papers" (documents given me by the Brazilian officials), "you may get there all right"; adding, "well, if the boat ever reaches home she will be a great curiosity," the meaning of which, I could readily infer, was, "and your chances for a snap in a dime museum will be good." This, after many years of experience as an American shipmaster, and also ship owner, in a moderate way, was interesting encouragement. By our Brazilian friends, however, the voyage was looked upon as a success already achieved.

"The utmost confidence," said the *Journal Opiz*, of Rio, "is placed in the cool-headed, audacious American mariner, and we expect in a short time to hear proclaimed in all of the journals of the Old and New World the safe arrival of this wonderful little craft at her destination, ourselves taking part in the glory." "Temos confianca na pericia e sangue frio do audaciauso marinhero Americano por isso esperamos que dentro em pouco tempo veremos o seu nome proclamado por todos os jornaes do velho e novo mundo.

"A nos tambem cabera parte da gloria."

With these and like kind expressions from all of our *friends*, we took leave of Rio, sailing on the morning of July 23d, 1888.

July 23d, 1888, was the day, as I have said, on which we sailed from Rio de Janeiro.

Meeting with head winds and light withal, through the day we made but little progress; and finally, when night came on we anchored twenty miles east of Rio Heads, near the shore. Long, rolling seas rocked us as they raced by, then, dashing their great bodies against defying rocks, made music by which we slept that night. But a trouble unthought of before came up in Garfield's mind before going to his bunk; "Mamma," cried he as our little bark rose and fell on the heavy waves, tumbling the young sailor about from side to side in the small quarters while he knelt seriously at his evening devotion, "Mamma, this boat isn't big enough to pray in!" But this difficulty was gotten over in time, and Garfield learned to watch as well as to pray on the voyage, and full of faith that all would be well, laid him down nights and slept as restfully as any Christian on sea or land.

By daylight of the second day we were again underway, beating to the eastward against the old head wind and head sea. On the following night we kept her at it, and the next day made Cape Frio where we anchored near the entrance to a good harbor.

Time from Rio, two days; distance, 70 miles.

The wind and tide being adverse, compelled us to wait outside for a favorable change. While comfortably anchored at this place, a huge whale, nosing about, came up under the canoe, giving us a toss and a great scare. We were at dinner when it happened. The meal, it is needless to say, was finished without dessert. The great sea animal—fifty to sixty feet long—circling around our small craft, looked terribly big. He was so close to me twice, as he swam round and round the canoe, that I could have touched him either time with a paddle. His flukes stirring the water like a steamer propeller appeared alarmingly close and powerful!—and what an ugly mouth the monster had! Well, we expected instant annihilation. The fate of the stout whale-ship *Essex* came vividly before me. The voyage of the *Liberdade,* I thought, was about ended, and I looked about for pieces of bamboo on which to land my wife and family. Just then, however, to the infinite relief of all of us, the leviathan moved off, without doing us much harm, having felt satisfied, perhaps, that we had no Jonah on board.

We lost an anchor through the incident, and received some small damage to the keel, but no other injury was done—even this, I believe, upon second thought, was unintentional—done in playfulness only! "A shark can take a joke," it is said, and crack one too, but for broad, rippling humor the whale has no equal.

"If this be a sample of our adventures in the beginning," thought I, "we shall have enough and to spare by the end of the voyage." A visit from this quarter had not been counted on; but Sancho Panza says, "when least aware starts the hare," which in our case, by the by, was a great whale!

When our breath came back and the hair on our heads settled to a normal level, we set sail, and dodged about under the lee of the cape till a cove, with a very enticing sand beach at the head of it, opened before us, some three miles northwest of where we lost the anchor in the remarkable adventure with the whale. The "spare bower" was soon bent to the cable. Then we stood in and anchored near a cliff, over which was a goat-path leading in the direction of a small fishing village, about a mile away. Sheering the boat in to the rocky side of the cove which was steep to, we leaped out, warp in hand, and made fast to a boulder above the tidal flow, then, scrambling over the cliff, we repaired to the village, first improvising a spare

209

anchor from three sticks and a stone which answered the purpose quite well.

Judging at once that we were strangers the villagers came out to meet us, and made a stir at home to entertain us in the most hospitable manner, after the custom of the country, and with the villagers was a gentleman from Canada, a Mr. Newkirk, who, as we learned, was engaged, when the sea was smooth, in recovering treasure that was lost near the cape in the British warship *Thetis,* which was wrecked there, in 1830. The treasure, some millions in silver coins and gold in bars, from Peru for England, was dumped in the cove, which has since taken the name of the ship that bore it there, and as I have said, came to grief in that place which is on the west shore near the end of the cape.

Some of the coins were given to us to be treasured as souvenirs of the pleasant visit. We found in Mr. Newkirk a versatile, roving genius; he had been a schoolmaster at home, captain of a lake schooner once, had practiced medicine, and preached some, I think; and what else I do not know. He had tried many things for a living, but, like the proverbial moving stone had failed to accumulate. "Matters," said the Canadian, "were getting worse and worse even, till finally to keep my head above water I was forced to go under the sea," and he had struck it rich, it would seem, if gold being brought in by the boat-load was any sign. This man of many adventures still spoke like a youngster; no one had told him that he was growing old. He talked of going home, as soon as the balance of the treasure was secured, "just to see his dear old mother," who, by the way, was seventy-four years old when he left home, some twenty years before. Since his last news from home, nearly two decades had gone by. He was "the youngest of a family of eighteen children, all living," he said, "though," added he, "our family came near being made one less yesterday, by a whale which I thought would eat my boat, diving-bell, crew, money and all, as he came toward us, with open mouth. By a back stroke of the oars, however, we managed to cheat him out of his dinner, if that was what he was after, and I think it was, but here I am!" he cried, "all right!" and might have added, "wealthy after all."

After hearing the diver's story, I related in Portuguese our own adventure of the same day, and probably with the same whale, the monster having gone in the direction of the diver's boat. The astonishment of the listeners was great; but when they learned of our intended voyage to *America do Norte,* they crossed themselves and asked God to lend us grace!

"Is North America near New York?" asked the village merchant, who owned all the boats and nets of the place.

"Why, America is *in* New York," answered the ex-schoolmaster.

"I thought so," said the self-satisfied merchant. And no doubt he thought some of us very stupid, or rude, or both, but in spite of manners I had to smile at the assuring air of the Canadian.

"Why did you not answer him correctly?" I asked of the ex-schoolmaster.

"I answered him," said Newkirk, "according to his folly. Had I corrected his rusty geography before these simple, impoverished fishermen, he would not soon forgive me; and as for the rest of the poor souls here, the knowledge would do them but little good."

I may mention that in this out-of-the-way place there were no schools, and except the little knowledge gained in their church, from the catechism, and from the fumbling of beads, they were the most innocent of this world's scheme, of any people I ever met. But they seemed to know all about heaven, and were, no doubt, happy.

211

After the brief, friendly chat that we had, coffee was passed around, the probabilities of the *Liberdade's* voyage discussed, and the crew cautioned against the dangers of the *balaena* (whale), which were numerous along the coast, and vicious at that season of the year, having their young to protect.

I realized very often the startling sensation alone of a night at the helm, of having a painful stillness broken by these leviathans bursting the surface of the water with a noise like the roar of a great sea, uncomfortably near, reminding me of the Cape Frio adventure; and my crew, I am sure, were not less sensitive to the same feeling of an awful danger, however imaginary. One night in particular, dark and foggy I remember, Victor called me excitedly, saying that something dreadful ahead and drawing rapidly near had frightened him.

It proved to be a whale, for some reason that I could only guess at, threshing the sea with its huge body, and surging about in all directions, so that it puzzled me to know which way to steer to go clear. I thought at first, from the rumpus made that a fight was going on, such as we had once witnessed from the deck of the *Aquidneck*, not far from this place. Our course was changed as soon as we could decide which way to avoid, if possible, all marine disturbers of the peace. We wished especially to keep away from infuriated swordfish, which I feared might be darting about, and be apt to give us a blind thrust. Knowing that they sometimes pierce stout ships through with their formidable weapons, I began to feel ticklish about the ribs myself, I confess, and the little watch below, too, got uneasy and sleepless; for one of these swords, they knew well, would reach through and through our little boat, from keel to deck. Large ships have occasionally been sent into port leaky from the stab of a sword, but what I most dreaded was the possibility of one of us being ourselves pinned in the boat.

212

A swordfish once pierced a whale-ship through the planking, and through the solid frame timber and the thick ceiling, with his sword, leaving it there, a valuable plug indeed. The point, it was found upon unshipping her cargo at New Bedford, even pierced through a cask in the hold.

July 30th, early in the day, and after a pleasant visit at the cape, we sailed for the north, securing first a few sea shells to be cherished, with the *Thetis* relics, in remembrance of a most enjoyable visit to the hospitable shores of Cape Frio.

Having now doubled Cape Frio, a prominent point in our voyage, and having had the seaworthiness of our little ship thoroughly tested, as already told; and seeing, moreover, that we had nothing to fear from common small fry of the sea (one of its greatest monsters having failed to capsize us), we stood on with greater confidence than ever, but watchful, nevertheless, for any strange event that might happen.

A fresh polar wind hurried us on, under shortened sail, toward the softer "trades" of the tropics, but, veering to the eastward by midnight, it brought us well in with the land. Then, "Larboard watch, ahoy! all hands on deck and turn out reefs," was the cry. To weather Cape St. Thome we must lug on all sail. And we go over the shoals with a boiling sea and current in our favor. In twenty-four hours from Cape Frio, we had lowered the Southern Cross three degrees—180 miles.

Sweeping by the cape, the canoe sometimes standing on end, and sometimes buried in the deep hollow of the sea, we sunk the light on St. Thome soon out of sight, and stood on with flowing sheet. The wind on the following day settled into regular south-east "trades," and our cedar canoe skipped briskly along, over friendly seas that were leaping toward home, doffing their crests onward and forward, but never back, and the splashing waves against her sides, then rippling along the thin cedar planks between the crew and eternity, vibrated enchanting music to the ear, while confidence grew in the bark that was HOMEWARD BOUND.

But coming upon coral reefs, of a dark night, while we listened to the dismal tune of the seas breaking over them with an eternal roar, how intensely lonesome they were! no sign of any living thing in sight, except, perhaps, the phosphorescent streaks of a hungry shark, which told of bad company in our wake, and made the gloom of the place more dismal still.

One night we made shelter under the lee of the extensive reefs called the Paredes (walls), without seeing the breakers at all in the dark, although they were not far in the distance. At another time, dragging on sail to clear a lee shore, of a dark and stormy night, we came suddenly into smooth water, where we cast anchor and furled our sails, lying in a magic harbor till daylight the next morning, when we found ourselves among a maze of ugly reefs, with high seas breaking over them, as far as the eye could reach, on all sides, except at the small entrance to the place that we had stumbled into in the night. The position of this future harbor is South Lat. 16° 48′, and West Long. from Greenwich 39° 30′. We named the place "PORT LIBERDADE."

The next places sighted were the treacherous Abrohles, and the village of Caravellas back of the reef where upon refitting, I found that a chicken cost a thousand reis, a bunch of bananas four hundred reis; but where a dozen limes cost only twenty reis—one cent. Much whaling gear lay strewn about the place, and on the beach was the carcass of a whale about nine days slain. Also leaning against a smart-looking boat was a gray-haired fisherman, boat and man relics of New Bedford, employed at this station in their familiar industry. The old man was bare-footed and thinly clad, after the custom in this climate. Still, I recognized the fisherman and sailor in the set and rig of the few duds he had on, and the ample straw hat (donkey's breakfast) that he wore, and doffed in a seaman-like manner, upon our first salute. *"Filio do Mar do Nord Americano,"* said an affable native close by, pointing at the same time to that "son of the sea of North America," by way of introduction, as soon as it was learned that we, too, were of that country. I tried to learn from this ancient mariner the cause of his being stranded in this strange land. He may have been cast up there by the whale for aught I could learn to the contrary.

Choosing a berth well to windward of the dead whale—the one that landed "the old man of the sea" there, maybe!—we anchored for the night, put a light in the rigging and turned in. Next morning, the village was astir betimes; canoes were being put afloat, and the rattle of poles, paddles, bait boxes, and many more things for the daily trip that were being hastily put into each canoe, echoed back from the tall palm groves notes of busy life, telling us that it was time to weigh anchor and be sailing. To this cheerful tune we lent ear and hastening to be underway, were soon clear of the port. Then, skimming along near the beach in the early morning, our sails spread to a land breeze, laden with fragrance from the tropic forest and the music of many songsters, we sailed in great felicity, dreading no dangers from the sea, for there were none now to dread or fear.

Proceeding forward through this belt of moderate winds, fanned by alternating land and sea-breezes, we drew on toward a region of high trade winds that reach sometimes the dignity of a gale. It was no surprise, therefore, after days of fine-weather sailing, to be met by a storm, which so happened as to drive us into the indifferent anchorage of St. Paulo, thirty miles from Bahia, where we remained two days for shelter.

Time, three days from Caravellas; distance sailed, 270 miles.

A few fishermen lounged about the place, living, apparently, in wretched poverty, spending their time between waiting for the tide to go out, when it was in, and waiting for it to come in when it was out, to float a canoe or bring fish to their shiftless nets. This, indeed, seemed their only concern in life; while their ill-thatched houses, forsaken of the adobe that once clung to the wicker walls, stood grinning in rows, like emblems of our mortality.

We found at this St. Paulo anything but saints. The wretched place should be avoided by strangers, unless driven there for shelter, as we ourselves were, by stress of weather. We left the place on the first lull of the wind, having been threatened by an attack from a gang of rough, half-drunken fellows, who rudely came on board, jostling about, and jabbering in a dialect which, however, I happened to understand. I got rid of them by the use of my broken Portuguese, and once away I was resolved that they should stay away. I was not mistaken in my suspicions that they would return and try to come aboard, which shortly afterward they did, but my resolution to keep them off was not shaken. I let them know, in their own jargon this time, that I was well armed. They finally paddled back to the shore, and all visiting was then ended. We stood a good watch that night, and by daylight next morning, Aug. 12th, put to sea, standing out in a heavy swell, the character of which I knew better, and could trust to more confidently than a harbor among treacherous natives.

Early in the same day, we arrived at *Bahia do todos Santos* (All Saints' Bay), a charming port, with a rich surrounding

country. It was from this port, by the way, that Robinson
Crusoe sailed for Africa to procure slaves for his plantation,
and that of his friend, so fiction relates.

At Bahia we met many friends and gentle folk. Not the least
interesting at this port are the negro lasses of fine physique seen
at the markets and in the streets, with burdens on their heads
of baskets of fruit, or jars of water, which they balance with
ease and grace, as they go sweeping by with that stately mien
which the dusky maiden can call her own.

At Bahia we refitted, with many necessary provisions, and
repaired the keel, which was found upon hauling out, had been
damaged by the encounter with the whale at Frio. An iron shoe
was now added for the benefit of all marine monsters wishing
to scratch their backs on our canoe.

Among the many friends whom we met at Bahia was Capt.
Boyd and his family of the Barque *H. W. Palmer.* We shall meet
the *Palmer* and the Boyds again on the voyage. They were old
traders to South America and had many friends at this port who
combined to make our visit a pleasant one. And their little son
Rupert was greatly taken with the "*Riberdade,*" as he called
her, coming often to see us. And the officials of the port taking
great interest in our voyage, came often on board. No one could
have treated us more kindly than they.

The venerable *Administradore* himself gave us special welcome to the port and a kind word upon our departure, accompanied by a present for my wife in the shape of a rare white
flower, which we cherished greatly as coming from a true
gentleman.

Some strong abolitionists at the port would have us dine in
an epicurean way in commemoration of the name given our
canoe, which was adopted because of her having been put
afloat on the thirteenth day of May, the day on which every

217

human being in Brazil could say, "I have no master but one."
I declined the banquet tendered us, having work on hand, forti-
fying the canoe against the ravaging worms of the seas we were
yet to sail through, bearing in mind the straits of my great
predecessor from this as well as other causes on his voyage over
the Caribbean Seas. I was bound to be strengthened against
the enemy.

The gout, it will be remembered, seized upon the good
Columbus while his ship had worms, then both ship and
admiral lay stranded among menacing savages; surrounded,
too, by a lawless, threatening band of his own countrymen not
less treacherous than the worst of cannibals. His state was critical, indeed! One calamity was from over high living—this I was
bound to guard against—the other was from neglect on the part
of his people to care for the ship in a seaman-like manner. Of
the latter difficulty I had no risk to run.

Lazy and lawless, but through the pretext of religion the in-
fected crew wrought on the pious feelings of the good Admiral,
inducing him at every landing to hold mass instead of cleaning
the foul ship. Thus through petty intrigue and grave neglects,
they brought disaster and sorrow on their leader and confusion
on their own heads. Their religion, never deep, could not be
expected to keep *Teredo* from the ship's bottom, so her timbers
were ravished, and ruin came to them all! Poor Columbus! had
he but sailed with his son Diego and his noble brother Barthol-
omew, for his only crew and companions, not forgetting the
help of a good woman, America would have been discovered
without those harrowing tales of woe and indeed heartrending
calamities which followed in the wake of his designing people.
Nor would his ship have been less well manned than was the
Liberdade, sailing, centuries after, over the same sea and
among many of the islands visited by the great discoverer—

sailing too, without serious accident of any kind, and without sickness or discontent. Our advantage over Columbus, I say, was very great, not more from the possession of data of the centuries which had passed than from having a willing crew sailing without dissent or murmur—sailing in the same boat, as it were.

A pensive mood comes over one voyaging among the scenes of the New World's early play-ground. To us while on this canoe voyage of pleasant recollection the fancied experience of navigators gone before was intensely thrilling.

Sailing among islands clothed in eternal green, the same that Columbus beheld with marvelous anticipations, and the venerable Las Casas had looked upon with pious wonder, brought us, in the mind's eye, near the old discoverers; and a feeling that we should come suddenly upon their ships around some near headland took deep hold upon our thoughts as we drew in with the shores. All was there to please the imagination and dream over in the same balmy, sleepy atmosphere, where Juan Ponce de Leon would fain have tarried young, but found death rapid, working side by side with ever springing life. To live long in this clime one must obey great Nature's laws. So stout Juan and millions since have found, and so always it will be.

All was there to testify as of yore, all except the first owners of the land; they alas! the poor Caribbees, together with their camp fires, had been extinguished long years before. And no one of human sympathy can read of the cruel tortures and final extermination of these islanders, savages though they were, without a pang of regret at the unpleasant page in a history of glory and civilization.

From Bahia to Pernambuco our course lay along that part of the Brazilian coast fanned by constant trade winds. Nothing unusual occurred to disturb our peace or daily course, and we pressed forward night and day, as was our wont from the first.

Victor and I stood watch and watch at sea, usually four hours each.

The most difficult of our experiences in fine weather was the intense drowsiness brought on by constantly watching the oscillating compass at night; even in the daytime this motion would make one sleepy.

We soon found it necessary to arrange a code of signals which would communicate between the tiller and the "man forward."

This was accomplished by means of a line or messenger extending from one to the other, which was understood by the number of pulls given by it; three pulls, for instance, meant "Turn out," one in response, "Aye, aye, I am awake, and what is it that is wanted?" one pull in return signified that it was "Eight bells," and so on. But three quick jerks meant "Tumble out and shorten sail."

Victor, it was understood, would tie the line to his arm or leg when he turned in, so that by pulling I would be sure to arouse him, or bring him somewhat unceremoniously out of his bunk. Once, however, the messenger failed to accomplish its purpose. A boot came out on the line in answer to my call, so easily, too, that I suspected a trick. It was evidently a preconceived plan by which to gain a moment more of sleep. It was a clear imposition on the man at the wheel!

We had also a sign in this system of telegraphing that told of flying-fish on board—manna of the sea—to be gathered up for the *cuisine* whenever they happened to alight or fall on deck, which was often, and as often they found a warm welcome.

The watch was never called to make sail. As for myself, I had never to be called, having thoughts of the voyage and its safe completion on my mind to keep me always on the alert. I can truly say that I never, on the voyage, slept so sound as to forget where I was, but whenever I fell into a doze at all it would be to dream of the boat and the voyage.

Press on! press on! was the watchword while at sea, but in port we enjoyed ourselves and gave up care for rest and pleasure, carrying a supply, as it were, to sea with us, where sail was again carried on.

Though a mast should break, it would be no matter of serious concern, for we would be at no loss to mend and rig up spars for this craft at short notice, most anywhere.

The third day out from Bahia was set fine weather. A few flying-fish made fruitless attempts to rise from the surface of the sea, attracting but little attention from the sea-gulls which sat looking wistfully across the unbroken deep with folded wings.

And the *Liberdade* doing her utmost to get along through the common quiet, made but little progress on her way. A dainty fish played in her light wake, till tempted by an evil appetite for flies, it landed in the cockpit upon a hook, thence into the pan, where many a one had brought up before. Breakfast was cleared away at an early hour; then day of good things happened—"the meeting of the ships."

> "When, o'er the silent seas alone
>   For days and nights we've cheerless gone,
> Oh, they who've felt it know how sweet,
>   Some sunny morn a sail to meet!
>
> "Sparkling at once is every eye,
>   'Ship ahoy! ship ahoy!' our joyful cry;
> While answering back the sound we hear,
>   'Ship ahoy! ship ahoy! what cheer? what cheer?'
>
> "Then sails are backed, we nearer come,
>   Kind words are said of friends and home,

221

And soon, too soon, we part with pain,
To sail o'er silent seas again."

On the clear horizon could be seen a ship, which proved to be our staunch old friend, the *Finance,* on her way out to Brazil, heading nearly for us. Our course was at once changed, so as to cross her bows. She rose rapidly, hull up, showing her lines of unmistakable beauty, the stars and stripes waving over all. They on board the great ship, soon descried our little boat, and gave sign by a deep whistle that came rumbling over the sea, telling us that we were recognized. A few moments later and the engines stopped. Then came the hearty hail, "Do you want assistance?" Our answer "No" brought cheer on cheer from the steamer's deck, while the *Liberdade* bowed and courtesied to her old acquaintance, the superior ship. Captain Baker, meanwhile, not forgetting a sailor's most highly prized luxury, had ordered in the slings a barrel of potatoes—new from home! Then dump they came, in a jiffy, into the canoe, giving her a settle in the water of some inches. Other fresh provisions were handed us, also some books and late papers. J. Aspinwill Hodge, D.D., on a tour of inspection in the interest of the Presbyterian Mission in Brazil—on deck here with his camera—got an excellent photograph of the canoe.*

One gentleman passed us a bottle of wine, on the label of which was written the name of an old acquaintance, a merchant of Rio. We pledged Mr. Gudgeon and all his fellow passengers in that wine, and had some left long after, to the health of the captain of the ship, and his crew. There was but little time for words, so the compliments passed were brief. The

* We had the pleasure of meeting this gentleman again on the voyage at Barbadoes, again at New London, and finally with delight we heard him lecture on his travels, at Newport, and saw there produced on the wall the very picture of the *Liberdade* taken by the doctor on the great ocean.

ample plates in the sides of the *Finance,* inspiring confidence in American thoroughness and build, we had hardly time to scan, when her shrill whistle said "good-bye," and moving proudly on, the great ship was soon out of sight, while the little boat filling away on the starboard tack, sailed on toward home, perfumed with the interchange of a friendly greeting, tinged though, with a palpable lonesomeness. Two days after this pleasant meeting, the Port of Pernambuco was reached.

Tumbling in before a fresh "trade" wind that in the evening had sprung up, accompanied with long, rolling seas, our canoe came nicely round the point between lighted reef and painted buoy.

Spray from the breakers on the reef opportunely wetting her sails gave them a flat surface to the wind as we came close haul.

The channel leading up the harbor was not strange to us, so we sailed confidently along the lee of the wonderful wall made by worms, to which alone Pernambuco is indebted for its excellent harbor; which extending also along a great stretch of the coast, protects Brazil from the encroachment of the sea.

At 8 P.M., we came to in a snug berth near the *Alfandega,* and early next morning received the official visit from the polite port officers.

Time from Bahia, five days; distance sailed, 390 miles.

Pernambuco, the principal town of a large and wealthy province of the same name, is a thriving place, sending out valuable cargoes, principally of sugar and cotton. I had loaded costly cargoes here, times gone by. I met my old merchant again this time, but could not carry his goods on the *Liberdade.* However, fruits from his orchards and a run among the trees refreshed my crew, and prepared them for the coming voyage to Barbadoes, which was made with expedition.

From Pernambuco we experienced a strong current in our

favor, with, sometimes, a confused cross sea that washed over us considerably. But the swift current sweeping along through it all made compensation for discomforts of motion, though our "ups and downs" were many. Along this part of the coast (from Pernambuco to the Amazon), if one day should be fine, three stormy ones would follow, but the gale was always fair, carrying us forward at a goodly rate.

Along about half way from Cape St. Roque to the Amazon, the wind which had been blowing hard for two days, from E. S. E., and raising lively waves all about, increased to a gale that knocked up seas, washing over the little craft more than ever. The thing was becoming monotonous and tiresome; for a change, therefore, I ran in toward the land, so as to avoid the ugly cross sea farther out in the current. This course was a mistaken one; we had not sailed far on it when a sudden rise of the canoe, followed by an unusually long run down on the slope of a roller, told us of a danger that we hardly dared to think of, then a mighty comber broke, but, as Providence willed, broke short of the canoe, which under shortened sail was then scudding very fast.

We were on a shoal, and the sea was breaking from the bottom! The second great roller came on, towering up, up, up, until nothing longer could support the mountain of water, and it seemed only to pause before its fall to take aim and surely gather us up in its sweeping fury.

I put the helm a-lee; there was nothing else to do but this, and say prayers. The helm hard down, brought the canoe round, bows to the danger, while in breathless anxiety we prepared to meet the result as best we could. Before we could say "Save us, or we perish," the sea broke over with terrific force and passed on, leaving us trembling in His hand, more palpably helpless than ever before. Other great waves came madly on,
224

leaping toward destruction; how they bellowed over the shoal!
I could smell the slimy bottom of the sea, when they broke!
I could taste the salty sand!

In this perilous situation, buried sometimes in the foaming
breakers, and at times tossed like a reed on the crest of the
waves, we struggled with might and main at the helm and the
sheets, easing her up or forcing her ahead with care, gaining
little by little toward deep water, till at last she came out of
the danger, shook her feathers like a sea bird, and rode on
waves less perilous. Then we had time and courage to look back,
but not till then.

And what a sight we beheld! The horizon was illumined with
phosphorescent light from the breakers just passed through.
The rainstorm which had obscured the coast was so cleared
away now that we could see the whole field of danger behind
us. One spot in particular, the place where the breakers dashed
over a rock which appeared awash, in the glare flashed up a
shaft of light that reached to the heavens.

This was the greatest danger we had yet encountered. The
elasticity of our canoe, not its bulk, saved it from destruction.
Her light, springy timbers and buoyant bamboo guards brought
her upright again and again through the fierce breakers. We
were astonished at the feats of wonder of our brave little craft.

Fatigued and worn with anxiety, when clear of the shoal
we hauled to under close reefs, heading off shore, and all hands
lay down to rest till daylight. Then, squaring away again, we
set what sail the canoe could carry, scudding before it, for the
wind was still in our favor, though blowing very hard. Nevertheless the weather seemed fine and pleasant at this stage of
our own pleased feelings. Any weather that one's craft can
live in, after escaping a lee shore, is pleasant weather—though
some may be pleasanter than other.

What we most wished for, after this thrilling experience, was sea room, fair wind, and plenty of it. That these without stint would suit us best, was agreed on all hands. Accordingly then I shaped the course seaward, clearing well all the dangers of the land.

The fierce tropical storm of the last few days turned gradually into mild trade winds, and our cedar canoe skipped nimbly once more over tranquil seas. Our own agitation, too, had gone down and we sailed on unruffled by care. Gentle winds carried us on over kindly waves, and we were fain to count fair days ahead, leaving all thoughts of stormy ones behind. In this hopeful mood we sailed for many days, our spirits never lowering, but often rising higher out of the miserable condition which we had fallen into through misfortunes on the foreign shore. When a star came out, it came as a friend, and one that had been seen by friends of old. When all the stars shone out, the hour at sea was cheerful, bright, and joyous. Welby saw, or had in the mind's-eye, a day like many that we experienced in the soft, clear "trades" on this voyage, when writing the pretty lines:—

> "The twilight hours like birds flew by,
>   As lightly and as free,
> Ten thousand stars were in the sky,
>   Ten thousand on the sea.

> "For every rippling, dancing wave,
>   That leaped upon the air,
> Had caught a star in its embrace,
>   And held it trembling there."

"The days pass, and our ship flies fast upon her way."

For several days while sailing near the line we saw the constellations of both hemispheres, but heading north, we left those of the south at last, with the Southern Cross—most beautiful in all the heavens—to watch over a friend.

Leaving these familiar southern stars and sailing towards constellations in the north, we hoist all sail to the cheery breeze which carries us on.

In this pleasant state of sailing with our friends all about us, we stood on and on, never doubting once our pilot or our ship.

A phantom of the stately *Aquidneck* appeared one night, sweeping by with crowning skysails set, that fairly brushed the stars. No apparition could have affected us more than the sight of this floating beauty, so like the *Aquidneck,* gliding swiftly and quietly by, from her mission to some foreign land —she, too, was homeward bound!

This incident of the *Aquidneck's* ghost, as it appeared to us, passing at midnight on the sea, left a pang of lonesomeness for a while.

But a carrier dove came next day, and perched upon the mast, as if to tell that we had yet a friend!

The lovely visitor remained with us two days, off and on, but left for good on the third, when we reached away from Avès Island, to which, maybe, it was bound. Coming as it did from the east, and flying west towards the island when it left, bore out the idea of the lay of sweet singer Kingsley's "Last Buccaneer."

> "If I might but be a sea dove, I'd fly across the main
> To the pleasant Isle of Avès, to look at it once again."

The old Buccaneer, it may have been, but we regarded it as the little bird, which most likely it was, that sits up aloft to look out for poor "Jack." *

* "There's a sweet little cherub that sits up aloft,
  To look out for a berth for poor Jack."—*Dibdin's Poems.*

227

A moth blown to our boat on the ocean, found shelter and a welcome there. The dove! we secretly worshipped.

With utmost confidence in our little craft, inspired by many thrilling events, we now carried sail, blow high, blow low, till at times she reeled along with a bone in her mouth quite to the mind of her mariners. Thinking one day that she might carry more sail on the mast already bending hopefully forward, and acting upon the liberal thought of sail we made a wide mistake, for the mainmast went by the board, under the extra press and the foremast tripped over the bows. Then spars, booms and sails swung alongside like the broken wings of a bird but were grappled, however, and brought aboard without much loss of time. The broken mast was then secured and strengthened by "fishes" or splints after the manner in which doctors fish a broken limb.

Both of the masts were very soon refitted and again made to carry sail, all they could stand; and we were again bowling along as before. We made that day a hundred and seventy-five miles, one of our best days' work.

I protest here that my wife should not have cried "More sail! more sail!" when, as it has been seen the canoe had on all the sail that she could carry. Nothing further happened to change the usual daily events until we reached Barbadoes. Flying-fish on the wing striking our sails, at night, often fell on deck, affording us many a toothsome fry. This happened daily, while sailing throughout the trade-wind regions. To be hit by one of these fish on the wing, which sometimes occurs, is no light matter, especially if the blow be on the face, as it may cause a bad bruise or even a black eye. The head of the flying-fish being rather hard makes it in fact a night slugger to be dreaded. They never come aboard in the daylight. The swift darting bill-fish, too, is a danger to be avoided in the tropics at night. They are

228

met with mostly in the Pacific Ocean; therefore South Sea Islanders are loath to voyage during the "bill-fish season."

As to the flight of these fishes, I would estimate that of the flying-fish as not exceeding fifteen feet in height, or five hundred yards of distance, often not half so much.

Bill-fish darting like an arrow from a bow, have, fortunately for sailors, not the power or do not rise much above the level of the waves, and can not dart further, say, than two hundred and fifty feet, according to the day for jumping. Of the many swift fish in the sea, the dolphin perhaps, is the most marvelous. Its oft told beauty, too, is indeed remarkable. A few of these fleet racers were captured, on the voyage, but were found tough and rank; notwithstanding some eulogy on them by other epicures, we threw the mess away. Those hooked by my crew were perhaps the tyrrhena pirates "turned into dolphins" in the days of yore.

On the 19th day from Pernambuco, early in the morning, we made Barbadoes away in the West. First, the blue, fertile hills, then green fields came into view, studded with many white buildings between sentries of giant wind-mills as old nearly, as the hills. Barbadoes is the most pleasant island in the Antilles; to sail round its green fringe of coral sea is simply charming. We stood in to the coast, well to windward, sailing close in with the breakers so as to take in a view of the whole delightful panorama as we sailed along. By noon we rounded the south point of the island and shot into Carlysle Bay, completing the run from Pernambuco exactly in nineteen days. This was considerably more than an hundred miles a day. The true distance being augmented by the circuitous route we adopted made it 2,150 miles.

Many old friends and acquaintances came down to see us

upon our arrival at Barbadoes, all curious to inspect the strange craft. While there our old friend, the *Palmer,* that we left at Bahia, came in to refit, having broke a mast "trying to beat us," so Garfield would have it. For all that we had beaten her time four days. Who then shall say that we anchored nights or spent much time hugging the shore? The *Condor* was also at Barbadoes in charge of an old friend, accompanied by a pleasant helpmeet and companion who had shared the perils of shipwreck with her husband the year before in a hurricane among the islands.

Meeting so many of this class of old friends of vast and varied experiences, gave contentment to our visit and we concluded to remain over at this port till the hurricane season should pass. Our old friend, the *Finance* too, came in, remaining but a few hours, however. She hurried away with her mails, homeward bound.

The pleasant days at Barbadoes with its enchantment flew lightly by; and on the 7th of October we sailed, giving the hurricane season the benefit of eight days. The season is considered over on the 15th of that month.

Passing thence through the Antilles into the Caribbean Sea, a new period of our voyage was begun. Fair breezes filled the sails of the *Liberdade* as we glided along over tranquil seas, scanning eagerly the islands as they came into view, dwelling on each, in our thoughts, as hallowed ground of the illustrious discoverers—the same now as seen by them! The birds, too, of "rare plumage," were there, flying from island to island, the same as seen by the discoverers; and the sea with fishes teemed, of every gorgeous hue, lending enchantment to the picture, not less beautiful than the splendor on the land and in the air to thrill the voyager now, the same as then; we ourselves had only to look to see them.

230

Whether it was birds with fins or fishes with wings, or neither of these that the old voyagers saw, they discovered yet enough to make them wonder and rejoice.

"Mountains of sugar, and rivers of rum and flying-fish, was what I saw, mother," said the son on his return home from a voyage to these islands. "John," said the enraptured mother, "you must be mistaken about the fish; now don't lie to me, John. Mountains of sugar, no doubt you saw, and even rivers of rum, my boy, but *flying-fish* could never be."

And yet the *fish* were there.

Among the islands of great interest which came in view, stretching along the Caribbean Sea, was that of Santa Cruz, the island famous for its brave, resolute women of days gone by, who, while their husbands were away, successfully defended home and happiness against Christian invaders, and for that reason were called fierce savages. I would fain have brought away some of the earth of the island in memory of those brave women. Small as our ship was, we could have afforded room in it for a memento thus consecrated; but the trades hauling somewhat to the northward so headed us off that we had to forgo the pleasure of landing on its shores.

Pushing forward thence, we reached Porto Rico, the nearest land in our course from the Island of Brave Women, standing well in with the southeast capes. Sailing thence along the whole extent of the south coast, in waters as smooth as any mill pond, and past island scenery worth the perils of ten voyages to see, we landed, on the 12th of October, at Mayaguez in the west of the island, and there shook the kinks out of our bones by pleasant walks in tropic shades.

Time, five days from Barbadoes; distance, 570 miles.

This was to be our last run among the trees in the West Indies, and we made the most of it. "Such a port for mariners

231

I'll never see again!" The port officials, kind and polite, extended all becoming courtesies to the quaint *"barco piquina."*

The American Consul, Mr. Christie, Danish Consul, Mr. Falby, and the good French Consul, vied in making our visit a pleasant one.

Photographers at Mayaguez desiring a picture of the canoe with the crew on deck at a time when we felt inclined to rest in the shade on shore, put a negro on board to take the place of captain. The photographs taken then found their way to Paris and Madrid journals where, along with some flattering accounts, they were published, upon which it was remarked that the captain was a fine-looking fellow, but "awfully tanned!" The moke was rigged all ataunto for the occasion, and made a picture indicative of great physical strength, one not to be ashamed of, but he would have looked more like me, I must say, if they had turned him back to.

We enjoyed long carriage drives over rich estates at Mayaguez. We saw with pain, however, that the atmosphere of the soldier hung over all, pervading the whole air like a pestilence.

Musketed and sabred, and uniformed in their bedticking suits; hated by the residents and despised by themselves, they doggedly marched, counter-marched and wheeled, knowing that they are loathsome in the island, and that their days in the New World are numbered. The sons of the colonies are too civil and Christianlike to be ruled always by sword and gun.

On the 15th of October, after three days' rest, we took in, as usual before sailing from ports, sufficient fresh supplies to carry us to the port steered for next, then set sail from pleasant Mayaguez, and bore away for the old Bahama Channel, passing east of Haiti, thence along the north coast to the west extremity of the island, from which we took departure for the headlands of Cuba, and followed that coast as far as Cardinas, where we took a final departure from the islands, regretting that we could not sail around them all.

The region on the north side of Cuba is often visited by gales of great violence, making this the lee shore; a weather eye was therefore kept lifting, especially in the direction of their source, which is from north to nor'west. However storms prevailed from other quarters, mostly from the east, bringing heavy squalls of wind, rain and thunder every afternoon, such as once heard will never be forgotten. Peal on peal of nature's artillery for a few hours, accompanied by vivid lightning, was on the cards for each day, then all would be serene again.

The nights following these severe storms were always bright and pleasant, and the heavens would be studded with constellations of familiar, guiding stars.

My crew had now no wish to bear up for port short of one on our own coast, but, impatient to see the North Star appear higher in the heavens, strung every nerve and trimmed every sail to hasten on.

Nassau, the place to which letters had been directed to us we forbore to visit. This departure from a programme which was made at the beginning was the only change that we made in the "charter party" throughout the voyage. There was no haphazard sailing on this voyage. Daily observations for determining latitude and longitude were invariably made unless the sun was obscured. The result of these astronomical observations were more reliable than one might suppose, from their being taken on a tittlish canoe. After a few days' practising, a very fair off-hand contact could be made, when the canoe rose on the crest of a wave, where manifestly would be found the best result. The observer's station was simply on the top of the

233

cabin, where astride, like riding horseback, Victor and I took the "sights," and indeed became expert "snap observers" before the voyage ended.

One night in the Bahama Channel, while booming along toward the Banks to the nor'west of us before stiff trades, I was called in the first watch by Victor, to come up quickly, for signs of the dread "norther" were in the sky. Our trusty barometer had been low, but was now on the cheerful side of change. This phenomenon disturbed me somewhat, till the discovery was made, as we came nearer, that it was but the reflection of the white banks on the sky that we saw, and no cause at all for alarm.

Soon after this phenomenon the faint glimmer of Lobos Light was descried flickering on the horizon, two points on the weather bow. I changed the course three points to windward, having determined to touch at the small Cay where the lighthouse stands; one point being allowed for leeway, which I found was not too much.

Three hours later we fetched in under the lee of the reef, or Cay, as it is commonly called, and came to in one and a half fathoms of water in good shelter.

We beheld then overhead in wonderful beauty what had awed us from the distance in the early night—a chart of the illuminating banks marked visibly on the heavens.

We furled sails and, setting a light in the rigging, turned in; for it lacked three hours yet of daylight. And what an interesting experience ours had been in the one short night! By the break of day my crew were again astir, preparing to land and fill water at a good landing which we now perceived farther around the point to leeward, where the surf was moderate.

On the Cay were stored some hundred thousand gallons of rain water in cisterns at the base of the iron tower which carried

the light; it was the one we saw from the canoe at a distance
of fourteen miles.

The keeper of the light, a hardy native of Nassau, when he
discovered the new arrival at his "island," hoisted the British
Board of Trade flag on a pole in the centre of this, his little
world, then he came forward to speak to us, thinking at first,
he said, that we were shipwrecked sailors, which indeed we
were, but not in distress, as he had supposed when hoisting the
flag, which signified assistance for distressed seamen. On learning our story, however, he regarded us with grave suspicions,
and refused water to Victor, who had already landed with
buckets, telling him that the captain would have to bring his
papers ashore and report. The mate's report would not be taken.
Thus in a moment was transformed the friend in need to *governor of an island*. This amused me greatly, and I sent back word
to my veritable Sancho Panza that in my many voyages to
islands my mate had attended to the customs reports; at which
his Excellency chafed considerably, giving the gunnels of his
trousers a fitful tug up now and then as he paced the beach,
waiting my compliance with the rules of the island. The governor, I perceived, was suspicious of smugglers and wreckers,
apparently understanding their ways, if, indeed, even he were
not a reformed pirate himself.

However, to humor the punctiliousness of his Excellency,
now that he was governor of an island, I placed my papers in
my hat, and, leaping into the surf, waded ashore, where I was
received as by a monarch.

The document I presented was the original *Passe Especial*,
the one with the big seal on it, written in Portuguese; had it
been in Choctaw the governor would have read it with the same
facility that he did this, which he stared at knowingly and said,
"all right, take all the water you want; it is free."

I lodged a careful report of the voyage with the governor and explained to his Excellency the whereabouts of the "Island of Rio," as his grace persistently called Rio de Janeiro, whence dated my papers.

Conversing on the subject of islands, which was all the world to him, the governor viewed with suspicion the absence of a word in my documents, referring even to an islet; this, in his mind, was a reprehensible omission; for surely New York to which the papers referred was built on an island. Upon this I offered to swear to the truth of my clearance, "as far as known to me," after the manner of cheap custom-house swearing with which shipmasters, in some parts of the world, are made familiar. "Not on the island!" quickly exclaimed the governor, " 'for thou shalt not disglorify God's name,' is written in the Bible."

I assured the governor of my appreciation of his pious sentiment of not over-swearing,—a laudable plan that even the Chinese adopt as a policy, and one that I would speak of on my return home, to the end that we all emulate the laws of the island; whereupon the governor, greatly pleased, urged me to take some more water, minding me again that it was free.

In a very few minutes I got all the water I wished for; also some aurora shells from the governor's lady, who had arisen with the sun to grace the day and of all things most appropriate held in her generous lap beautiful aurora shells for which—to spoil the poem—I bartered cocoanuts and rusty gnarly yams.

The lady was on a visit only to her lord and master, the monarch of all he surveyed. Beside this was their three children also on a visit, from Nassau, and two assistant keepers of the light which made up the total of this little world in the ocean.

It was the smallest kingdom I had ever visited, peopled by happy human beings and the most isolated by far.

The few blades of grass which had struggled into existence,

not enough to support a goat, was all there was to look at on the island except the lighthouse, and the sand and themselves.

Some small buildings and a flagstaff had once adorned the place, but together with a coop of chickens, the only stock of the islanders—except a dog—had been swept away by a hurricane which had passed over the island a short time before. The water for which we had called being now in the canoe, and my people on board waiting for me, I bade the worthy governor good-bye, and, saluting his charming island queen in a seaman-like manner, hastened back to my own little world; and bore away once more for the north. Sailing thence over the Great Bahama Banks, in a crystal sea, we observed on the white marl bottom many curious living things, among them the conch in its house of exquisite tints and polished surface, the star-fish with radiated dome of curious construction, and many more denizens of the place, the names of which I could not tell, resting on the soft white bed under the sea.

"They who go down to the sea in ships, they see the wonders of the Lord," I am reminded by a friend who writes me, on receipt of some of these curious things which I secured on the voyage, adding: "For all these curious and beautiful things are His handiwork. Who can look at such things without the heart being lifted up in adoration?"

For words like these what sailor is there who would not search the caves of the ocean? Words too, from a lady.

Two days of brisk sailing over the white Bahama Banks brought us to Bimini. Thence a mere push would send us to the coast of our own native America. The wind in the meantime hauling from regular nor'east trade to the sou'west, as we came up to Bimini, promising a smooth passage across, we launched out at once on the great Gulf Stream, and were swept along by its restless motion, making on the first day, before the wind

237

and current, two hundred and twenty miles. This was great getting along for a small canoe. Going at the same high rate of speed on the second night in the stream, the canoe struck a spar and went over it with a bound. Her keel was shattered by the shock, but finally shaking the crippled timber clear of herself she came on quite well without it. No other damage was done to our craft, although at times her very ribs were threatened before clearing this lively ocean river. In the middle of the current, where the seas were yet mountainous but regular, we went along with a wide, swinging motion and fared well enough; but on nearing the edge of the stream a confused sea was met with, standing all on end, in every which way, beyond a sailor's comprehension. The motion of the *Liberdade* was then far from poetical or pleasant. The wind, in the meantime, had chopped round to the nor'east, dead ahead; being thus against the current, a higher and more confused sea than ever was heaped up, giving us some uneasiness. We had, indeed, several unwelcome visitors come tumbling aboard of our craft, one of which furiously crashing down on her made all of her timbers bend and creak. However, I could partially remedy this danger by changing the course.

"Seas like that can't break this boat," said our young boatswain; "she's built strong." It was well to find among the crew this feeling of assurance in the gallant little vessel. I, too, was confident in her seaworthiness. Nevertheless, I shortened sail and brought her to the wind, watching the lulls and easing her over the combers, as well as I could. But wrathful Neptune was not to let us so easily off, for the next moment a sea swept clean over the helmsman, wetting him through to the skin and, most unkind cut of all, it put out our fire, and capsized the hash and stove into the bottom of the canoe. This left us with but a *damper* for breakfast! Matters mended, however, as the day

238

advanced, and for supper we had a grand and glorious feast. Early in the afternoon we made the land and got into smooth water. This of itself was a feast, to our minds.

The land we now saw lying before us was hills of America, which we had sailed many thousands of miles to see. Drawing in with the coast, we made out, first the broad, rich forests, then open fields and villages, with many signs of comfort on every hand. We found it was the land about Bull's Bay on the coast of South Carolina, and night coming on, we could plainly see Cape Roman Light to the north of us. The wind falling light as we drew in with the coast, and finding a current against us, we anchored, about two miles from the shore, in four fathoms of water. It was now 8 P.M., October 28, 1888, thirteen days from Mayaguez, twenty-one days from Barbadoes, etc.

		Days.	Distance.
From Paranagua to Santos - - - -		1	150
" Santos to Rio de Janeiro (towed by *Finance*) - - -		¾	200
" Rio to Cape Frio - - - - -		2	70
" Cape Frio to Carvellas - - -		4	370
" Carvellas to Saint Paulo - - -		3	270
" Saint Paulo to Bahia - - - -		½	40
" Bahia to Pernambuco - - - -		5	390
" Pernambuco to Barbadoes - - -		19	2,150
" Barbadoes to Mayaguez - - -		5	570
" Mayaguez to Cape Roman - - -		13	1,300
		53¼	5,510

Computing all the distances of the ins and outs that we made would considerably augment the sum. To say, therefore, that the *Liberdade* averaged a hundred and three miles a day for fifty-three days would be considerably inside the truth.

239

This was the voyage made in the boat which cost less than a hundred dollars outside of our own labor of building. Journals the world over have spoken not unkindly of the feat; encomiums in seven languages reached us through the newspapers while we lay moored in Washington. Should the same good fortune that followed the *Liberdade* attend this little literary craft, when finished, it would go safe into many lands. Without looking, however, to this mark of good fortune, the journal of the voyage has been as carefully constructed as was the *Liberdade,* and I trust, as conscientiously, by a hand, alas! that has grasped the sextant more often than the plane or pen, and for the love of doing. This apology might have been more appropriately made in the beginning of the journal, maybe, but it comes to me now, and like many other things done, right or wrong, but done on the impulse of the moment, I put it down.

No one will be more surprised at the complete success of the voyage and the speedy progress made than were we ourselves who made it, with incidents and events among which is the most prominent of a life at sea.

A factor of the voyage, one that helped us forward greatly, and which is worthy of special mention, was the ocean current spoken of as we came along in its friendly sway.

Many are the theories among fresh water philosophists respecting these currents, but in practical sailing, where the subject is met with in its tangible form, one cause only is recognized; namely, the action of the wind on the surface of the water, pushing the waves along. Out on the broad ocean the effect at first is hardly perceptible, but the constant trades sending countless millions of waves in one direction, cause at last a mighty moving power, which the mariner meets sometimes as an enemy to retard and delay, sometimes as a friend, as in our case, to help him on his way. These are views from a practical experience with no theory to prove.

By daylight on the twenty-ninth, we weighed anchor and set sail again for the north. The wind and current were still adverse but we kept near the land making short boards off and on through the day where the current had least effect. And when night came on again we closed in once more with Cape Roman light. Next day we worked up under the lee of the Roman shoals and made harbor in South Santee, a small river to the north of Cape Roman, within range of the light, there to rest until the wind should change, it being still ahead.

Next morning, since the wind had not changed, we weighed anchor and stood farther into the river looking for inhabitants, that we might listen to voices other than our own. Our search was soon rewarded, for, coming around a point of woodland, a farmhouse stood before us on the river side. We came alongside the bank and jumped ashore, but hardly had we landed when, as out of the earth a thousand dogs, so it seemed, sprung up threatening to devour us all. However, a comely woman came out of the house and it was explained to the satisfaction of all, especially to a persistent cur, by a vigorous whack on the head with a cudgel, that our visit was a friendly one; then all was again peaceful and quiet. The good man was in the field close by, but soon came home accompanied by his two stalwart sons each "toting" a sack of corn. We found the Andersons— this was the family name—isolated in every sense of the word, and as primitive as heart could wish. The charming simplicity of these good people captivated my crew. We met others along the coast innocent of greed, but of all unselfish men, Anderson the elder was surely the prince.

Purchasing some truck from this good man, we found that

241

change could not be made for the dollar which I tendered in payment. But I protested that I was more than content to let the few odd cents go, having received more garden stuff than I had ever seen offered for a dollar in any part of the world. And indeed I was satisfied. The farmer, however, nothing content, offered me a coon skin or two, but these I didn't want, and there being no other small change about the farm, the matter was dropped, I thought, for good, and I had quite forgotten it, when later in the evening I was electrified by his offering to carry a letter for us which we wished posted, some seven miles away, and call it "square," against the twenty cents of the morning's transaction. The letter went, and in due course of time we got an answer.

I do not say that we stuck strictly to the twenty-cent transaction, but I fear that not enough was paid to fair-dealing Anderson. However all were at last satisfied and warming into conversation, a log fire was improvised and social chat went round.

These good people could hardly understand how it was, as I explained, that the Brazilians had freed the slaves and had no war, Mr. Anderson often exclaiming, "Well, well, I d'clar. Freed the niggers, and had no wah. Mister," said he, turning to me after a long pause, "mister, d'ye know the South were foolish? They had a wah, and they had to free the niggers, too."

"Oh, yes, mister, I was thar! Over thar beyond them oaks was my house."

"Yes, mister, I fought, too, and fought hard, but it warn't no use."

Like many a hard fighter, Anderson, too, was a pious man, living in a state of resignation to be envied. His years of experience on the new island farm had been hard and trying in the extreme. My own misfortunes passed into shade as the harder luck of the Andersons came before my mind, and the resolution which I had made to buy a farm was now shaken and finally dissolved into doubts of the wisdom of such a course. On this farm they had first "started in to raise pork," but found that it "didn't pay, for the pigs got wild and had to be gathered with the dogs," and by the time they were "gathered and then toted, salt would hardly cure them, and they most generally tainted." The enterprise was therefore abandoned, for that of tilling the soil, and a crop was put in, but "the few pigs which the dogs had not gathered came in at night and rooted out all the taters." It then appeared that a fence should be built. "Accordingly," said he, "the boys and I made one which kept out the stock, but, sir, the rats could get in! They took every tater out of the ground! From all that I put in, and my principal work was thar, I didn't see a sprout." How it happened that the rats had left the crop the year before for their relations—the pigs—was what seemed most to bother the farmer's mind. Nevertheless, "there was corn in Egypt yet;" and at the family circle about the board that night a smile of hope played on the good farmer's face, as in deep sincerity he asked that for what they had they might be made truly thankful. We learned a lesson of patience from this family, and were glad that the wind had carried us to their shore.

Said the farmer, "And you came all the way from Brazil in that boat! Wife, she won't go to Georgetown in the batto that I built because it rares too much. And they freed the niggers and had no wah! Well, well, I d'clar!"

Better folks we may never see than the farmers of South Santee. Bidding them good-bye next morning at early dawn we sailed before a light land wind which, however, soon petered out.

The S.S. *Planter* then coming along took us in tow for

Georgetown, where she was bound. We had not the pleasure, however, of visiting the beloved old city; for having some half dozen cocoanuts on board, the remainder of small stores of the voyage, a vigilant officer stopped us at the quarantine ground. Fruit not being admitted into South Carolina until after the first of November, and although it was now late in the afternoon of the first, we had to ride quarantine that night, with a promise, however, of *pratique* next morning. But there was no steamer going up the river the next day. The *Planter* coming down though supplied us with some small provisions, such as not procurable at the Santee farm. Then putting to sea we beat along slowly against wind and current.

We began now to experience, as might be expected, autumn gales of considerable violence, the heaviest of which overtaking us at Frying-pan Shoal, drove us back to leeward of Cape Fear for shelter. South Port and Wilmington being then so near we determined to visit both places. Two weeks at these ports refreshed the crew and made all hands willing for sea again.

Sailing thence through Corn-cake Inlet we cut off Cape Fear and the Frying-pan Shoals, being of mind to make for the inlets along the Carolina coast and to get into the inland waters as soon as practicable.

It was our good fortune to fall in with an old and able pilot at Corn-cake Inlet, one Capt. Bloodgood, who led the way through the channel in his schooner, the *Packet,* a Carolina pitch and cotton droger of forty tons register, which was manned solely by the captain and his two sons, one twelve and the other ten years old. It was in the crew that I became most interested, and not the schooner. Bloodgood gave the order when the tide served for us to put to sea. "Come, children," said he, "let's try it." Then we all tried it together, the *Packet* leading the way. The shaky west wind that filled our sails as we

244

skimmed along the beach with the breakers close aboard, carried us but a few leagues when it flew suddenly round to nor' east and began to pipe.

The gale increasing rapidly inclined me to bear up for New River Inlet, then close under our lee with a treacherous bar lying in front, which to cross safely, would require great care.

But the gale was threatening, and the harbor inside, we could see, was smooth. Then, too, cried my people: "Any port in a storm." I decided prompt; put the helm up and squared away. Flying thence, before it, the tempest-tossed canoe came sweeping in from sea over the rollers in a delightfully thrilling way. One breaker only coming over us, and even that did no harm more than to give us all the climax soaking of the voyage. This was the last sea that broke over the canoe on the memorable voyage.

The harbor inside the bar of New River was good. Adding much to our comfort too, was fish and game in abundance.

The *Packet*, which had parted from us made her destined port some three leagues farther on. The last we saw of the children, they were at the main sheets hauling aft, and their father was at the helm, and all were flying through the mist like fearless sailors.

After meeting Carolina seamen, to say nothing of the few still in existence further north, I challenge the story of Greek supremacy.

The little town of South Port was made up almost entirely of pilots possessing, I am sure, every quality of the sailor and the gentleman.

Moored snug in the inlet, it was pleasant to listen to the roar of the breakers on the bar, but not so cheerful was the thought of facing the high waves seaward. Therefore the plan suggested itself of sufficiently deepening a ditch that led through the

245

marshes from New River to Bogue Sound to let us through, thence we could sail inland the rest of the voyage without obstruction or hindrance of any kind. To this end we set about contrivances to heave the canoe over the shoals, and borrowed a shovel from a friendly schooner captain to deepen the ditch which we thought would be necessary to do in order to ford her along that way. However, the prevailing nor'east gales had so raised the water in the west end of the sound as to fill all the creeks and ditches to overflowing. I hesitated then no longer, but heading for the ditch through the marshes on a high tide before a brave west wind, took the chances of getting through by hook or by crook or by shovel and spade if required.

The *Coast Pilot,* in speaking of this place, says there is never more than a foot of water there, and even that much is rarely found. The *Liberdade* essayed the ditch, drawing two feet and four inches, thus showing the further good fortune or luck which followed perseverance, as it usually does, though sometimes, maybe, it is bad luck! Perhaps I am not lucid on this, which at best must remain a disputed point.

I was getting lost in the maze of sloughs and creeks, which as soon as I entered seemed to lead in every direction but the right one. Hailing a hunter near by, however, I was soon put straight and reassured of success. The most astonished man, though, in North Carolina, was this same hunter when asked if he knew the ditch that led through where I wished to go.

"Why, stranger," said he, "my gran'ther digged that ditch."

I jumped, I leaped! at thought of what a pilot this man would be.

"Well, stranger," said he, in reply to my query, "stranger, if any man kin take y' thro' that ditch, why, I kin"; adding doubtfully, however, "I have not hearn tell befo' of a vessel from Brazil sailing through these parts; but then you mout get through, and again ye moutent. Well, it's jist here; you mout and you moutent."

A bargain was quickly made, and my pilot came aboard, armed with a long gun, which as we sailed along proved a terror to ducks. The entrance to the ditch, then close by, was made with a flowing sheet, and I soon found that my pilot knew his business. Rush-swamps and corn-fields we left to port and to starboard, and were at times out of sight among brakes that brushed crackling along the sides of the canoe, as she swept briskly through the narrows, passing them all, with many a close hug, though, on all sides. At a point well on in the crooked channel my pilot threw up his hat, and shouted, with all his might:

"Yer trouble is over! Swan to gosh if it ain't! And ye come all the way from Brazil, and come through gran'ther's ditch! Well, I d'clar!"

From this I concluded that we had cleared all the doubtful places, and so it turned out. Before sundown my pilot was looking for the change of a five-dollar-piece; and we of the *Liberdade* sat before a pot-pie, at twilight, the like of which on the whole voyage had not been tasted, from sea fowl laid about by our pilot while sailing through the meadows and marshes. And the pilot himself, returning while the pot-pie was yet steaming hot, declared it "ahead of coon."

A pleasant sail was this through the ditch that gran'ther dug. At the camp fire that night, where we hauled up by a fishing station, thirty stalwart men talked over the adventures of their lives. My pilot, the best speaker, kept the camp in roars. As for myself, always fond of mirth, I got up from the fire sore from laughing. Their curious adventures with coons and 'gators recounted had been considerable.

Many startling stories were told. But frequently reverting to the voyage of the *Liberdade,* they declared with one voice that "it was the greatest thing since the wah." I took this as a kind of complimentary hospitality. "When she struck on a sand reef," said the pilot, "why, the captain he jumped right overboard and the son he jumped right over, too, to tote her over, and the captain's wife she holp."

By daylight next morning we sailed from this camp pleasant, and on the following day, November 28, at noon, arrived at Beaufort.

Mayor Bell of that city and many of his town folk met us at the wharf, and gave me as well as my sea-tossed crew a welcome to their shores, such as to make us feel that the country was partly ours.

"Welcome, welcome home," said the good mayor; "we have read of your adventures, and watched your progress as reported from time to time, with deep interest and sympathy."

So we began to learn now that prayers on shore had gone up for the little canoe at sea. This was indeed America and home, for which we had longed while thousands of miles across the ocean.

From Beaufort to Norfolk and thence to Washington was pleasant inland sailing, with prevailing fair winds and smooth sea. Christmas was spent on the Chesapeake—a fine, enjoyable day it was! with not a white-cap ripple on the bay. Ducks swimming ahead of the canoe as she moved quietly along were loath to take wing in so light a breeze, but flapping away, half paddling and half flying, as we came toward them, they managed to keep a long gun-shot off; but having laid in at the last port a turkey of no mean proportions, which we made shift to roast in the "caboose" aboard, we could look at a duck without wishing its destruction. With this turkey and a bountiful plum duff, we made out a dinner even on the *Liberdade.*

248

Of the many Christmas days that come crowding in my recollections now—days spent on the sea and in foreign lands, as falls to the lot of sailors—which was the merriest it would be hard to say. Of this, however, I am certain, that the one on board the *Liberdade* on the Chesapeake was not the least happy of them all.

The day following Christmas found us on the Potomac, enjoying the same fine weather and abundant good cheer of the day before. Fair winds carried us through all the reaches of the river, and the same prosperity which attended our little bark in the beginning of the voyage through tempestuous weather followed her to the end of the voyage, which terminated in mild days and pleasant sunshine.

On the 27th of December, 1888, a south wind bore us into harbor at Washington, D. C., where we moored for the winter, furled our sails and coiled up the ropes, after a voyage of joys and sorrows; crowned with pleasures, however, which lessened the pain of past regrets.

Having moored the *Liberdade* and weather-bitted her cables, it remains only to be said that after bringing us safely through the dangers of a tropical voyage, clearing reefs, shoals, breakers, and all storms without a serious accident of any kind, we learned to love the little canoe as well as anything could be loved that is made by hands.

To say that we had not a moment of ill-health on the voyage would not tell the whole story.

My wife, brave enough to face the worst storms, as women are sometimes known to do on sea and on land, enjoyed not only the best of health, but had gained a richer complexion.

Victor, at the end of the voyage, found that he had grown an inch and had not been frightened out of his boots.

Little Garfield—well he had grown some, too, and continued

249

to be a pretty good boy and had managed to hold his grip through many ups and downs. He it was who stood by the bow line to make fast as quick as the *Liberdade* came to the pier at the end of the voyage.

And I, last, as it should be, lost a few pounds' weight, but like the rest landed in perfect health; taking it altogether, therefore, only pleasant recollections of the voyage remain with us who made it.

With all its vicissitudes I still love a life on the broad, free ocean, never regretting the choice of my profession.

However, the time has come to debark from the *Liberdade*, now breasted to the pier where I leave her for a time; for my people are landed safe in port.

So ends Captain Joshua's narrative.

About the middle of April the *Liberdade* cast loose her moorings from the dock at Washington, and spreading sail before a brave west wind, bent her course down the Potomac with the same facility she experienced in December coming up before a wind from the south. Then, shaping her course for New York through inland passages, the voyage was turned into a pleasure excursion. The animation of spring clothed the landscape on all sides in its greatest beauty; and the voyagers found the northern forest no less charming than the tropic shade of foreign climes.

At Battery Basin, New York, the writer detached himself from the *Liberdade*, joined the *Finance*, and returned to Brazil. The *Liberdade* and rest of the crew transported to Boston where all spent the winter again amongst friends. With the return of spring the *Liberdade* was refitted and retraced her course to Washington where she was placed on view temporarily in the Smithsonian Institution. There she remained until about 1909 when the Captain, with a view to taking her as tender to the *Spray*, removed her from Washington. Taken apart to facilitate handling, the *Liberdade* was shipped and stored, presumably somewhere near New Bedford, there to await the return of the *Spray* from her own last voyage—that never was. As the Captain inadvertently had neglected to advise any of his family where the boat had been stored, what became of the *Liberdade* has remained a mystery ever since.

CHAPTER 13

The *Destroyer:*

Captain Joshua Goes to War

WHEN Captain Slocum was given command of the semi-undersea fighting craft *Destroyer,* bound for South America, it proved the most hazardous experience of his career up to that time. But it suited his adventurous nature, and seemed the climax of a dramatic sea life. This was just before the *Spray* voyage, and to battle with the ocean was his idea of a good time.

On completing his part of the contract, he secured passage back to New York on a German bark. The skipper was congenial and his sense of humor so stimulating that during the leisurely sail across the doldrums the passenger wrote a book. It was entitled: "The Voyage of the *Destroyer* from New York to Brazil." 37 pp. 1894. Private publication. The issue (for private circulation) was 500 copies. One copy is in the files of the Smithsonian Institution, Washington, D. C.; the only other copy I know of is in my possession.

Since it is not feasible to re-print the book in full here, I shall try to present the reader with an abridged re-arrangement, with such historical annotations as may be felt necessary after this lapse of time to clarify certain points. It is my aim as well to preserve some of the flavor of the Captain's inimitable pen.

In the year following the loss of the *Aquidneck* and our departure in the *Liberdade* from Brazil, the country had changed from an empire into a republic. The change was made by the voluntary abdication of the good Dom Pedro II. Fonseca was then elected president with Piexoto serving as vice president. All members of the group in control of politics were either generals or admirals; among them in this ring were Admirals Mello and Wandenkolk.

Fonseca's particular brand of democracy became odious to Piexoto and Mello, and they managed to make short work of him. Piexoto was then made president. Secure in this high office, he took on the character of a dictator and laid plans for his own re-election. Wandenkolk, by political intrigue, thereupon engineered a bill through Congress aimed at the president's personal ambition. President Piexoto immediately threw Wandenkolk into prison on political charges, and kept him there indefinitely, without trial. Wandenkolk's friend, Admiral Floriano Mello, commander in chief of the Brazilian Navy, headed a revolt against these arbitrary proceedings.

On the night of September 5, 1893, boarding the flagship *Aquidaban* he took possession of the ships *Republica, Javary, Irajano* and the *Marcilio Diaz*, with all the gun boats, torpedo boats and most of the Brazilian merchantmen in the harbor. Mello then began a bombardment of the city and the forts, which remained loyal to the Government. During this bombardment the ironclad *Javary*, the heaviest turret ship in the fleet, was sunk by a single shell striking her deck.

The next step taken by the legal Government was to declare the insurrectionists rebels, outlaws and enemies of the United States of Brazil. Piexoto needed a fleet, and as Mello had led practically the whole of the Brazilian Navy into rebellion, he was obliged to send abroad to obtain means of opposing him. Agents were commissioned both in Europe and the United States of America for the purchase and delivery of war materiel. In Germany they bought the torpedo boat *Aurora* which arrived off the coast of Brazil on November 22. Mello, to avoid being bottled up, put out with the announced purpose of giving battle to his new enemies in the open sea. The coming conflict, according to the papers, promised to settle the question of the efficiency of the torpedo against the battleship in modern warfare.

Piexoto's New York agents, under the direction of his minister, bought two merchant steamers and a few torpedo boats of various types and sizes. Three of the smaller ones were sent to Brazil on the decks of the larger vessels. The first ship to be armed and made ready for the war was the *Nictheroy*, which sailed from New York November 22 and arrived in the West Indies, flying the Brazilian flag, on the 28th. Her principal armament was the huge Zalinski pneumatic gun which was expected to rain dynamite on the rebel forts in Rio. Mello was said to have sent the cruiser *Republica* to intercept the *Nictheroy*, but she failed to do so. The *Republica*, however, was at sea somewhere between Rio and the West Indies, as was later determined.

The next armed steamer sent out from New York was the *America*, equipped with a Sims-Edison electric torpedo guided by remote control by means of a cable which fed out as it advanced towards the target. The third in order was the Ericsson torpedo vessel *Destroyer*, with a submarine gun built into her extreme bottom. She was in charge of Captain Joshua Slocum, "a seaman of large experience who had commanded many sailing ships and was accustomed to peril."

The *Destroyer* was lying up in Newport when bought by Piexoto's agents from the Ericsson Coast Defence Company, which held the vessel for market. Ericsson's partner, Delameter, put up $100,000 on the venture and to conduct the subsequent tests which proved that it was an entire success. "Destroyer" was a type name which was adopted as the permanent one upon documenting the vessel at the Custom House. She was a double-ended steamer, 150 feet long, of 1000 indicated horse power and with a trial trip speed of 18 knots to her credit. Nothing that Mello had could do more than 12 knots. The *Destroyer's* principal feature was a brass submarine gun, 43 feet long, built into the bow. It was a breech loader and operated as simply as any other piece of breech loading ordnance. This gun was 8 feet below the water line. The 35-foot projectile carried a charge of 350 pounds of gun-cotton in the war head. The propelling charge was 50 pounds of gun powder and experiments proved that the projectile could be shot through two torpedo nets. Both engine and gun crews, on going into action, were protected by a heavy breast armor incline to deflect any enemy gunfire. In addition to rudder steering, the direction of her head could be controlled by water jets. Before Captain Ericsson died (1889), he had proved that his destroyer, when advancing head-on to a distance of 200 yards, could sink anything afloat.

After her layup of a number of years, waiting for a market, she was still efficient and Mello's ironclads, ponderous and slow, were of the very type that Ericsson had in his mind when he designed his latest war engine.

The personnel, with the exception of three departments,

(Above) A portrait of the Spray under sail by Benjamin Aymar Slocum, second son of Capt. Joshua.

(Below) The Spray in Providence harbor, Rhode Island, September 1906, after its voyage around the world.

The Providence Portraits

[*Data on Photographs of Captain Joshua Slocum and Sloop*
Spray *Taken at Providence, R. I., September, 1906 by E. P.*
McLaughlin]

Sometime in September, 1906, I was at Providence, R. I., with
The Kodak Exhibition put on the road by the Eastman Kodak
Co. to advertise and demonstrate the photographic goods manu-
factured by them. As we were open afternoons and evenings
only, our forenoons were our own, to do as we pleased, so being
salt water born, I took my camera and made a beeline for the
waterfront. Coming around the end of a dock I was delighted
to sight the old *Spray* tied up alongside the pier. I had of course
read "Sailing Alone Around the World" by Captain Slocum and
before going on board started taking various shots of the good
old boat.

I then went aboard myself to gam with the Captain and sat
with him in the little cabin that had been his quarters on his
long voyage around the world. I gave him an entrance card to
our exhibition and invited him to attend the lecture and demon-
strations that evening, which he did. When it came time to make
my flashlight demonstration on the stage I invited him to act
as my subject, using the same 3¼ x 5½ camera I had used to take
the *Spray.—E. P. McLaughlin.*

Captain Joshua Slocum, photographed by E. P. McLaughlin whose comments on the photograph face this page.

A stern view of the Spray *in Providence Harbor, photographed by E. P. McLaughlin.*

were recruited from a regular sailor's shipping office on South Street. The skipper we are acquainted with. John Wildgoose was chief engineer; Hamilton, second engineer. The military department in charge of the gun, rated as "specialists," were variously qualified to meet the enemy. We shall later hear more of this department of non-seagoing professionals, which in the meantime took passage down on a larger and more comfortable ship. The *Destroyer* did not have room even for her coal. After a technical overhauling, "largely on paper," and the construction of some sponsons intended to be water-tight to help float the narrow vessel on her trip to the Southern Hemisphere, the *Destroyer* was given a spin about the harbor to test her machinery. She was then declared by the agents to be ready for sea but no insurance company would take a risk on a life on board. Partly to compensate for this disadvantage, the Brazilian Minister, Senor Mendonca, increased the very substantial emolument offered by his government. To encourage the men he told them that the sea to the south of the Gulf Stream was "like a lake," but what lake he failed to say.

Having a very limited steaming radius she was to be taken to Brazil by the large ocean towboat *Santuit*, which had sufficient bunker and tank capacity for both vessels. The *Destroyer* took on a ton of gun-cotton, but the *Santuit* carried the heavy projectiles for the submarine gun and a small Yarrow torpedo boat which was to be attached to the *Destroyer* in Brazilian waters. Captain Sturges, "king of towboat men," commanded the *Santuit* while Colonel Burt, representing the agents, had charge of the whole expedition until reaching the scene of war.

On December 7, 1893, the *Destroyer* left New York in tow of the *Santuit*, bound for Brazil. She towed smoothly and steadily enough, gliding along by the channel buoys, marking a fair rate of speed. Off Sandy Hook, clear of the shoals, the tow was stopped that they might readjust the thimble in the towline, a sharp point having pressed against the rope threatening to cut it off. This event, though small in itself, was the beginning of a series of mishaps which came soon enough. The sailors climbed out on the beak of the bow with tackle, crowbar and sledge, fixed up the defective thimble, as far as a job of that kind could be remedied, and wondered, while working, what long-shore riggers would do without old tars to finish their work at sea.

The propeller at this point was disconnected, as steam was to be used only for pumps and whistle. A system of signals was arranged between the two vessels: rockets and lights for the night, and code flags for the day. The thimble repaired, all seemed well, and the *Destroyer* was again headed on her course. The wind was west to nor'west, blowing a moderate breeze. The sea was smooth. The ship was making good head-way, skirting the coast with the land close aboard, as far as Winter Quarter Shoal; whence, taking her departure, she headed boldly away for the Gulf Stream. At 6 A.M., December 8, the light on the shoal was visible abeam and by noon a 220-mile run had been made in 28 hours. The wind had veered to the north-northeast, and the sea was not so smooth. All things considered, the *Destroyer* behaved well, though she showed a tendency to roll down low in the water in spite of her newly built sponsons, and took short cuts clean through the waves. Steam had been kept up since leaving New York. The vessel was making water and the steam pumps were at work. One calamity had already overtaken the vessel. The top seams were opening and the starboard sponson was water-logged. All hands were baling and pumping to keep the ship afloat, but the water was gaining steadily. By midnight it was washing the fires and putting them out. Steam must be kept up or they would go down. The sea became rougher. Rounds of fat pork were heaped upon the struggling fires. Hardbread smeared with fish oil was hurled into the furnace by the barrel, and all available light stuff which would burn on top of the dead coals was thrown on the fires. The rising water had cut off the draft, but the furniture, after a while, made a joyful fire that sent steam into the tubes to yield a giant's strength. Danger signals of rockets and blue lights had been shown through the night. The *Santuit* responded to all of the signals and handled the *Destroyer* with great care in the rough sea.

The storm continued through the 9th, but with energy taxed to the utmost, they gained mastery over the sea, and by daylight the water was so reduced that coals again would burn on the grates. A number of holes and leaks were located through which the water had been streaming all night. These were caulked, some with cotton waste, while others were plugged with pine wood. They signalled the towboat to go ahead, that they were "all right." The first danger had passed.

A stout canvas bag was now made which could hold a barrel of water and a sheers was rigged for a hoisting purchase. Hardly was this completed when it was sorely needed. All of the next night this bag was kept constantly going as fast as it could be filled, hoisted and emptied by eight pairs of strong arms. The rest of the men were driving the steam pumps, repairing defective valves and making new ones, working as fast as they could. The cook throughout the storm kept the coffee pot hot; there were no idlers around during these hours of danger and toil. After awhile, the steam pumps were again in action and along with them were many long and strong pulls at the big canvas bucket, without rest, for five long hours before the ship had free bilges again. Four more days of incessant care, anxiety and toil were passed before the sea ran more regularly, as they proceeded southward, nearing the regions of the trade winds which promised some respite. But good weather failed them on making the trades and the *Destroyer* began to make water again, which, in the hold, was kept down from one to three feet. Now and then a rolling suck was gained which they were glad to call a free bilge. Great quantities of water went over the ship. She still washed heavily, often going under the seas, like a great duck fond of diving. Everything was wet, with never a dry place in the ship. They were literally sailing under the sea.

When the *Destroyer* came out of the storm she was decked from the top of the smokestack down to the lifelines in Sargasso weed. All along the man ropes, fore and aft, the flowers of the sea were hanging in clusters, a rare and beautiful sight.

After the sea had quieted, coal, water and antiseptics were procured from the *Santuit,* as well as irons which were used to secure to a stanchion one of the stokers, named Brennan, for refusing duty and for making a brutal attack on Mr. Hamilton, the engineer on watch. Mr. Hamilton, already partly disabled by falling through the engine room skylight to the floor plates, was set upon by Brennan, who had shown earlier signs of mutiny. He first kicked the elderly officer and then, jumping upon him, had bitten him like a wild beast. The Captain said it was the worst exhibition of savagery he had ever seen and prompt action was taken upon it. Stoker and victim were to be taken care of upon meeting with the fleet.

On December 14, the ship was heading for Mona Passage with no great distance to go. The trades were very strong and a heavy cross sea was encountered as they neared the windward capes. Twenty miles northwest of Mona Passage the rudder was disabled, but it could still be put two spokes to port, and half of its proper angle to starboard. With this she was kept fairly well in the wake of the towboat. Early on the following day, they entered and passed through the Passage and in the afternoon they hauled in under the lee of the southwest point of Porto Rico to receive more coal and water from their supply ship, the *Santuit*. Thence proceeding to sea, they headed directly for Martinique. Here, in the Caribbean Sea, they found the trades strong and fierce, where times out of mind they had all seen it smooth.

This night was a dangerous one, for the storm continued wild and with a high sea. The port sponson as well as the starboard was now water-logged, making them both worse than useless. The crew gallantly struggled to keep the ship afloat. The water again put out the furnace fires. With all their work at hoisting the big canvas bucket they could not keep the water down. The crew had not seen the storm as their Captain had looked upon it; all they knew was hard work and salt water; but they toiled on like the stout loyal men that they were.

The Captain at the wheel, facing the sea, *felt her going down*. The hull was now a foot under water. The *Destroyer* seemed just about ready to make her last dive under the sea. Only the tank on deck buoyed her up; and the base of that was well submerged, when Big Alec of Salem, spoke up: "Captain, steam in the men is going down too; we can't keep it up much longer." But the first streak of dawn cheered every soul on board, and the men, with a wild yell, flew to their work with redoubled energy, for the storm was breaking away.

So they saved the *Destroyer*, and probably their own lives as well, for it is doubtful if any small boat could have lived in the sea that was then raging. The *Santuit* had seen their signals of distress and stood in as near as was prudent in the gale.

Twice in the night the Captain, who held a good grip, was washed from the wheel, for the constant pelting of the sea made him reel with dizziness. Mentally all he could realize was that the voyage was a fact, and that the iron tank which they were driving through the waves had, in reality, a bottom to it somewhere under the sea.

By daylight the storm went down as suddenly as it had come up in the night. Under the lee of a small island they found shelter. It was the Island of Caja Muertos, adjacent to Porto Rico, which gave them this comfort. Here they cast anchor at 9 A.M. and lay for eleven hours before sailing again on the perilous voyage.

At Caja Muertos the *Santuit's* crew lent a liberal hand to straighten things up on board the *Destroyer*. Colonel Burt, who came aboard to inspect the big canvas bucket, gave ample signs of his appreciation of a good crew. The *Destroyer* had free bilges before casting anchor at the island.

There is little to say about the remainder of the voyage through the Caribbean Sea. The *Santuit* took a circuitous route, the sooner to gain the lee of the islands. Proceeding under moderate speed and changing her course from time to time to accommodate the *Destroyer* to the run of the sea, she went bravely on. On December 18 the best steam pump broke down beyond all possibility of repair, for only new parts could replace those which were broken. Happily, enough of the sea had gone down so they suffered little from leakage. The kind influence of the islands was with them, and they would soon be in still smoother water. So it was full ahead with no rough seas to hinder.

December 19 at daybreak, the islands of Guadaloupe, Marie Galante and Dominique, hove in sight. The *Santuit* and her tow were heading directly for Martinique. They raised the

island soon, and at 4 P.M. of that day, came to anchor in the
Port of St. Pierre, with the *Destroyer* still in a leaky condition.
Here, at St. Pierre, they found the *America,* also bound for
Brazil and war. The stoker, Brennan, kicker and biter, was
transferred to that ship where his mutinous conduct could
be conveniently restrained in the brig which she rated. Mr.
Hamilton, in a very sore condition, was also transferred to the
America, where there was a good hospital in which to lay up
and an excellent surgeon to dress his wounds.

All of the *Destroyer's* stores were re-sorted at the island,
dried and repacked; then, moving to Fort de France Bay, repair work was continued until January 5, 1894, on which date
the *Destroyer* sailed at early daylight. The Old Year had been
escorted out and the New Year ushered in at Fort de France
Bay by the crews of all the ships in a glorification ashore worthy of the importance of the timely occasion. William, one of
the smartest of the *Destroyer's* crew, came on board from the
hospital some days later, minus a piece of his liver, which
Quiet John, the fireman, had snipped off in an argument over a
bottle. New Year's Eve had transformed John, the silent
drudge who "wouldn't say bah to a goose," into a truculent
roisterer, but there were no arrests made. An understanding
gendarme brought on board a sheath knife found at the
scene of the fray with the reasonable request that "when the
crew goes ashore let them leave their knives behind."

Sea conditions had improved and the *Destroyer,* benefited
by her late repairs, went with some degree of safety now. The
trade winds were still blowing very strong, and although towing in the teeth of the wind, the ship was kept free, and handled
in all respects without the wear and tear on a man's soul that
had been suffered in the early part of the voyage.

Two transfers were made from the fleet to the *Destroyer*

at Martinique. The first was that of Mr. Kuhn, an engineer from the *America,* who took the place of Mr. Hamilton. The second, of lesser importance by far but the most talked of, was that of "Sir Charles, the hero of the Soudan," whose real status was third gunner's mate. All South American imbroglios attracted free lance soldiers from various parts of the world and this enthusiast had seen service in the British Royal Marine Artillery. He rated an enormous sword stamped on one side as a gift from "Her Majesty Queen Victoria" and on the other side with an American eagle. This was the famous sword which, buckled over a dashing red coat, secured for him his position. The sight of this rig and the cut of his sails did the trick, for it must be borne in mind that the *Destroyer* had to make a strong warlike appearance when she came to Brazil. The sailors made due note of the awe-inspiring weapon, taking special notice of the engraving of the Unmistakable Bird spreading his wings over the Queen's gift. Sir Charles had a predilection for dueling, and an affair of honor with the African cook, involving the destruction of the *Santuit's* best flapjack griddle against the steam winch, came to Captain Sturges' attention. The red-coated warrior was called to the bridge for an interview which could be heard all over the harbor, to the effect that "any more such work on board here, sir, and I'll make shark bait of your damned carcass, d'ye hear? Now go forward." Sir Charles went.

Colonel Burt at this point, with a twinkle of humor, sent him to the *Destroyer* to "stand by the Captain." This was opportune, for the crew of the *Destroyer,* having had a very salt time of it, was ready for anything fresh; and the hero of many battles dropped into the vacancy like one born for the place. A duel on the *Destroyer* came to a focus in no time, and had not Sir Charles' friend and countryman, Mr. Wildgoose, extracted all of the cartridges from the revolvers, some one on board might have been hurt.

Mr. Kuhn, while bathing over the side at Fort de France, had a narrow escape from a 20-foot shark which was shot at the proper instant by Mr. Brown, the cool-headed engineer of the *Santuit*. The bullet passed through the shark's head and the brute shot past his intended victim with closed jaws and lay lifeless on the water. The American Consul who was on board, had just remarked, "Oh, there are no sharks in here," when Brown fired. Kuhn, an athletic young man, upon reaching the vessel's side, landed on deck like a flying fish in a gale of wind. The waters were now filled with other monsters who tore at the slain shark and grabbed greasy planks, butter firkins and even a ship's bucket, by way of dessert. There was no further need of cautioning the crews to keep on the inside of the rail.

On January 18 the *Destroyer* arrived at the penal Island of Fernando de Noronha where all hands were busy for the day, taking in coal and water again from the *Santuit*. A heavy surf was running, but dispatches were safely brought out to them by convicts in one-man canoes which they skillfully managed. There was no report of the rebel cruiser *Republica* but it was learned that a batch of Piexoto's political prisoners had been landed on this island the day before the *Destroyer's* arrival. At 7 P.M. she sailed with orders for Pernambuco, where she arrived without further incident on January 20. A pilot with a harbor tug took her into the inner harbor, where she was moored to the reef. This finished the worst part of the hardest voyage that the Captain ever made.

In Pernambuco the *Destroyer* fell in with the Loyal fleet of the new Brazilian Navy. Passing under the lee of the *Nictheroy*, that noble ship gave the little Ericsson gun vessel three rousing cheers. The Loyal Admiral, Gonçalves, was in Pernambuco on his old ark, the wooden flagship *Paranahyba,* armed with muzzle-loading smoothbores which were just good enough for salutes. This seemed to the crew of the *Destroyer* to be a waste of valuable powder, but it suited Gonçalves' idea of pomp and circumstance.

It was in Pernambuco that the chief gunner who had come on the *Santuit* took charge of the submarine gun. This was the member of the crew who was on the ship's articles "principally as Count." He was a "specialist" and "torpedo expert" and while the *Destroyer* was in Erie Basin he had the job of balancing the projectiles and making them ready for use. The Captain tossed him off as a "brand new sailor and a good judge of a hotel." It turned out that he had undoubted ballistic credentials as a graduate of the French Government Torpedo School, and a personal acquaintance with the great John Ericsson himself. His name was M. Nils Gustave de Foch. Without consulting anyone on the *Destroyer* he decided to fire the submarine gun. First, from his hotel, he wrote a note to Admiral Duarte, begging him to witness the coming exploit with the *cannon.* There were several other admirals about, but for special reasons Duarte had Foch's sympathy, so he invited him to the show. The note was written in the politest French, but the Admiral did not come; neither did the gun go off. The only trouble was that the powder got wet. The vessel was then grounded at the risk of springing another leak to unload the projectile from the outboard end of the tube since it would not discharge by fire.

It was now "hurrah for the war, boys, get a cargo of powder in and be off." There was no time to be lost. The *Destroyer* now carried powder for the whole fleet, which had previously burnt all they had saluting the Admiral. The *Destroyer* already had enough gun-cotton in to make a noise, but Gonçalves wanted more thunder of his own old-fashioned sort, so they filled her chock-a-block with the stuff to make it. The submarine gun was stowed all over with barrels of powder and was not accessible during the rest of the voyage to Bahia. In fact, powder was casually scattered all about. Three barrels of it found passage in the Captain's room. One was stowed abaft the galley near the cook's stove.

Before leaving Pernambuco, the organization of the *Destroyer* was changed by the Brazilian Commander of Forces who had received the vessel and all of her equipment from the Ericsson Estate. Captain Joshua, after being towed over (and under) a large portion of two oceans, found himself putting his hand to Articles of War. Notwithstanding his peaceful disposition he was expected to fight, and in gold braid at that, which would be something new for him. He says, confidentially, that while he was joining the Brazilian Navy in an official capacity, he was also, for a private reason "burning to get a rake at Mello," for it was he who illegally expelled the *Aquidneck* with her cargo of Argentine hay from the quarantine station at Ilha Grande, some time previously. It was the *Aquidaban* who turned her gun on him, so that he had formed a good idea of the enemy's characteristics and armament, and it would have been a great joke on Mello to find that the hitherto helpless Yankee skipper had dynamite aboard this time instead of hay.

The Captain still had with him the best of his fine crew which had shipped in New York. The Yarrow torpedo boat, perfect in every respect, which had been brought out on the *Santuit*, was named the *Moxoto* and attached to the *Destroyer*. The *Destroyer* was re-named the *Pirating*, a Brazilian place name, it was explained, which had no bearing on the character of the crew. For the purpose of our narrative we shall continue to use the Ericsson name, *Destroyer*, which, now in alien hands, will need our sympathies.

In due time the powder which the *Destroyer* carried was delivered in good order to the various ships in Bahia. For this she came into disfavor with all of the naval authorities except his Excellency, Senor Netto, Minister of Marine, who found himself in a delicate position. He alone was loyal to the Piexoto government, for the State of Bahia, with that flexible state of mind peculiar to South American revolutions, was on the point of going over to the rebels. Later, a portion of this same cargo of powder, forwarded to Rio, was laid in a mine to blow up the rebel *Aquidaban*, but by "mistake" was not fired until after the great battleship got by and well out of the way of it.

There was funereal stillness when they arrived at Bahia. Often the doughty Gonçalves, a passive traitor to Piexoto, was seen in his barge on the bay, passing to and fro, always to the music of a band. But, says Captain Slocum, "a skipper of my grade and a foreigner to boot, got no music in Brazil."

All was quiet and serene save for the pop of the champagne cork at the "Paris" on the hill and the boom of the sunset gun. The rising sun had to take care of itself. The average Brazilian naval man was an amphibious being, never dangerous, spending his time equally between hotel and harbor. The quietness of Bahia was astonishing, for there was not even target practice. The further from New York, the less it was like war. There was, to be sure, torpedo practice one day. A Howell torpedo was launched, but boomerang-like, it returned, hitting the ship again. The only thing lacking to make the drill a howling success was the dynamite which these remarkable warriors forgot to put in.

A trial trip of the Yarrow torpedo boat, *Moxoto*, observed

from the deck of the *Destroyer,* brought a blush to the Captain's pen. A crockery-ware clerk had been put in command of her and she was sent among the ships in the bay. To the poor clerk and his earthern-ware crew, this was all strange and dangerous, but they managed to make things hum. They got plenty of steam up; and then found they did not know how to stop her. The skipper-clerk hailed a foreign steamer and shouted to the engineer that he would give 20 mil reis ($10) to be stopped. She was going full speed. The vice-admiral's brig, an old craft which had been anchored there for many years, came in for the first ram in the collisions that followed. But the *Moxoto,* not hitting her fair, glanced off, second best in the battle. Then she made for Brig. No. 2, not far away, aground on her own beef bones, and gave her a blow in the quarter that brought the crew on deck in a hurry. The crew at first supposed that the shock came from an earthquake, and as nothing less could move them to action they all went below again, taking no notice of the *Moxoto,* which by some miracle brought her propeller to a stop.

On the following day Gonçalves and his staff, under a false pretext, withdrew both the *Destroyer* and the *Moxoto* from active service. Against this overt conspiracy Senor Netto was apparently powerless, but he always had a warm hand clasp for the Captain whenever they met alone. There was a mutual understanding of what was about to take place. The great Ericsson cannon, which alone could have settled the revolt, was next dismantled and rendered useless. In New York, guards had been placed on it to keep people away, but in Bahia, while the cannon was in order, it was impossible to get anyone to go near it. "Should that double on us like the Howell torpedo," they declared, "it would be worse than the yellow fever around here."

Gonçalves then revoked Captain Slocum's contract (and commission) made by the Commander of Forces at Pernambuco. With this official act vanished all prospect of promised prize money as far as the crew of the *Destroyer* was concerned. It was to have been a handsome sum of gold.

The officers then proceeded to revile the *Destroyer*, not only for bringing the powder so quickly upon their heels, thus cutting into their quiet in port and hastening them to the front, but for still greater personal reasons. It was well known that the ships of Gonçalves were manned by peaceful people, "harmless as jaybirds." Mello's outfit was the same. Why should they kill each other? The *Destroyer*, then, the most formidable ship of all, must be disposed of. This went without saying.

In addition there were other reasons for being disgruntled over the *Destroyer*, for when she first came to Bahia it was reported that she was the long hoped for "money ship" that was to follow the fleet and pay the bills. The size of the large iron "tank" in which the crew lived measured up to their expectations of the money chest from which they would all get rich. But instead of bank notes pouring forth they beheld seabegrimed mariners tumbling out of the tank, and worse yet, barrels of gun powder.

On February 28 the American sailors were discharged, and the *Destroyer*, seasoned by many storms, changed her crew to give up the fight in a summer sea. The upland navigators at the Arsenal of Bahia, having observed the New York crew put the vessel in and out of the Basin with dispatch, thought they might be able to do the trick themselves on the principle of "monkey see, monkey do." In doing so they "accidentally" stove a hole in her bottom on a rock. Before this her best steam pump was removed and landed under a tree at the arsenal, together with the breech-block of the Ericsson gun.

Captain Slocum, from the top of the hill, watched all of these maneuvers to the last and saw the *Destroyer*, which had been designed to upset navies and make them impotent, now lying undone, herself, in the Basin; the tide ebbing and flowing through her broken hull, a rendezvous for eels and crayfish.

The rebel navy, without a land base, soon weakened and the *Aquidaban* was sent by Mello from Rio to the southern State of Santa Catharina where he still dominated. Here she was caught at anchor on a foggy morning and torpedoed by the *Aurora*, and after some wild firing the great ship settled in the mud.

In the *Paranahyba*, Gonçalves took up the position formerly occupied by Mello in Rio, and went on with the business of burning powder in noisier salutes than ever.

The revolt began in Rio September 1893, and the "funny war," so far as the Navy was concerned, ended of itself in March 1894. As Captain Slocum wrote, "No historian can ever say more about the Mello Rebellion in Brazil."

CHAPTER 14

The Building of the *Spray*

WHEN, in 1891, my father changed his residence from Boston to Fairhaven, he had already taken an interest in the reconstruction of an historic sloop called the *Spray*. The circumstance of the acquirement reached into the past as do many things in our lives. The ancient vessel had been the property of Eben Pierce, a whaling captain of New Bedford, whom my father had met but a short time before in Boston, and who was a relative of the talented Captain Drew of Gardiner, Maine, who had the ship *Sea Witch* in Manila at the time the *Northern Light* was there. While talking about the past and about ships, Captain Pierce had said in a jocular way, "Come to Fairhaven and I will *give* you a ship."

The sad and dejected hull of the old sloop, awaiting the hand of rehabilitation, was affectionately blocked up in an Oxford Village pasture, not far from the water and near the residence of Captain Pierce himself. "She needs some repairs," he further commented as he and the new owner made a fresh survey. That was plain to them both. There was something in her lines which suggested to the new owner a round-the-world ship. Mystery surrounded the origin of the *Spray*. Nobody exactly knew where she came from and for seven years the neighbors had been wondering what "Captain Eben" was going to do with the old boat and if he did anything, would it "pay."

They all averred that she had been built in the year one, when Adam was a small boy. There was no record in the customhouse of where she was built. She was once a sword-fisherman out of Noank and afterwards in New Bedford. Next we see her blocked up in the Oxford Village pasture.

On a smaller scale she greatly resembled Amundsen's exploring ship *Gjøa*, which he said was a Norwegian herring boat before he took her through the Northwest Passage. The writer saw the *Gjøa* blocked up in Golden Gate Park, San Francisco, where she may be seen at the present day; the resemblance of the *Spray* to the *Gjøa* was very striking, particularly in the apple bow and broad square stern.

Oxford Village is that part of Fairhaven which is to the northward of the bridge leading from New Bedford. It is the resting place of John Cook who was the last surviving Pilgrim on the *Mayflower* and the first white man to settle in Fairhaven (1659) when they bought the place from the Indians. The spot where the *Spray* was hauled out was but a few steps to the eastward of the present Cook Monument. For seven years the neighbors asked, "I wonder what Captain Eben is going to do with the old *Spray?*" And when the actual work began, they all thought she was to be broken up. Great was the amazement of the thrifty and observant ones who wondered if it would ever "pay." It was made to pay.

There is nothing alike in building and rebuilding a vessel of any size. The processes are entirely different, and a man might start in courageously to rebuild a larger job than he would think of building from scratch. It may be just as hard or even harder, but it does not look so from the start. The chief advantage in rebuilding the *Spray* was the excellent model which could thereby be reproduced and preserved. Timber by timber and plank by plank were replaced without changing either dimensions or shape, but at no savings of expense.

In the first place, the old job was a centerboarder, and that had to be replaced first, as a centerboard box weakens a hull and is very sure to leak, no matter what. To take that out, the floor timbers were sawed across without disturbing the garboard, and the old keel removed in sections without disturbing either the stem forward or the sternpost or deadwoods aft. The new keel was a solid stick of "pasture" white oak cut down not far from the work.

A word about pasture oak, as it was then called, for it is now, and more's the pity, no more. It was employed by the New England builders of small craft when they wanted something lasting and tough. What made the pasture oak tough? It was because it grew up in the middle of an open pasture and from the time it was but an acorn sprout it had to fight the four winds to survive; as it grew to size its sinews were hardened by the many gales which bent its trunk and twisted its branches. The life history of the pasture white oak was much different from its cousin white oak which might have grown to much greater size in the protecting contiguity of forest neighbors. Pasture white oak was at one time common to the shores of New England. It made a solid keel, stem or sternpost. For steam-bent frames it excelled. A pasture white-oak, steam-bent frame, good and hot, could be tied in a knot. When they became cold, they became as hard as rock. And that was the kind of frame that went into the *Spray*. But we are ahead of the story.

The new keel, trimmed with a broadax, was pushed into the place of the old one, and a whole new set of floor timbers installed. These were of pasture oak and steamed and reaching across the keel to tie the frames when they came to be put in. The old garboards were then temporarily fastened to the new floor timbers. The frame timbers were then steamed, pre-bent and put in place, for about a third of the length of the vessel, against the old planking and held with temporary fastenings. At this stage, the new keel was in place and one-third of the new floor timbers and frames in place. The next job was the stem and the apron for receiving the fore-hood ends.

It must be borne in mind that, while all this tearing out and replacing is being done, the deck and upper works have not been disturbed, and that they remain to serve as a brace against changing the shape of anything below. The elements of the new stem were made of the butt of a pasture oak and this same butt was to cleave a coral head in twain at the Keeling Islands. The elements of the stem consisted of the stem piece, the stem knee and the apron all through-bolted together before it was shoved into the place where the old one was.

It was a great day in the *Spray* shipyard when the new stem was set up and bolted to the keel. Whaling captains worked along up over the bridge from New Bedford to survey it. When one hove in sight, the builder rested on his adz for a gam. They never came too often for him. In their opinion it was fit to smash ice, and they saw no reason why the *Spray* should not yet cut in bowhead off the coast of Greenland.

On the placement of the new stem and apron the displaced ends of the old plank were tacked up to keep them in place, and then the builder's attention was given to the deadwoods,

276

the sternpost and to the transom which formed the stern. All of the parts were removed and replaced on the same principle as the operation on the bow, but the results were not so dramatic. There was something about the bow that was symbolic; it was a challenge.

The keel and the ends of the new vessel secure, all the attention of the builder could be directed towards the installing of the rest of the frame timbers to get ready for the planking. The

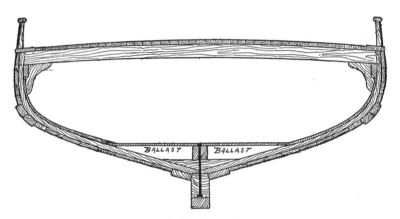

Cross-section of the Spray's *construction*

fore ends of the planking as well as the frame and the breast hooks had to be steamed, and for that purpose a steam box was rigged with a whaler's trypot hung under it by a chain. The whole outfit was out-of-doors and alongside the job. The planks for the new vessel were of Georgia pine an inch and a half thick. The operation of putting them on was tedious. The hardest was putting on the thick wales around the turn of the bilges to take the place of the usual inside stringers. They were of Georgia pine but twice as thick as the planking elsewhere. They were put on first and the knuckles of the frame drawn down

277

to them by means of large screw clamps. In that way the integrity of her diagonals was assured. The planking was copper-riveted to the frames while the butts were through-fastened right through the skin with screw bolts with nuts set up on washers. There was never any complaint from the butts. A thousand screw bolts entered into the entire construction, for it was the purpose of the builder to make his vessel stout and strong.

The bulwarks were built up of white oak stanchions, fourteen inches high, and covered with seven-eighth-inch white pine. These stanchions, morticed through a two-inch oak covering board, were caulked with thin cedar wedges and they remained tight ever after. The deck was made of one-and-a-half-inch by three-inch white pine, spiked to beams of Georgia pine placed three feet apart.

The deck inclosures were one over the main hatch, six feet by six feet, for a cooking galley, and a trunk farther aft, about ten feet by twelve, for a cabin. Both of these rose about three feet above the deck and were sunk sufficiently into the hold to afford head room. In a space along the starboard side of the cabin a berth was arranged to sleep in, and shelves for small storage, not forgetting a place for the medicine chest. In the midship hold, which was five feet fore and aft by the entire width of the vessel under decks (the space between the cabin and the galley), was room for provision of water, salt beef, and other heavy stores ample for many months. Forward of the galley and under the foredeck there were two bunks which gave room for the stowage of spare sails and other gear as well as for the anchor chains and for a spare anchor.

When caulking was finished and the seams payed with a filling cement, the underwater surface was given two coats of copper paint and two coats of white lead on the topsides and bulwarks; the rudder was then shipped and painted. On the following day the *Spray* was launched. As she rode again to an anchor she sat on the water like a swan.

The *Spray's* dimensions when finished were: thirty-six feet nine inches long over all, fourteen feet two inches wide, and

*"It'll crawl!" remarked Fairhaven neighbors when
they watched Captain Slocum caulking the* Spray

four feet two inches deep in the hold; her tonnage was nine tons net and twelve and seventy-one hundredths tons gross.

Under a sheers farther down the harbor, the mast, a live New Hampshire spruce stick, was stepped and stayed. It was fitted with a square doubling with crosstree cap and topmast. Both boom and gaff were fitted with jaws to the mast and there were mast hoops to hold the sail to the mast. When first rigged, the *Spray* was a double-head rigged sloop with a long bowsprit

279

and a boom about as long as she was on the deck. There was plenty of muslin for a fairly strong breeze. Later on during the voyage, the rig and some of the spar dimensions were modified, as we shall see.

In the equipment and appurtenances of the little vessel, simplicity was the rule. The steering was by a wheel, and a drum, with two gun tackles at the deck between the tiller and the bulwarks. The tiller led aft towards the transom so as to be out of the way. The compass was a dry card set inside the cabin and with a window so as to be seen from the wheel. In this way there was no difficulty keeping a light in the binnacle in a gale of wind. For ground gear she carried three anchors weighing, respectively, forty pounds, one hundred pounds, and one hundred and eighty pounds. The windlass was of the crab type; a ratchet operated by a handspike, a very unhandy device if one had much heaving to do like fifty fathoms of chain out, up and down. The ballast was concrete cement, stanchioned down securely to ensure it against shifting should the vessel be hove on her beam-ends. There was no outside ballast whatever. The *Spray* could have been self-righting if hove down on her beam-ends, a fact that was proven, since, by an experiment on an exact duplicate of the original boat and ballasted just like her. The test boat was hove down with mast flat to the water and when released righted herself. My father never knew of that test. Of the *Spray's* unusual self-steering qualities we shall see farther along in the story of her voyage.

"I did not know the center of effort in her sails, except as it hit me in practice at sea, nor did I care a rope yarn about it. Mathematical calculations, however, are all right in a good boat, and *Spray* could have stood them. She was easily balanced and easily kept in trim."

With these words Captain Joshua dismisses the technique of *Spray's* design.

Charles D. Mower, the marine architect, took off a set of lines which were used to illustrate the editions of "Sailing Alone Around the World." These, in turn, were more carefully analyzed by C. Andrade Jr., an engineer and yacht designer in December 1908. His article about the balance of the *Spray* hull and sail plan make interesting reading. It appeared in *The Rudder* from which I am happy to reprint it with the permission of the proprietors.

To quote Mr. Andrade:

One of the most remarkable things about *Spray* is her ability to hold her course for hours or days at a time with no one at the helm. Had she not possessed this quality, Slocum's performance would have been a physical impossibility. For example, she ran from Thursday Island to the Keeling Cocos Islands, 2,700 miles, in twenty-three days. Slocum stood at the helm for one hour during that time. Her average distance made good for the run was over 117 miles a day or about 5 miles an hour. This was a fair cruising speed for *Spray,* and she maintained that speed of 5 knots for twenty-three consecutive days, or 552 consecutive hours. The impossibility of steering a boat for that time, or for any considerable portion of that time, is of course obvious. There are well-known men right here in New York City who have seen boats do the same thing for comparatively short distances. Thus, Mr. Day records that after he had converted *Sea-Bird* into a keel boat and had lengthened her keel, he laid her on a course and she held that course for an hour and a half, at the end of which time there came a change in the wind. Now if a boat will hold her course alone for an hour and a half, she will hold it for a year and a half, *provided always* that the wind and sea remain unchanged.

Examine an ocean chart of *Spray's* voyage, and you will see that Slocum systematically ran down the trades, not only for hundreds but for thousands of miles, and his wind and sea conditions for whole days and weeks must have been practically constant. This is one of the reasons for *Spray's* phenomenal runs. Perfect balance is the other reason.

After a thorough analysis of *Spray's* lines, I found her to have a theoretically perfect balance. Her balance is marvelous—almost uncanny. Try as I would—one element after the other—they all swung into the same identical line. I attacked her with proportional dividers, planimeter, rota-meter, Simpson's rule, Froude's coefficients, Dixon Kemp's formulæ, series, curves, differentials, and all the appliances of modern yacht designing, and she emerged from the ordeal a theoretically perfect boat. For when she is underway, every element of resistance, stability, weight, heeling effort, and propulsive force is in one transverse plane, and that plane is the boat's midship section. I know of no similar case in the whole field of naval architecture, ancient or modern. There may be similar cases in existence, but it has not been my good fortune to know of them.

Before passing to a critical analysis of the figures, I shall take up a few general questions concerning this unusual boat.

Spray's lines appear, in much reduced size, at the end of Slocum's book, "Sailing Alone Around the World." When I first looked at them, and read Slocum's statement that this hull had been driven at a speed of 8 knots, I thought he must be mistaken.

Slocum, however, is an accurate historian; and I therefore set to work with proportional dividers, and laid *Spray* out to a scale of ½ inch to the foot, in order to acquire an intimate personal knowledge of her lines—merely looking at them in a book will not always suffice. I next swept in two diagonals (*A* and *B* in the half-breadth plan), which are omitted from the lines as published in Slocum's book, and then I realized that he was justified in his claim of 8 knots.

If you will look at the drawings, you will see that *Spray's* real working line is the diagonal *B*, which is a normal practically the whole length of the boat. On the half-breadth plan, you will see that diagonal *B* is marked by a little cross between stations 3 and 6. At this point she takes the water. From the cross to station 6, there is a very coarse angle of entrance, of which I shall have more to say in a moment. From station 6 to the transom, a run of over 27 feet, diagonal *B* is as clean a line, as fine drawn, easy running and fair as you will find in any racer of the Larchmont fleet—and that is the line that bears her; it is the line she runs on, and it is the measure of her speed.

Now let us take up that coarse entrance angle of diagonal *B* from the cross to station 6—a matter of some two feet.

Twenty years ago, Mr. Herreshoff announced that hollow bow lines were not essential to speed.

The Whitehead torpedo, which travels at about 30 knots, has a nose as round as a cannon-ball.

Some of the little scow boats on the Western lakes develop great speed, and they hold this speed through rough water (that is, rough for their size and length), and their bows show hard curves, and in some cases even flat transoms.

Viewing all these things with impartial eyes, I should say that the two feet of diagonal *B* in *Spray* from the cross to section 6 would be no detriment whatever to her speed.

Let us now consider that portion of diagonal *B* which lies forward of the cross. This portion of the diagonal runs up to the stem-head at an angle somewhere in the neighborhood of

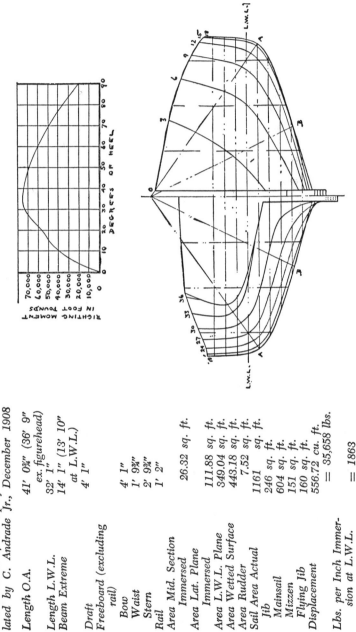

284

The elements of the Spray's hull as calculated by C. Andrade Jr., December 1908

Length O.A.	41' 0¾" (36' 9" ex. figurehead)
Length L.W.L.	32' 1"
Beam Extreme	14' 1" (13' 10" at L.W.L.)
Draft	4' 1"
Freeboard (excluding rail)	
Bow	4' 1"
Waist	1' 9¾"
Stern	2' 9¾"
Rail	1' 2"
Area Mid. Section Immersed	26.32 sq. ft.
Area Lat. Plane Immersed	111.88 sq. ft.
Area L.W.L. Plane	349.04 sq. ft.
Area Wetted Surface	443.18 sq. ft.
Area Rudder	7.52 sq. ft.
Sail Area Actual	1161 sq. ft.
Jib	246 sq. ft.
Mainsail	604 sq. ft.
Mizzen	151 sq. ft.
Flying Jib	160 sq. ft.
Displacement	556.72 cu. ft. = 35,658 lbs.
Lbs. per Inch Immersion at L.W.L.	= 1863

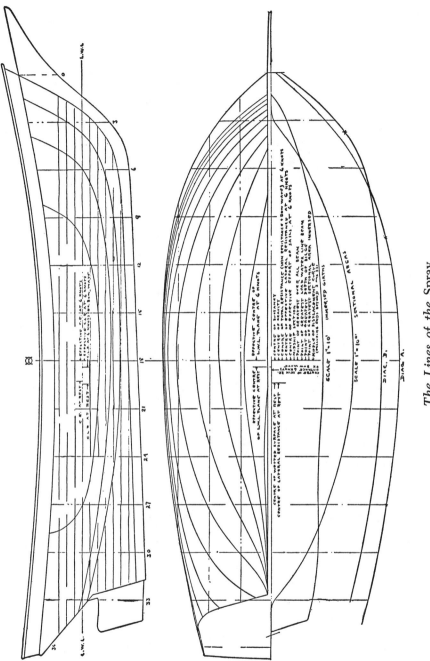

The Lines of the Spray

45°. The water-lines do the same and the buttock lines do the same. The result is a bow of terrific power. With her thirty-five thousand odd pounds of dead-weight and a few more thousand sail pressure on top of that, *Spray* can go coasting down the side of a roller, and then when she turns from the long downgrade up-hill again, instead of running under, or carrying a ton or so of water aft along her decks, that bow will lift her. And it is the only bow that would lift her.

Spray's stern is the best that my limited experience could suggest. There is just enough rake in her transom to lift her handsomely over any following sea. Her transom is broad enough and deep enough to hold her water-lines and buttocks easy to the very last moment. And the practice of dropping the bottom of her transom below the water-line finds support in such examples as Mr. Crane's *Dixie II* and Mr. Herreshoff's *Sea Shell,* and many other master designed craft. It does ease up the buttock lines so; and contrary to popular superstition, it does not create any material drag of dead-water. The Crosbys have been building catboats this way for years. By dropping the transom below the water-line, the water lifts the boat to the very end of the run, and one of the resultants of that lift on the buttock lines is a forward thrust. On the other hand, where the knuckle of the transom is above the water-line, the exact opposite takes place, and the water, instead of lifting the boat and thrusting her forward, is lifted by the boat and holds her back.

Spray's midsection, at first glance, would seem much wider and shallower than a seagoing model would require.

But like everything else about her, there is a very good reason for *Spray's* form of midsection; in fact there are several good reasons.

Firstly: I have heard it said, that her immunity from loss is due to the fact that when she is hove to she yields and gives to the sea, constantly easing away to leeward; whereas a deeper, more ardent model, holding in uncompromising fashion to the wind, would be battered and strained into destruction.

Secondly: *Spray's* great breadth gives her no end of deck room. Now when you are living on a boat weeks and months and years, deck room becomes not only important, but essential. Without adequate deck room for walking and exercise, a man could not exist for that length of time. He would fall ill of some sickness and die.

Thirdly: The form of *Spray's* midship section insures that she will never heel to an uncomfortable angle. She would rarely go down much below 10° of heel, and in good sailing breezes, she would probably not exceed 5°. Now equally with deck room, this matter of heel is most essential to the comfort and, in the long run, the health of the crew. The strain of living on a boat at 25 or 30° of heel may be borne for the brief period of a race, maybe a race as far as Bermuda. But when it comes to living on a boat thus for weeks at a time, no human being could stand it.

Fourthly: *Spray* is a much better boat to windward than her form of midsection would at first glance indicate. To the casual observer, it would seem almost impossible to drive her to windward at all without a centerboard (and she has no centerboard). But on careful analysis it will appear that there are three reasons why *Spray* should be a fairly good boat to windward.

In the first place, she has an unusually hard bilge and an unusually flat vertical side, and the result is that even at a small angle of heel, her lee side acts as an efficient leeboard of very considerable area.

In the second place, she has a long, fairly deep keel and as

287

this keel rakes downward from the forefoot to the rudder, it is constantly entering solid water at every portion of its length, and is very much more efficient than if the keel were horizontal.

In the third place, *Spray* has a large lateral plane proportion to her sail spread.

Therefore, like everything else about her, I should say that her form of midsection was fully justified.

For a boat of 32 feet water-line, *Spray's* displacement is enormous—35,658 lb. Of course, this is essential in her design. Being an oceangoing cruiser, her construction is heavy, 1½-inch yellow pine planking. Her great breadth requires heavy deck beams, 6-inch by 6-inch yellow pine; and her construction in other particulars is equally massive. All this means displacement. Then her crew, even one man, consumes a good deal of water, food and fuel in the course of several months. She must carry a large supply of spare gear and stores. Her large displacement then is necessary, unavoidable; and, besides, it gives her power to carry on through a sea.

By reason of her large water-line plane, her displacement per inch immersion at the load water-line is very large, 1,863 lb. This is a good feature, as it makes little difference in her trim whether she has a ton or so more or less of stores on board. This feature is still another advantage accruing from her wide shallow form of midship section.

We now come to the inner mystery of *Spray's* design.

I suppose that the extraordinary focusing of her centers is the result of chance. *Spray* was laid down about the year 1800. Analytic boat designing, as we understand it, was unknown at that time. *Spray's* perfection of balance, then, must be purely empirical, but it is none the less marvellous for that.

To begin with, *Spray's* center of buoyancy is located exactly at the boat's midship section. This is unusual. In fact, at the

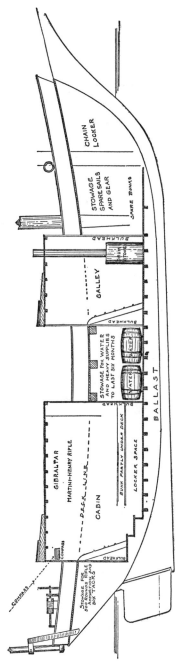

Cabin profile of the Spray

moment I do not recall any other design that has even this peculiarity. Axiomatically, the center of gravity and the center of buoyancy must lie in the same vertical line; and thus at the very outset of our investigations we find that the center of gravity, the center of buoyancy, the greatest breadth, the greatest depth of bilge, and the maximum point in the boat's curve

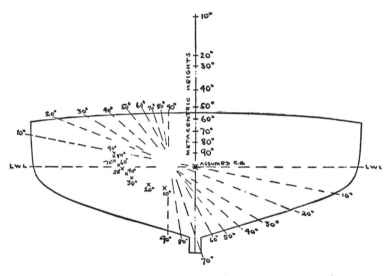

Transverse metacenters, load water lines and centers of buoyancy of the Spray. *Calculated by C. Andrade Jr.*

of displacement, all fall exactly on the same line, which happens to be station 18.

And what is still more unusual, it will be observed that station 18, containing within itself all these elements, falls at exactly the effective middle point of the boat's curve of displacement. A glance at the curve of displacement will show that for all practical purposes the portion lying forward of station 3, and aft of station 33, can be disregarded. In other words, for all practical purposes, the curve begins at station 3 and ends at station 33, and exactly midway between station 3 and station 33 lies station 18, at which are focused all the points abovementioned.

Let us now examine station 18 with reference to its position on the load water-line. The old school of designers who pinned their faith to the wave-line theory, held that the maximum point in the curve of displacement (station 18 in *Spray*) should be .60 of the L. W. L. aft from the forward point of immersion. Modern practice has discarded the coefficient .60, and says that it should be .55; and the measurement rule now in force adopts this coefficient of .55. *Spray's* coefficient, however, instead of being .60 or .55, is only .506; which means that her midsection is somewhat forward of the position which has been decreed by modern practice.

Now, all displacement curves under the wave-line rule and under the modern practice show a marked hollow at the bow. Obviously, where the bow portion of the displacement curve is hollow, it is essential that the boat's center of gravity should be thrown as far aft as possible, in order to keep her head from burying when running under a press of sail; and this entails putting the midship section as far aft as possible; all of which doubtless had much to do with the adoption of the coefficients .60 and .55 above-mentioned.

But in the case of *Spray*, it will be noted that the displacement curve of the boat's entrance is not hollow at all, but convex. Therefore, there is no reason for throwing her center of gravity very far aft, because her bow is powerful enough to lift her at all times and under all circumstances. On the other hand, in *Spray*, there is a very good reason for not throwing the center of gravity very far aft of the middle of the L. W. L. And the reason is this: To throw the center of gravity aft, is to throw the midship section aft, and as the boat of necessity has great displacement, the placing of the midship section very far aft would result in hard lines (either buttocks, water-lines, or diagonals), and would produce a form of run that would inevitably create a heavy stern wave and make a slow boat.

The next element to be considered is the center of lateral resistance. This center lies .044 of the L. W. L. aft of station 18 when the boat is at rest. And here it is well to remember that the position of the C.L.R. is not always thoroughly appreciated in all its aspects. The C. L. R. as laid out on the drawings represents the point on which the boat (rudder and all) would balance if pushed sideways through the water. Take the case now under discussion. Suppose you were to make a working model of *Spray* and put her in a tank of still water. Then suppose you took the point of a knife, and pressed it against the side of the model at the exact point marked "C. L. R. at rest" in the drawing. Now, if you pushed the model sideways, at right angles to her keel, she would just balance on the knife point, the boat moving bodily sideways, without turning either the stern or the bow. And that is all that is meant by the C. L. R. as shown on the plans.

The instant, however, that the boat starts to move forward, the C. L. R. starts to move forward toward the bow of the boat. This is in obedience to a well-known law. As the bow works in solid water, and the stern dead-wood in broken water, the bow holds on better than the stern, and a square foot of lateral plane at the bow holds better than a square foot of lateral plane at the stern. The net result is that the effective C. L. R. moves forward. The question of *just how far* the C. L. R. moves forward when the boat begins to move ahead is a question involving some rather tedious calculation. Froude compiled a set of figures, showing the change of resistance per square foot at vari-
292

ous portions of a surface located at various distances aft from the leading edge. (They relate specifically to skin resistance, but I assume that the lateral resistance would vary in the same ratio.) A table of these coefficients is given at page 135 of Mackrow's Pocket Book. Froude gives the figures for 2, 8, 20 and 50 feet. By interpolation, using a variable differential to satisfy the points established by Froude, it is possible to get the correct coefficient for any intermediate point. Then by applying the appropriate coefficients to the various stations of the immersed lateral plane, and applying Simpson's formula, it is possible to find how far the C. L. R. will move forward for any predetermined speed. In the specific case of *Spray,* moving at a speed of 6 knots, the C. L. R. moves, from a point 1.45 feet aft of station 18, to a point .4 of a foot aft of station 18, a forward movement of 1.05 feet. This gives us the actual working location of *Spray's* C. L. R. at 6 knots, *disregarding the bow wave.* In order to make our calculation complete, we must further reckon with the bow wave. The question of stern wave may be disregarded, because, from the pictures and photographs of *Spray* underway, it clearly appears that the boat creates no sensible stern wave—she has too clean a run for that. She does raise a moderate bow wave, and the effect of that bow wave is of course to bring her effective C. L. R. a little bit forward.

The question of just exactly how far forward the bow wave will carry the C. L. R. is a matter beyond the ken of precise calculation. Judging from the height of the bow wave as shown on *Spray's* pictures, I should say it would amount to a little over 1% of the L. W. L., and if that assumption is correct, it would bring *Spray's* effective working C. L. R. exactly on station 18. Of course, every heave of the sea, every slant of wind, every touch on the helm throws this center a little bit forward or aft —it is no more fixed and stable than her angle of heel is fixed and stable. Constantly it plays forward and aft, but the central average point of its play must be station 18 or within a fraction of an inch of it.

In order to make my analysis of *Spray's* hull quite complete, I also calculated a center that is seldom considered at all in yacht design, and yet which must have some significance—that is, the center of wetted surface. In other words, I determined the effective center of her curve of immersed girths by Simpson's formula. To my surprise, this center worked out to a hair on identically the same line as the C. L. R. at rest, viz., 1.45 feet aft of station 18—another of the extraordinary coincidences in *Spray's* design.

Now exactly the same considerations which apply to the C. L. R. apply also to this center of wetted surface. In other words, when the boat begins to move forward, the focal point of her skin resistance begins to move forward from the place occupied by the center of wetted surface at rest. Thus, by applying Froude and Simpson, as in the case of the lateral plane, we find that at a speed of 6 knots, *Spray's* center of skin resistance moves forward from a point 1.45 aft of station 18, to a point .6 of a foot aft of station 18, a forward movement of .85 foot—that is, leaving the bow wave out of account. To complete our calculation, we must again reckon with the bow wave.

Now the bow wave will have a more potent effect in carrying forward the center of skin resistance, than in carrying forward the center of lateral resistance. And for this reason—the boat throws off two bow waves, one from the weather bow and one from the lee bow. Both of these waves affect the wetted surface, whereas only the lee wave affects the lateral plane. Of course, the wave on the lee bow is heavier than the wave on the weather bow, and therefore we may safely say that the two bow waves will *not* move the center of skin resistance forward twice as far as the lee-bow wave moves the C. L. R. forward. We thus reach the conclusion that the boat's wave action will throw the center of skin resistance forward further than the C. L. R. is thrown forward, and yet not so much as twice that distance. We have already seen that the wave action throws her C. L. R. forward .4 of a foot. Therefore the wave action will throw her center of skin resistance forward between .4 and .8 of a foot, say .6 of a foot as a mean. And when we do move her center of skin resistance forward .6 of a foot, we land again exactly to a hair on station 18. Another in the series of coincidences.

Even the effective center of the L. W. L. plane falls only .4 foot aft of station 18 when the boat is at rest; and the piling up of the bow waves under the bow, when she is underway, must bring this center also just about on station 18. (Unlike the C. L. R. and the center of skin resistance, the effective center of the L. W. L. plane is not affected by the forward motion of the boat—it is affected only by the bow wave.)

From an inspection of the L. W. L. plane, the almost perfect symmetry of the curve of displacement with reference to station 18 as an axis, and the symmetry of the boat's ends, it is quite evident that the longitudinal metacenter for a given angle of pitch forward will be at practically the same height as for an equal angle of pitch aft.

I know of no other conceivable factor of weight, displacement, buoyancy or resistance that can be calculated for a hull, so far as longitudinal balance is concerned, and I shall leave the discussion of *Spray's* hull with the statement that every one of these factors, when she is underway, is concentrated exactly at her midship section (station 18). So much for *Spray's* hull.

Let us now examine her sail plan.

At the outset, it should be remarked that the flying jib will be eliminated from the discussion of sail balance, as it is a light-weather sail, set standing on a light bamboo jibboom, which is merely lashed to the bowsprit when the flying jib is set, and is stowed when the flying jib is stowed, and is never used on the wind.

When *Spray* is on the wind, she carries three sails only, the jib, mainsail and mizzen. The combined center of effort of these three sails at rest falls about .17 of a foot forward of the C. L. R. at rest. This .17 of a foot is only a little over .5 of 1% of the L. W. L. Modern practice calls for from 1 to 3% of the L. W. L. But it must be remembered that the 1 to 3% coefficient is used for sloops with large mainsails and small jibs, whereas *Spray* is a yawl with an unusually large jib and a comparatively small mainsail. On this state of facts no less an authority than Dixon Kemp uses the following language ("Yacht Architecture," Third Edition, page 100): "In the case of yawls it is generally found that the calculated center of effort requires (relatively to the center of lateral resistance) to be a little further aft than in either cutters or schooners, as the mizzen is not a very effective sail on a wind, the eddy wind of the mainsail causing it to lift; also a yawl's mainmast is usually farther forward than a cutter's, and it should be noted that the position of the center of effort of the largest driving sail influences the position of the general C. E. more than the calculation shows."

Spray's center of effort is therefore amply justified by authority, and the authority, in turn, is justified by *Spray's* actual performance under the sail plan shown. For Slocum says of her: "Briefly, I have to say that when close-hauled in a light wind under all sail she required little or no weather helm. As the wind increased I would go on deck, if below, and turn the

296

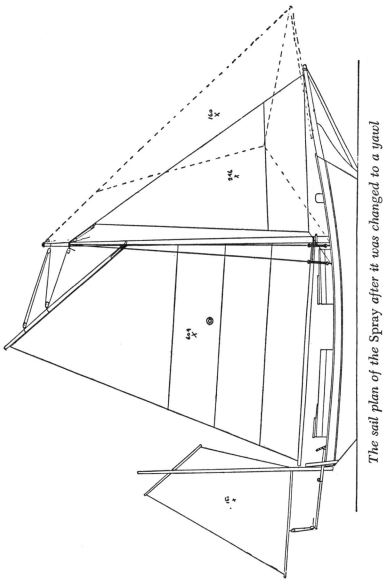

The sail plan of the Spray after it was changed to a yawl

297

wheel up a spoke more or less, relash it, or as sailors say, put it in a becket, and then leave it as before."

Of course, in order to attain this balance, *Spray's* efficient center of effort must be over her effective C. L. R. And as we have already seen that the effective C. L. R. at 6 knots falls exactly on station 18, so her efficient center of effort also at that speed must fall exactly on station 18.

It is obvious that, just as the effective C. L. R. moves forward as the boat moves forward so the efficient center of effort moves forward on the sail plan when the boat sails forward. This has long been known by naval architects; and the recent activity in aeroplane flight has led to much experiment on the subject. The C. E. seems to move forward more slowly than the C. L. R. as the boat's speed increases; and the result is that although the C. E. at rest is forward of the C. L. R., yet when the boat is at her normal speed, these two centers, advancing at unequal rates, come into exact balance; and when the boat's speed is increased still more by a harder wind, the C. L. R. continuing to work forward faster than the C. E. makes the boat carry a harder and harder weather helm as the wind increases. This is matter of common observation.

The curve of stability shows that *Spray* is theoretically uncapsizable, because of 90° of heel, she still has left a righting moment of over 20,000 foot-pounds or over 9 foot-tons. This is most remarkable for a boat of her shallow draft; doubly remarkable in view of the fact that she carries no outside ballast whatever, and even her inside ballast consists merely of cement blocks. (All boatmen of experience say that stone or cement ballast makes a livelier, "corkier" boat than the same weight of lead or iron.) Her maximum stability is at about 35° of heel, where she has a righting moment of 75,000 foot-pounds or over 33 foot-tons.

298

As she should never be sailed much lower than 10° of heel, it will be seen that she has an ample margin of safety at all times.

In plotting the curve of stability, I assumed the center of gravity to lie exactly at the L. W. L., which, I think, is conservative.

I have also plotted the transverse L. W. L., transverse center of buoyancy, and metacentric height for each 10° of heel up to 90°.

I conclude my analysis of *Spray's* lines with a feeling of profound admiration and respect. She is not only an able boat, but a beautiful boat; using the term "beautiful" as defined by Charles Elliott Norton, "that form most perfectly adapted to perform its allotted work"—beautiful in the same sense that Sandow, or the Farnese Hercules is beautiful. From the man who loves boats and the sea, and in some measure understands them (for it has been given to no one yet to know all their ways), *Spray* will receive the recognition that is her due.

She is the perfection of her type—a perfection demonstrated not only on paper, but by the ordeal of actual achievement. She is an oceangoing cruiser, in the largest sense of that term. After sailing 46,000 miles, and weathering a hundred gales, some of which foundered great ships in his near vicinity, Slocum says of her: "I have given in the plans of *Spray* the dimensions of such a ship as I should call seaworthy in all conditions of weather and on all seas." These words coming from such a source are not lightly to be disregarded.

So ends Mr. Andrade's masterful analysis.

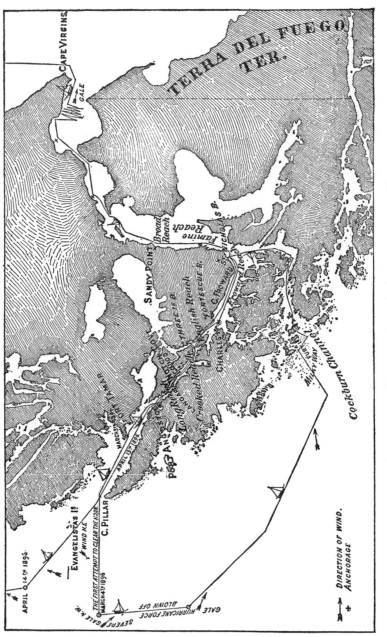

The course of the Spray through the Strait of Magellan

CHAPTER 15

The *Spray:*
Around the World Single-handed

The first leg of the *Spray's* great voyage was her shakedown between Boston and Yarmouth, the point selected for the departure. As I lived in Boston at that time my father talked over with me the problems he expected to meet, the principal one being how to handle the steering so as not to lose too much time at night lying-to.

As I saw it, the sea anchor was his best chance against sea wear. The sea anchor he always had and frequently used. Between Boston and Yarmouth the *Spray* made several stops. The first was in Gloucester where he remained several days to purchase some supplies there best obtained. Being again ready for sea he stood out to the eastward, but having a mind for some nice fresh fish, he let his sheets flow to try a line and sinker on Cashes Ledge, in thirty fathoms. Some cod, haddock, and a fat little halibut were soon flapping on the deck. Finding that the tide was setting against the wind and thinking that it might be a good thing to heave to and fish the next day as well, he doused sail with sea anchor out ahead, put a light in the rigging and turned in. It was his first night alone at sea.

In the morning and after a good breakfast, he found that the weather had changed; it had begun to blow and kick up a rough cross sea which made it unpleasant to resume the fishing. Tripping the sea anchor and heaving it on board, he again made sail. He called in at Westport, Brier Island, before stopping in Yarmouth and in both places he renewed acquaintance with many long-forgotten landmarks.

In Yarmouth he took in some well-salted butter for the voyage, a barrel of potatoes, and filled six barrels of water. He set up his rigging, sent down his topmast and made all a-taunto for sea. That he secured all below as well goes without saying. He was in high spirits and ready for the coming adventure. He was ready for the boisterous Atlantic and merely waited for the local bad weather to clear up and a slant to come from the northwest.

He sailed on July 1st. The wind was northwest and the head sea had gone down. Everything was right. It was his last hold upon America. The big mainsail bellied out and the single jib pulled like a "sojer." On passing Cape Sable he found that he was going eight knots and that was top going for such a small craft. He fell in with a large schooner bound eastward out of Liverpool; the *Spray* put her hull down in five hours. Two days after leaving Yarmouth he passed Sable Island, and would soon be clear of all dangers and shoals. He was now sailing into the unbounded sea and keeping a charter party with himself. While riding to his sea anchor on Cashes Ledge he had thrashed that all out with himself. He had taken little advice from anyone; there was now no turning back.

The wind was fair and he crowded on all sail in order to lose no time passing the track of liners which were a menace at night to small sailing vessels with oil-burning lights only. For them he always had his flare ready for self-protection. A dense fog set in for days. He could almost sit on it.

When at last the sun came out he observed a meridian altitude and called out "eight bells," as was customary on the sea, but now it was to an imaginary man at the wheel. He gave orders to an imaginary crew and then went and did it himself. Finding that his voice sounded hollow in the empty air, he dropped the practice, for it made him feel his solitude the more acutely.

About the fourth day out the *Spray* gave him a surprise. Realizing that there was only a crew of one, she began to steer herself. That was much better, for one man could never steer a vessel all the way around the world by himself. The *Spray* knew that as well as anyone. She was still going eight knots, her very best speed. Her long boom was broad off with jib sheet hauled flat. The mainsail had a reef tucked for the wind had increased to a moderate gale. All looking well, my father lashed the helm and went below.

That was all there was to it; his vessel kept her course. It was to be expected that a fore-and-aft vessel could hold a course trimmed close to the wind, but here was a fore-and-after holding to it with boom broad off in a stiff breeze with lumpy sea. And she kept it up. Of course the *Spray's* skipper was thoroughly wind- and sea-conscious and, whether awake or sleeping, he knew what was happening on deck.

On July 10th, the position of the *Spray* was fifteen hundred miles east of Cape Sable and that was one hundred and fifty miles a day. As the wind became lighter she could easily overhaul heavy-laden and foul freighters and sometimes it was amusing. The larger vessels were always surprised to see a smaller one sail so much faster and could never figure out the reason why. They beheld the small speeding sloop in wonderment.

The first one was a Spaniard. When the *Spray* got up close to the Spaniard's port quarter, she received a heaving line which became the means for transferring a bottle of very good wine accompanied by the Spanish captain's card bearing his compliments. The stranger was the *La Vaguisa* of Vigo, whither she was bound from Philadelphia, Captain Juan Gantes. He must have been a pious man for when the *Spray* hauled off him and when he realized that my father was alone, he crossed himself and disappeared. He must have thought that he had handed a bottle of wine to the devil.

The next ship passing occurred when the wind had dropped, but the light *Spray* was still ghosting along in her own way. It was an English ship, the *Java* of Glasgow, rolling in her barnacles.

"How long has it been calm around here?" hailed the Britisher from his high quarterdeck.

"Dunno, Cap," came the reply, "I haven't been around here long enough to find out."

At this, the mate on the forecastle could not help a broad grin at the expense of his chief who after further hearing that the smaller vessel was only fifteen days from Cape Sable, burst forth again.

"Listen to the Yankee liar, listen to the Yankee liar!" And the *Spray* passed on.

The human contact, even though bearish, was welcome and the acute pain of solitude which my father felt at first never returned. The third vessel he encountered on the way to the Azores was a steamer which gave him longitude 34:50 west. It was a good position, and it was proved by sighting the high peak of Flores the very next morning.

304

On the morning of the next day the *Spray* raised Pico looming above the clouds on the starboard bow. Only those who have seen the Azores from the deck of a vessel realize the beauty of the midocean picture. Nineteen days out from Yarmouth the *Spray* came to anchor in Fayal. She was eighteen

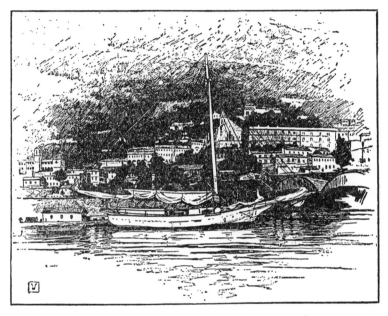

The Spray *at anchor off Gibraltar. From a drawing by George Varian*

days from Cape Sable, making a distance of 1,650 miles which was very good for a start. He remained four days in Fayal.

Fayal to Gibraltar is 1,130 miles. Sailing from Fayal on July 24th, he made Gibraltar in eleven days. He had a boisterous trip, half a gale on the port quarter and close-reefed; the *Spray* still doing her best and no human hand at the helm. The Captain felt by this time he had a self-steering ship so his mind was at rest as far as future navigation was concerned.

305

It was like having three extra men on board standing regular watches.

The *Spray* fell among friends in Gibraltar, but it did not look so good at first when he encountered the peppery quarantine officer who threatened to "put him in the fort" for not having his bill of health in order. But they got along very well after "a deuce of a row" which the Captain says you must first have with every Englishman, anyway, to succeed. Anchored inside of the lines, the *Spray* became the guest of the British Navy and attended the Admiral's "at home."

The first intention of Captain Slocum was to reach the Indian Ocean by way of the Suez Canal, but on the advice of the British admiral this plan was altered, for in his opinion a lone voyager on the north coast of Africa might fare badly at the hands of the Berber pirates who were then much in evidence. The Captain noticed for himself, on an excursion in a torpedo boat across the strait from "Gib" to Tangiers, that small arms were kept at hand on deck.

When the *Spray* first came to an anchor it was at the old mole, among the native craft where it was rough and uncomfortable but the next morning it was different. A steam launch came alongside, with the compliments of the senior naval officer, Admiral Bruce, with the word there was a berth for her at the arsenal and among battleships such as the *Collingwood*, *Barfleur* and *Cormorant*, which were at that time stationed there.

"Put it thar, as Americans say," was the salute that the skipper got from Admiral Bruce when he called at the Admiralty to thank him for the courtesy of the berth. "Say, old man," the admiral continued, "you must have knocked the devil out of her coming over alone in twenty-nine days. But we'll make it smooth for you here."

Not one of Her Majesty's ships was better looked after than the *Spray* at Gibraltar. Later in the day, Mrs. Bruce went on board, "to shake hands with the *Spray*," and on the following day, the governor of Gibraltar, with other high officials of the garrison and all the commanders of the battleships, came on board and signed their names in the *Spray's* logbook.

Monday, August 25, 1895, the *Spray* sailed from Gibraltar. A tug belonging to the arsenal towed the sloop into a steady breeze clear of the mount, where her sails caught a violent wind which carried her once more into the Atlantic, where it rose rapidly to a gale. The Captain's plan was to haul offshore to avoid pirates, when he made out a native felucca leaving the nearest port. The *Spray* changed her course. The felucca did the same, both vessels sailing very fast, but the distance growing less between them. At the moment when the felucca became dangerously near, out went her mast and down came the great yard with its sail. They had been carrying too great a load of sail for a squall which suddenly hit, and broached to. The *Spray* had carried away her boom at the same moment but was able to continue her distance while the felucca rolled in the trough of the sea with its wreckage.

After fishing the boom and furling the sail, the sloop laid to for the night; there was a supper of fresh flying fish and tea. She headed now for the channel between Africa and the island of Fuerteventura, the easternmost of the Canary Islands. On September 4th the island came into view. It is twenty-seven hundred feet high and in this fine weather it was visible for many miles. It was grand sailing. The wind was fresh and blew from the north-northeast which was exactly astern. The sea surged along with the sloop. A reminder that he was heading for South America occurred about noon on September 4th, when a steamship, a bullock-droger from the River Plate, hove

307

in sight. She was a stale one, rolling and plunging into the head sea and making bad weather of it. She did not answer the *Spray's* signal. From the way that she yawed, my father humorously imagined that a wild steer was at the wheel. Two days later he passed another droger, on the same track, rolling as badly and steering as wildly as the first one. There were no reefers in those days and live cattle were transported from the Argentine to Europe "on the hoof," as they called it. It was an unromantic business. The landfall of the island of St. Antonio, the northwesternmost of the Cape Verdes, was very true. Then leaving the Cape Verde Islands out of sight astern, my father found himself once more sailing a lonely sea and in a solitude supreme all around. When he slept, he dreamed that he was alone. That feeling never left him; but sleeping or waking, he seemed always to know the position of the sloop, and he saw his vessel moving across the chart, which became a picture before him.

One night while he sat in the cabin under that spell, the profound stillness was broken by human voices alongside. A white bark under full sail was passing under his lee. The sailors on board of her were singing out on the ropes, bracing the yards which just cleared the sloop's mast as she swept by. No one hailed from the white-winged flier. He sat long on the deck that night, thinking of ships and watching the constellations on their voyages. On the following day, a large four-masted ship passed some distance to windward, heading north. The day after another lofty ship was seen from the masthead, heading north.

The *Spray* now entered the gloomy region of the doldrums to battle with squalls and be harassed by fitful calms; the rain poured down in torrents day and night. She was ten days making the three hundred miles through the doldrums when she hit the southeast trades four degrees north of the line. At that point, on September 23rd, she met the schooner *Nantasket* of Boston, from Bear River, Nova Scotia, for the River Plate, with a cargo of lumber. The *Spray* crossed the equator in 29:30 west longitude. The trades now gave her sails a stiff, full breeze, sending her handsomely over the sea towards the coast of Brazil where, on the 5th of October, she cast anchor in Pernambuco, forty days from Gibraltar.

At this point, my father said that instead of tiring of the voyage he was never in better trim in his life, and that he was eager for the more perilous experience of rounding the Horn. It was not at all strange in a life common to sailors that, having already crossed the Atlantic twice and now being half way from Boston to the Horn, he should still find himself among friends. His determination to sail westward from Gibraltar not only enabled him to escape the pirates of the Red Sea, but in bringing him to Pernambuco, landed him on familiar shores. He had made many voyages to this and other ports in Brazil. The reader will recall that my father was employed as master in 1894 to take the famous Ericsson ship *Destroyer* from New York to Brazil to go against the rebel Mello and his party. In the same expedition went the *Nictheroy*, the ship purchased by the United States Government during the Spanish War and renamed the *Buffalo*. The *Destroyer*, with her enormous submarine cannon, was in many ways the better ship of the two, but the Brazilians in their curious war sank her themselves at Bahia.

Now, within two years, oddly enough, the Mello Party was again in power in Brazil. On clearing his vessel at the customhouse, my father encountered one of the unforgiving Mello faction in the person of the collector himself, who charged the *Spray* full tonnage dues notwithstanding that she sailed with

309

a yacht license and should have been exempt from port charges. Our consul reminded him of that fact and rather tactlessly stated that it was the captain of the *Spray* who brought the *Destroyer* to Brazil.

"Oh, yes," replied the bland collector. "We remember it very well." In a small way, it was now his turn.

While at Pernambuco, the boom which had been broken when the sloop escaped the pirates off Morocco, was shortened. Four feet came off the inboard end and the jaws were refitted.

On October 24, 1895, the *Spray* sailed, having had abundant good cheer. On his way south the captain did not miss the chance to view the resting place of his beloved *Destroyer*. The top of her smokestack being awash in Bahia, it was more than likely that she still rested on the bottom.

On November 5th, the *Spray* arrived at Rio de Janeiro and anchored near Villaganon to await the official port visit and, then, with a number of old shipmasters on board, sailed about the harbor of Rio the day before she put to sea. As my father had decided to give the *Spray* a yawl rig for the tempestuous waters of Patagonia, he here placed on the stern a semicircular brace to support a jiggermast. These old captains inspected the *Spray's* rigging, and each one contributed something to her outfit. One gave her an anchor and another a cable to go with it. The anchor and cable stood a strain on a lee shore while the cable itself, when towed off Cape Horn, helped to break combing seas astern which threatened to board her.

The *Spray* sailed from Rio de Janeiro November 28th, running first into a gale of wind which did considerable damage along the coast, and then met with a surprising adventure at Maldonado on the shore of Uruguay.

Down the coast a barkentine hove in sight and for several

days the two vessels sailed along together. Right here a current was found setting to the northward, and to avoid it the *Spray,* being the light draft, hugged the shore entirely too close, so that at daybreak on the morning of December 11th, she ran hard and fast on the beach. That was annoying, but it was found that the sloop was in no great danger. The false appearance of the sand hills under a bright moon had deceived

A *double surprise*

him. As the tide was dropping there was nothing to do but to run out an anchor into deeper water and wait for high water. In doing this the dory capsized, a chilly reminder that he could not swim. Righting the dory after sinking and getting under it three times, he managed to get into it and to roll sufficient water out of it to enable him to reach the beach where he stretched out to recover. Hearing the patter of a horse's hoofs he roused himself in time to stop a young horseman from dragging off the dory on his lariat. Being convinced after considerable argument that both sloop and dory were the property of the

311

bearded individual he discovered reclining in a clump of bushes, he made off very much disgruntled.

The exact spot where the *Spray* was stranded was at the Castillo Chicas, about seven miles south of the dividing line of Uruguay and Brazil, and of course the natives there speak Spanish. A coast guard from Fort Teresa appeared on the scene, "to protect the stranger from the natives of the plains"—he had seen a sample. Early in the day came a despatch from the port captain of Montevideo commanding the coast guards to render the *Spray* every assistance. The same messenger brought word that he would despatch a steam tug to tow the *Spray* to Montevideo. The officer was as good as his word; a powerful tug arrived the next day only to meet the sloop sailing before the wind.

The *Spray,* upon arriving in Montevideo, was greeted by steam whistles until her skipper felt embarrassed and wished that he could have come in unobserved. The voyage so far alone may have seemed to the Uruguayans a feat worthy of some recognition; but there was so much of it yet ahead, and of such an arduous nature, that any demonstration at this point seemed to him like premature boasting. The *Spray* had hardly come to anchor when the agents of the Royal Mail Steamship Company sent word that they would dock and repair her free of expense and give her skipper twenty pounds sterling, which they did to the letter and more besides. The caulkers at Montevideo paid very careful attention to the work of making the sloop tight, while the carpenters and painters looked to the damaged keel and to the upper works respectively.

Christmas of 1895 found the *Spray* refitted even to a wonderful makeshift stove which was contrived from a large iron drum of some sort punched full of holes to give it a draft; the pipe reached straight up through the forecastle. It would burn anything. It burned even green wood and on cold, wet days off Tierra del Fuego it stood the captain in good stead. The *Spray* was now ready for sea. Her course, however, was diverted up the River Plate to Buenos Aires from whence she sailed January 26, 1896.

My father had not for many years been south of the River Plate. It was a region where he did not expect fine sailing on the course for Cape Horn direct, but while he worked at the rigging he thought only of onward and forward. It was when he anchored in lonely places that a feeling of awe crept over him. At the last anchorage of that sort, on the monotonous and muddy river, he resolved that he would anchor no more north of the Strait of Magellan. With a fair wind the *Spray* bore away under all sail, pressing farther and farther towards the wonderland of the South till she forgot the blessings of the milder North.

While the *Spray* was making her fourteen-hundred-mile distance to the entrance to the Strait and was giving the Patagonian coast a wide berth, she encountered a rebounding tidal wave which evidently, for reasons best known to itself, had impinged against the land to return to its starting point. While it was thus amusing itself, the *Spray* just happened to get in the way and had to take it. By good luck she had three reefs tucked in so the gaff and the peak halyards were handy to get at for her skipper to climb and to reach the crosstrees before the thing struck. The top spume nearly reached him at his perch while the hull beneath him was entirely submerged under green water for fully a minute, as it seemed to the skipper. It was not exactly the kind of an occasion for getting out the stop watch as some navigators might have done, but his guess was good. After the big one got by and was succeeded by several smaller rollers, the Captain descended to the deck and found

313

everything, except for the washing, in order. Pushing back the companionway slides he found that hardly a bucketful had gotten below. Then he began to think of the adventure in the light of a test and a shakedown making him feel all the more confident of his vessel's complete seaworthiness. He knew of the terrific tide races which swirled in and out of the gulfs and around the headlands of the Patagonian coastline which are dangerous even for large ships. At the River Gallegos just north of the Virgins there is a tidal rise and fall of forty feet or more, according to the controlling conditions of moon and wind, which is comparable to the Bay of Fundy or Cook Inlet.

The *Spray* had a gloomy time of it approaching Cape Virgins. It was blowing a northeast gale. Feather-white spume was sent from a sea such as would swamp an ill-appointed ship. As the sloop neared the entrance to the strait it was observed that two great tide races made ahead, one very close to the land and one further offshore. Between the two, in a sort of channel, went the *Spray* with close-reefed sails. But a rolling sea followed her a long way in, and a fierce current swept around the cape against her; but this she stemmed and was soon running into smoother water. Long trailing kelp from sunken rocks waved forebodingly under her keel and the wreck of a great steamship smashed on the beach abreast did not lend a cheerful aspect to the scene. As soon as the promontory of the Virgins was rounded the gale shifted from the fair northeast to the foul northwest. It now became one of the blackest of nights all around, except in the southwest where rose the old familiar white arch, the terror of Cape Horn, rapidly pushed by a southwest gale. It struck the *Spray* like a shot from a cannon and for thirty hours it kept on blowing hard. In the height of the squalls she doused all sail and held on; she was not to be blown out of the strait at the very start of the transit. The weather moderating, she beat through the Narrows and anchored at Sandy Point (Punta Arenas), February 14, 1896.

The *Spray* found Sandy Point to be a Chilean coaling station with a mixed population of about two thousand engaged in other activities besides bunkering ships. What with sheep farming, gold mining, and hunting, the settlers in this dreary land seemed not the worst off in this world. Patagonian and Fuegian natives were about. The recent massacre of a schooner's crew was spoken of as well as the resultant punitive expedition sent to scatter a Fuegian settlement somewhere else. The port captain, a Chilean naval officer, told my father that if he could not wait until he could be towed through by a gunboat to at least ship some hands to fight Indians. My father did neither. He acquired a box of Birmingham carpet tacks instead, and loaded his guns. The port captain finding that the *Spray* was bound to go, set up no further objections but advised her skipper, in case the savages tried to surround him with their canoes, to shoot straight and to begin shooting in time.

With these simple injunctions, the officer gave him his port clearance free of charge and he sailed on the same day, February 19, 1896. It was not without thoughts of strange and stirring adventure beyond all that he had yet encountered that he now sailed into the country and very core of the savage Fuegians. They told him at Punta Arenas (Sandy Point) that he might expect to meet savages at any time, but during the first night at anchor under a high mountain near St. Nicholas Bay he saw or heard nothing of them, not even the barking of their dogs.

Here he had his first experience with the terrific squalls called williwaws—compressed gales of wind that come over the hills in chunks. A full-blown williwaw will throw a ship

315

even under bare poles on her beam ends. The only good thing about them is that they do not last long.

On the next day the sloop held the wind fair while she ran thirty miles more on her course, which brought her to Fortescue Bay, and at once the natives' signal fires blazed up on all sides. Clouds flew over the mountain from the west all day; at night the good east wind failed, and in its stead a gale from the west soon came on. That was not so good as it was a head wind. The *Spray* gained an anchorage at twelve o'clock that night under the lee of an island. By daylight the *Spray* was again under way, beating hard against the new west wind; but she came to in a cove in Charles Island and remained undisturbed for two days with both anchors down in a bed of kelp. Had not the wind moderated, she might have remained there indefinitely; for during those two days it blew so hard that no boat could venture out upon the strait. The natives being away to other hunting grounds made the anchorage safe.

The *Spray* found that heavy weather meant safety from Indians and easy sailing meant annoyance coupled with the likelihood of danger. Canoes manned by savages from Fortescue went in pursuit of the *Spray* next day when she got her anchors and sailed out upon the strait. The wind falling light, they gained on the sloop rapidly till coming within hail. At eighty yards the *Spray* fired a shot across the bows of the nearest canoe, at which they all stopped and called out in Spanish that they were not advancing in the direction of the vessel but that they intended to go around the island. *"Bueno, jo via Isla!"*

While in Sandy Point, the port captain had told my father to shoot a certain renegade mongrel on sight. He was "Black Pedro," a leader in several bloody massacres. My father knew that it was this same Black Pedro who hailed him, by his

Spanish lingo and by his beard, for all the natives have smooth faces. Pedro made for the island now, and the others followed him and disappeared.

So much for the first day among savages. The *Spray* came to anchor at midnight in Three Island Cove. There were signal fires on the opposite side of the Strait, the barking of dogs, but no other sign of savages. Birds and seals avoid savages, and when they are seen about one may feel pretty sure there are no Indians. Seal are never plentiful in the Strait waters, but the presence of one in Three Island Cove made the place seem secure. On the next day the wind was again blowing a gale and although she was in the lee of the island the sloop dragged her anchors so that he had to get her under way and beat farther into the cove, where he came to a landlocked pool. At another time or place this would have been a rash thing to do, and it was safe now solely for the fact that the gale which drove him to shelter would keep Indians from crossing the Strait.

Seeing that was the case he went ashore, just like Robinson Crusoe with gun and axe, where he could not in any event be surprised, and there felled trees and split about a cord of firewood, which loaded his small boat several times. While he carried the wood, though he was morally sure there were no savages near, he never once went to or from the skiff without his gun. The scattering of trees on the island was of a type of beech and stunted cedar, both of which made good fuel. Even the green limbs of the beech, which seemed to possess a resinous quality, burned readily in the great Montevideo stove. In his method of wooding up and in all other particulars of the voyage, he took great care against all kinds of surprises. In the Strait of Magellan the greatest vigilance was necessary. In this instance, he had all about him the greatest danger of the whole

317

voyage and that was the treachery of cunning savages for which he had to be particularly on the alert.

Sailing from Three Island Cove, in due time the *Spray* fetched Borgia Bay where vessels had anchored from time to time and had nailed boards on trees ashore with name and date of visit carved or painted. Nothing else could he see to indicate that civilized man had ever been there. He had taken a survey of the gloomy place with his spyglass and was getting his boat out to take notes when the Chilean gunboat *Huemel* came in; its officers, coming on board, advised him to leave the place at once, a thing which required not much more than a hint to do. In tow of the *Huemel* the *Spray* reached Notch Cove, eight miles farther along, where he should be clear of the worst of the Fuegians. Both vessels anchored in the cove about dark and the wind came down in fierce williwaws from the mountains. An instance of Magellan weather was afforded when the *Huemel*, a well-appointed gunboat of great power, after attempting on the following day to proceed on her voyage, was obliged by sheer force of the wind to return and take up anchorage again and remain until the gale had abated; and they considered themselves in luck to get back. Meeting this vessel was a godsend to the *Spray*. She was commanded and officered by a high type of sailors and gentlemen. While anchored at the Notch they got up an impromptu entertainment. A talented midshipman sang popular songs in French, German and Spanish, and one in Russian. It was an evening of merriment.

He was left alone the next day when the *Huemel* put to sea on her voyage, the gale having abated. He spent a day taking in wood and water; by that time the weather was fine. Then he sailed from that desolate place. On the rest of the *Spray's* first passage through the strait she anchored and weighed many times till she gained anchorage and shelter for the night at Port

Tamar, with Cape Pillar in sight to the west. Here he felt the throb of the great ocean that lay before him, he knew now that he had put a world behind him and that he was opening up another world ahead. He had passed the haunts of savages. Great piles of granite mountains of bleak and lifeless aspect were now astern; on some of them not a speck of moss had ever grown. Such a land was not a place to enjoy solitude. Throughout the whole of the strait west of Cape Froward he saw no animals except dogs owned by Indians. Those he saw often enough, and heard them yelping night and day. Birds were not plentiful. The scream of a loon startled him with its piercing cry. The steamboat duck was sometimes seen scurrying out of danger. There also was a sort of swan, smaller than a Muscovy duck, which might have been brought down with the gun, but in the loneliness of life about the dreary country he found himself in no mood to make one life less, except in self-defense.

On emerging into the Pacific the *Spray* encountered one of Cape Horn's equinoctial gales which threatened to blow her east-about into the Atlantic again. With the wind northeast the *Spray* sailed direct from Port Tamar to Cape Pillar with the hope that it would hold that way until she well cleared the land, but there was no such luck. The wind freshened and she tucked in three reefs. It was a gathering storm with a confused and treacherous sea. She ran all night with a free sheet but on the morning of March 4th the wind shifted to southwest and then suddenly from northwest and blew with terrific force. The *Spray,* stripped of her sails, bore off under bare poles. Knowing that this storm might continue for many days and that it would be impossible to work back to the westward along the coast outside of Tierra del Fuego, there seemed to be nothing to do but to keep on before the wind. She was running now with a reefed fore-staysail with the sheets flat amidships, with a haw-

319

ser veered out astern to break the following seas. Her helm was lashed amidship. In this trim she ran before it and never shipped a sea. When all had been done that he could do for the safety of the vessel, the Captain got to the forescuttle, and made a good Irish stew and coffee over a wood fire. He insisted on warm meals.

The first day of the storm gave the *Spray* her actual test in the worst sea that Cape Horn or its wild regions could kick up, and in no part of the world could a rougher sea be found than off Cape Pillar, the grim sentinel of the Horn. On the fourth day of the gale, rapidly nearing the pitch of the Cape, the Captain got out his chart to prick off course and distance to the Falklands in the Atlantic, for it looked to him then that that was the place he was headed for; east about after all. Then through a rift in the clouds he saw a high mountain. It was about twenty miles distant on the port beam. The gale to some extent had moderated. Bending on some random canvas in place of the lost mainsail he brought the sloop at once to the wind heading for the land which now appeared to be an island in the sea. So it turned out, but not the one he had supposed. There was a prospect of once more entering the Strait of Magellan and beating through again to the Pacific. There was a mountainous sea. When the sloop was in the fiercest squalls, with the nondescript trysail and reefed fore-staysail set, even that small area of sail shook her as though the mast would come out when the staysail shivered by the leech. She made for the land like a race horse while her skipper was at the helm to ease her over the crests of the waves.

Night closed down before the sloop reached land, leaving her to feel her way in the pitchy darkness. The Captain saw breakers ahead before long. At this he wore ship and stood off-shore, but was immediately startled by the tremendous roaring of breakers again and on the lee bow. This puzzled him, for there should have been no broken water where he supposed himself to be. He kept off a good bit, then wore around, but finding broken water there also, threw her head again offshore. In this way, amid danger, he spent the rest of the night. Hail and sleet cut into his flesh.

At daylight he saw that the sloop was in the midst of the Milky Way of the sea, which is northwest of Cape Horn, and it was the white breakers of a huge sea over sunken rocks which had threatened to engulf her during the night. It was Fury Island he had sighted and steered for, and what a panorama was before him now and all around. During the height of the gale and in the blackness of night she had cruised and tacked in the Milky Way, one of the worst death traps to be found at sea anywhere on the surface of the globe. Now that it was day he filled away among the breakers to find a channel between them. Since the *Spray* had escaped the rocks through the night, surely she could find her way by daylight. My father said that this was the greatest sea adventure of his life and that God alone knew how his vessel escaped.

The only known vessel to come through the Milky Way, other than the *Spray,* and live to tell the tale was the H.M.S. *Beagle,* Captain Fitzroy, R.N. Fitzroy in his description of the place cut short his remarks with the observation that it would have been of no practical use since no one but he would be very likely to see it after he was there in his expedition. He did not figure on the *Spray* which came sixty years after the *Beagle.* The great naturalist, Darwin, looked over this seascape from the deck of the *Beagle,* and wrote in his journal, "Any landsman seeing the Milky Way would dream of shipwreck and disaster for a week." He might have added "or seaman" as well.

The *Spray* was now in Cockburn Channel which leads into

the Strait of Magellan at a point opposite Cape Froward. The night of March 8th she was thankfully at anchor in a snug cove at the Turn. But she was not to be undisturbed for long. There were going to be more Indians and worse than the last ones. But they were going to step on something.

During the night there was a rumpus on the deck accompanied by unmistakable sounds of human surprise and agony. The savages had boarded the sloop thinking to get it as well as the crew below, but immediately changed their minds, thinking that something else had them. The tacks were working better than all the fighting men and dogs in Tierra del Fuego. The Captain encouraged their precipitate departure with his gun but tried not to hit any of his speeding guests. Then he turned in once more, feeling sure that he would not again be disturbed by people who left in so great a hurry.

The Fuegians, being cruel, are naturally cowards; they regard a rifle with superstitious fear. The only real danger from their quarter would be in allowing them to surround one within bow-shot, or in anchoring within range of where they might lie in ambush. As for their coming on deck at night, even if there were no tacks scattered about, they could be cleared off by shots from cabin and hold. The greatest danger from the savages was the use of fire. Every dugout canoe had a clay fireplace and a fire in the bottom. Nothing was thought of that; it was both for comfort and for smoke signals. An apparently harmless brand lying in the bottom of their canoes might in a moment be ablaze in one's cabin if not on the alert. The port captain at Sandy Point had spoken of this method of attack by the Canoe Indians. Only a short time before they had fired a Chilean gunboat by throwing firebrands in through the stern ports.

On the following morning, the sail-making department, after

a refreshing sleep and a warm breakfast of venison stew, got out palm and needle and turned to sewing a peak on a square tarpaulin for a jury mainsail to be set as soon as ready. The venison stew, by the way, was from a generous quantity of dried venison put aboard of him at Sandy Point by his friend Captain Pedro Samblich, a good Austrian of wide experience in the region. It was Samblich who also put the carpet tacks on board, maintaining stoutly that my father would have use for them. "You must use them with discretion," he said. "That is to say, don't step on them yourself." With that remote hint about the use of the tacks, he got on all right as we have seen; it was a way to clear the decks without the care of watching.

While he was working on the tarpaulin the weather was fine with light winds and everything promising well, and he wondered why no trees grew on the slope abreast his anchorage. Half minded to lay aside his sail-making and to land with his gun to inspect a boulder on the beach near a brook, down came a williwaw with such terrific force as to carry the sloop, with two anchors down, away into deep water. No wonder trees did not grow on that side of the hill; a tree would have to be all roots to hold against such a furious wind. From the cove to the nearest land was a long drift, so there was ample time to weigh both anchors before the sloop came near any danger, so no harm came of it. There were no more savages that day or the next; they probably had some sign by which they knew of the coming of williwaws. At least they were wise in not being afloat even on the second day, for the wind, after the anchor was again down, picked the sloop up and flung her seaward with a vengeance as before. This fierce wind, peculiar to the Magellan country, continued throughout the day, and swept the sloop by several miles of steep bluffs and precipices overhanging a bold shore of wild and uninviting appearance.

The *Spray* sailed on until she reached St. Nicholas Bay nineteen days after she had been anchored there the first time through. The distance oversailed was five hundred and sixty miles. She had circumnavigated the wildest part of desolate Tierra del Fuego, namely, Desolation Island, Santa Ines Island, Clarence Island, Capitan Aracena Island—a mass of insular formation forming the southwestern side of the strait. Of the smaller groups outside she passed Landfall Island, Rice Trevor Island, The Graftons (a trace of Fitzroy), Noir Island, and by great good luck she did not shave Tower Rocks too closely for it was near them that she first sighted Fury Island at the entrance to Cockburn Channel.

With the view of again making Sandy Point to get a new mainsail and otherwise refit, the *Spray* was kept before the southwest gale which fell and cat's-paws took the place of williwaws while she drifted slowly eastward. She came in sight of the ships at anchor when the wind came out from the northeast. That was a fair wind for the Pacific, so her prow was turned westward once more to traverse a second time her first course through the strait. There were two hundred miles to go, with the assurance of Magellan-like adventures as well. To these adventures and mishaps, the Captain was becoming accustomed and was beginning to like them. Since the gale which drove him south, his attitude towards the entire transit of the strait had changed. It was now: "If you want to play ball, come on. I am ready for you and I can beat you at your own game."

He became, in a measure, inured to the life, and began to think that the strait, if perchance the sloop should be blown off again, would make him the aggressor, and put the Fuegians entirely on the defensive. This feeling was forcibly borne in on him at Snug Bay, where he anchored one gray morning after passing Cape Froward to find, when broad daylight arrived, that two canoes which he had eluded by sailing all night were now stealthily entering the same bay under the shadow of a high headland. The canoes were well manned and the savages were well armed with spears and bows. At a shot from his rifle, both turned aside into a small creek out of range. In danger now of being flanked by the savages in the bush close aboard, he was obliged to hoist the sails and make across to

The brush with the Fuegians

the opposite side of the strait, a distance of six miles. He had trouble getting his anchor because of an accident to the wind-lass. He set sail and filled away, first hauling short by hand. The sloop carried her anchor away as though it was meant to be towed that way underfoot, and with it she towed a ton or more of kelp from a reef in the bay as she went in the strong breeze.

A sample incident, which might discourage a man and

dampen his ardor, occurred as he was clearing Magdalene Sound and entering Froward Reach. It was rough as usual and the sloop was plunging into the storm. The parting of the staysail sheet sent him forward in time to see a dark cliff ahead and breakers so close under the bows that he felt surely lost. He sprang aft again, unheeding the flapping sail, and threw the wheel over, expecting as the sloop came down into the hollow of a wave to feel her timbers crash under him on the rocks. But at the touch of her helm she swung clear of the danger, and in the next moment was in the lee of the land. It was a small island in the middle of the bay for which the sloop had been steering and which she made with such unerring aim as nearly to run it down. Further along in the bay was the anchorage, but before the anchor could be let go, another squall caught the sloop and carried her away. Still further to leeward was a great headland and he bore off for that. He was soon under the lee of the mountain, where the sea was as smooth as a millpond, and the sails flapped and hung limp while she carried her way in.

Here he thought that he would anchor and wait until morning, the depth being eight fathoms very close to the shore. The anchor did not reach bottom before another williwaw struck down from the mountain and carried the sloop off faster than the cable could be paid out. Therefore, instead of resting, he had to man the windlass and heave up the anchor with fifty fathoms (six feet to a fathom) of cable hanging straight up and down in deep water. The *Spray* had nothing but a small crab windlass with a lever and a "crab" pawl which slowly dragged the chain in link by link. Starting at midnight, it was daybreak by the time the anchor was at the hawse. At another time he did not bother with the anchors at all but tied up to a prehensile tree to keep from being blown out of the wrong end on the strait.

As the *Spray* turned again into the northwestward reach of the strait, her skipper set to work with palm and needle at every opportunity, when at anchor and when sailing. He was determined to rely upon his own resources to repair the damages of the great gale which drove him southward toward the Horn, after he had passed from the Strait of Magellan out into

"Yammerschooner." A call from Black Pedro

the Pacific. It was slow work on the sail; but little by little the squaresail on the boom expanded to the dimensions of a serviceable mainsail with a peak to it and a leech besides. If it was not the best setting sail afloat, it was at least very strongly made and would stand a hard blow. A ship meeting the *Spray* long afterwards reported her as wearing a mainsail of some improved design and patent reefer; that was not the case.

The *Spray* for the first few days after the storm enjoyed

327

some good weather, but good weather meant canoe Indians again. On comparatively fine days they ventured forth on their marauding expeditions; in boisterous weather they disappeared from sight. This being so, the Captain enjoyed gales of wind as never before and the *Spray* was never long without them during her struggles about Cape Horn.

It was under the lee of the Charles Islands, in the middle of the strait that the *Spray* was at last to meet Black Pedro face to face. From his canoe, alongside, he stuck up the point of his spear to get a box of matches he had asked for. The *Spray* who knew a trick twice as good as that passed them to him on the muzzle of a gun. It was a delicate exchange of compliments conducive to a perfect understanding all around. Even his two squaws in the canoe smiled at their chief's discomfiture at finding that he had to take the matches the *Spray's* way. Very likely he had beaten them up that very morning for not finding mussels enough for his breakfast. On first being allowed by the Captain to come alongside, one of the squaws had made a signal of warning to him lest Black Pedro do him harm. For that friendly gesture they were tendered some biscuits and meat, for which in return they handed over the *Spray's* rail some rather large lumps of tallow. (More about tallow later.)

From the outset Black Pedro registered indignation. It was "*Muy malo*," declared he, still feeling his ear, for the *Spray* to shoot at him when passing through the strait three weeks before. To prove his respectability he mentioned that he had many friends at Sandy Point. Some of those friends had recommended that he should be shot on sight for a murderer. The parley with the savages had begun at daylight when they lighted a signal fire from the top of the bluff and then got into their canoes. They had been gathering at Charles ever since the sloop had passed there the first time, the fine weather bringing them out of their haunts among the intricacies of Barbara Channel. During the parley the *Spray* kept under sail. The main body of the canoes was motioned to keep its distance. They well knew what would come their way if they did not, for they had a deeply rooted superstitious fear of powder and ball since experiencing their effect.

The *Spray* had signalled for only one canoe to advance and Pedro accepted the option. Being a halfbreed, the Spanish, or whatever else there was in him besides Indian, made him more intelligent than his tribe and not so easily fooled. The ruse of a Dummy crew, which three weeks before had been improvised on deck in an attempt to conceal the fact that the sloop had a one-man crew, did not entirely fool the wily savage. While he was alongside, Pedro asked the Captain where his crew was and he was told that they were below and asleep. At this misinformation, the savage gave him a cunning look. "*Hombre valiente*," he muttered in a sarcastic way, as much as to say, "There is something phony about all this and I know it; however, since you have that gun ready, I think I had better push off." And he did; but not for long, for he was not to be so easily discouraged.

Finding the *Spray* in Fortescue Bay the next day and in company with a steamer, he beamed with friendliness and begged my father to lend him his best rifle to shoot a guanaco for him. He was told that if he was in port next day, he would, and for his professed interest he received a cooper's drawknife and a few other articles which could be useful in canoe making. With the presents went a hint that he get out. He then went alongside of the steamer which was the *Colombia,* without faring so well. The *Colombia* that night made the bay cheerful with her electric lights and, on leaving in the morning, saluted

329

the *Spray* with three long blasts of her steam whistle. It sounded good enough in that dreary place. A few miles farther along was a large steamer, ashore, bottom up.

Then it fell entirely calm in the strait. Signal fires at once sprang up on all sides, and soon after more than twenty canoes hove in sight, all heading for the *Spray*. She fired a gun. All of the canoes then stopped and drew up in a semicircle, keeping outside eighty yards, which in the *Spray's* self-defense would have been the death-line.

On the following day and for the second time, she anchored in Borgia Bay. In Langara Cove she came upon some wreckage

Salving Wreckage

and goods cast up from the sea. The bulk of the goods was tallow in casks, and imbedded in the seaweed was a barrel of wine, which he also towed alongside and hoisted in with the throat halyards, which he took to the windlass. He worked on till the *Spray* was loaded with a full cargo.

330

It was a twenty-six mile run in a snowstorm from Langara to Port Angosto, where he found a safe harbor to refit and stow his cargo. He did not run the *Spray* into the harbor of Port Angosto, but came to inside of a bed of kelp, under a steep bluff on the port hand going in and this was the place from whence the *Spray* was to sail to Cape Pillar direct. And that is what she did on the 13th day of April 1896, having done about everything else in the strait except climb a tree.

When the *Spray* cleared Cape Pillar for the second time on her voyage, the hardest and most dramatic part of it had been accomplished. Her total distance: 9,600 miles.

There was a fair wind for it was from the southwest—the first winter wind of the season. Clearing the great tiderace off Cape Pillar and the Evangelistas, the Captain remained at the helm for a single trick of thirty hours. It was not that the sloop could not steer a straight course; he did not want her to. He had to humor his vessel in the cross seas. It was necessary to change her course in the combing seas, to meet them with what skill he could when they rolled ahead, and to keep off when they came up abeam. On the following day only the tops of the highest mountains were in sight.

The albatross dropped out of sight as he always does when you leave his latitudes or lay in too close to the land. In his place came the gulls to follow in the vessel's wake for scraps of food. The wind and sea decreasing, the *Spray* shook out a reef, and a few days later came under full sail. For the first time she set her jigger. The wind still held southwest, and rapid changes took place in both sea and weather while the sloop headed for the tropics. The first harbinger of warmer seas was a shark, which was promptly harpooned. The Captain's sailor instinct could not be restrained when he saw the sinuous thing near his vessel. It is instinctive for a sailor to destroy a single cruising shark on sight; but since there are countless millions of them in the oceans, what is the use?

From Cape Pillar he steered for Juan Fernandez which he made April 26, 1896. The blue hills of the island could be seen thirty miles off. When he first saw the island, the Captain, in adoration, made a salaam to the deck in the manner of the Orientals as the only means of expressing his emotions. He could find no other way. He did not reach the island until night on the northeast side where it fell calm and remained so all night. He saw the twinkling of a light, fired a gun but received no answer. He heard the sea booming against the cliffs all night and realized that the ocean swell was still great, although from the deck of his little ship it was still small.

From the sounds of animals in the hills he judged that he was dangerously near the shore, for the land being very high, appearances were deceptive. At daylight a boat pulled out; it held six oarsmen who pulled in oarlocks after the manner of trained seamen. He then knew that they belonged to a civilized race and that there was no occasion for fear as to their coming alongside. They were soon on board. One of the boat's crew, whom the others called the "king," spoke English; the rest spoke Spanish only. They had all heard of the voyage of the *Spray* through the Valparaiso papers and they told him of a war between Chile and the Argentine that he had not heard about when he was there. He had just visited both countries and he told them that, according to the latest reports while he was in Chile, their own island had sunk.

He had already made a pot of coffee and a batch of doughnuts fried in the Magellan tallow. They took the coffee for granted but the doughnuts were in strongest favor. His guests thought the doughnuts were extra nice and did he have any more of that tallow? Their handicap in regard to doughnuts was an entire shortage of fats to fry in, for there was nothing on the island but goats and they, at best, were but lean beasts.

Once at the anchorage, the steelyards were rigged up under the *Spray's* boom and the trade in tallow began. Before the sun went down, the islanders had become doughnut experts—thanks to some cooking lessons given on shore. He did not charge a high price for what he sold; but the ancient coins he got in payment, some of them from the wreck of a galleon sunk in the bay no one knew when, he sold afterwards to antiquarians for more than face value. In this way, he made a reasonable profit. He took away money of all denominations from the island—nearly all there was, as far as he could make out.

The *Spray* found Juan Fernandez, as a port of call, to be a lovely spot. The valleys are well wooded and fertile with streams of pure water pouring down through the many ravines.

The domestic economy was simplicity itself. There was neither policeman, lawyer or doctor. The people are all healthy and the children all beautiful. There were forty-five souls on the island all told. The adults were mostly from the mainland of South America. One of the inhabitants, a beautiful lady, made a flying jib for the *Spray,* and took her pay in tallow.

The architecture of the settlement wore a maritime look accounted for by a ship which had arrived there some time before on fire, and which had been stranded at the head of the bay. The sea smashed her to pieces on the rocks. After the fire was drowned, the islanders picked up the timbers and utilized them in the construction of their houses, which naturally came to have a ship-like appearance. The house of the king, besides resembling the ark, sported a polished brass knocker on its only door, which was painted green. In front of this gorgeous entrance was a flag mast, all a-taunto.

Of course the Captain made a pilgrimage to the old lookout place at the top of the three-thousand-foot mountain where Selkirk spent many days peering into the distance for the ship which came at last. From a tablet set into the face of the rock he copied these words:

IN MEMORY
OF
ALEXANDER SELKIRK
MARINER

A native of Largo in the County of Fife, Scotland, who lived on this island in complete solitude for four years and four months. He was landed from the *Cinque Ports* galley, 96 tons, 18 guns, A.D. 1704, and was taken off in the *Duke*, privateer, 12th February, 1709. He died Lieutenant of H.M.S. *Weymouth*, A.D. 1723, aged 47. This tablet is erected near Selkirk's lookout, by Commodore Powell and the officers of H.M.S. *Topaze*, A.D. 1868.

The cave in which Selkirk dwelt while on the island is at the head of the bay now called Robinson Crusoe Bay. The Captain visited Robinson Crusoe Bay in a boat. He entered the cave and found it dry and inhabitable. There are no serpents on the island. The island is about fourteen miles in length and eight miles in width. Its distance from Chile, to which country it belongs, is three hundred and forty miles.

On the morning of May 5th, 1896, the *Spray* sailed from Juan Fernandez, having feasted on many things but nothing sweeter than the adventure itself of a visit to the home and the very cave of Robinson Crusoe. And the last day she spent at the island was the pleasantest day of the whole voyage.

It must be borne in mind that the tracks of sailing ships were projected in accordance with general winds which blow from the tropical belts of low pressure towards the equatorial belt of high pressure, in the northern hemisphere from the northeast, and in the southern hemisphere from the southeast. These are called the "northeast trades" and the "southeast trades" which blow in their respective oceans. These trade winds have their northern and southern limits which are known to the sailing navigator. The southern limit of the southeast trade wind the *Spray* found and entered upon passing north of St. Felix Island. They seemed slow in reaching their limits, and it was for this navigational advantage in crossing the Pacific that the islands were reached from the southward before squaring away. In order to more fully understand the *Spray* tracks around the world it is well to study the wind charts of the globe. They may be found in a good commercial atlas.

The *Spray*, under reefs, now ran before a gale for a great many days, sometimes with a bone in her mouth, towards the Marquesas in the west, which she made in forty-three days from Juan Fernandez. The distance was thirty-eight hundred miles thus far. Fair going for a twelve-tonner. The high and beautiful Island of Nukahiva, easternmost of the Marquesas, the *Spray* merely used to check on her longitude which was found to be correct within practical limitations. They permit, in sailing vessels, an error of from two minutes of arc to a quarter of a degree. Two minutes is regarded by Bowditch as excellent practice.

With a free wind, day after day, the *Spray* bowled along on the remaining nineteen hundred miles to Samoa where the Captain had a mind to visit the home of Tusitala, the teller of tales. During these two runs, while his ship steered herself, her skipper found nothing could be easier and restful than a voyage in the trade winds. To have been alone for forty-three days as he was from Juan Fernandez to Nukahiva, would seem a long time, but in reality the moments flew lightly by.

It was easy for him to decide not to haul into Nukahiva, which he could have made as well as not, and to go on to Samoa without stopping. That made twenty-nine days more or seventy-two days in all. He was not distressed in any way during that time. There was no end of companionship; the very coral reefs kept him company, or gave him no time to feel lonely, which was the same thing, and there were many of them in his course to Samoa.

First among the incidents of his voyage from Juan Fernandez was an encounter with a sperm whale which was absentmindedly sculling the ocean at night, when he was below. The noise of the commotion he made in the sea at the approach of the sloop roused him on deck in time to see the whale throw up his flukes to sound and get out of the way. If whales do sleep, that was very likely what he was doing and why he was startled, for whales are very sensitive to noise. There must have been a pod of whales migrating east, for another was sighted soon after, headed east like the first one.

Hungry sharks came about the sloop when she neared islands or coral reefs. A number of birds were always about. Ships were less common than formerly and the *Spray* sighted not one in the many days of crossing the Pacific.

People have wondered what there could have been to eat on long passages in such a small vessel and where there was no icebox. There was no refrigeration even on large sailing vessels in those days. The foundation of the *Spray's* menu, like any long-voyage sailing ship, was the sea biscuit (hardtack) and salted beef (salt-horse) packed in brine in a cask. Salted pork came the same way. Potatoes were popular and they were carried as long as they kept edible. Properly stowed and ventilated, a potato might last three months. There was salt cod, beans which could be baked with salt pork, coffee, tea, sugar, molasses, and flour. There were hot biscuits made two or three times a week on the *Spray* and plenty of fruit preserves. Down in the hold and safely under the deck was a six-months' supply of fresh water in barrels.

The attractiveness of the above supply list depended largely

First exchange of courtesies in Samoa

on the adaptability and skill of the cook who was sometimes helped out with incidentals like sea turtle, flying fish and dried venison as was obtainable in the Strait of Magellan. At tropical stops there was always an abundance of fruit and fresh vegetables put on board. The objection to carrying small livestock on board was that it was next to cannibalism to kill and eat a fowl or animal one came to be in such close relation

337

with as on a small vessel. The idea was pronounced to be most repulsive.

The skipper of the *Spray* got on fairly well in the matter of provisions even on long voyages across the Pacific. He found always some small stores to help the fare with luxuries; what he lacked of fresh meat was made up in fresh fish, at least while in the trade winds, where flying fish crossing on the wind at night would hit the sails to fall on the deck, sometimes two or three of them, sometimes a dozen. Every morning, except when the moon was full, he got a supply by merely picking them up from the lee scuppers. All canned meats went begging.

On the 16th of July, 1896, he cast anchor at Samoa. The vessel being moored, he spread an awning, and instead of going on shore at once he sat under it till late listening to the musical voices of Samoan men and women. A canoe with some young native women in it rested her paddles abreast of the sloop.

"Schooner come Melike?" On being answered in the affirmative, the captain of the crew further inquired: "You man come 'lone?" Affirmative again.

"I don't believe that. You had other mans, and you eat 'em!" That rather disconcerting sally was followed by: "What for you come long way?" They were off, chanting a boat song in thirds as all Polynesians do when group singing.

It was a night of enchantment for the "ancient mariner," as United States Consul Churchill called him when he came ashore to report. He visited the Vailima mansion and entered the hall on the floor of which the "Writer of Tales," according to the Samoan custom, was wont to sit. He hobnobbed with King Malietoa who was of a dynasty two thousand years old. His people had not eaten a missionary in a hundred years, they said. He had only to take ava with the royal family and be ready for sea. His Majesty's beautiful daughter, Faamu-Sami ("to make the sea burn"), presided over the national beverage. The concluding treat was to hear a young native pupil of the L.M.S. School, a lad of nine or ten, read Basil Hall's fine description of Cape Horn. It was well done.

The *Spray* had hardly cleared the Samoan Islands when a sudden burst of the trades brought her down to close reefs. Finding a rough sea, her skipper swung her off free and sailed north of Fiji and coasted down the west side of the archipelago. Thence he sailed direct for New South Wales, passing south of New Caledonia, and arrived at Newcastle after a passage of forty-two days from Apia. There were severe gales all the way which foundered the American clipper ship *Patrician* further south and blew the French mail steamer from Noumea considerably out of her course. The French mail steamer had seen the little *Spray* in the thick of the storm and did not know what became of her. The *Spray* was snug, lying to under a goose-winged mainsail while the liner was rolling her funnel under.

After beating many hours off Seal Rocks, to weather them at last, the *Spray* arrived in Newcastle in the teeth of a gale of wind. It was their stormy season. The first visitor on board was the United States Consul, Mr. Brown. Nothing was too good for the *Spray* in Newcastle. All government dues were remitted. After she had rested a few days, she made along the coast towards the harbor of Sydney, where she arrived on the following day, October 10, 1896.

Summer was approaching and the harbor of Sydney was blooming with yachts. The typical boat was a handy sloop of great beam and enormous sail-carrying power. Everybody owned a boat. If a boy in Australia has not the means to buy him a boat, he builds one.

In Sydney the *Spray* shed her Joseph's coat, the Fuego mainsail, and, wearing a new suit, she was flagship of the Johnston's

339

Bay flying squadron, when the circumnavigators of Sydney harbor sailed in their annual regatta. They recognized the *Spray* as belonging to a club of her own and gave her credit for her record. Besides yachtsmen, the *Spray* was visited by the Royal Navy. Frequently, the officers of H.M.S. *Orlando* were aboard. Captain Fisher, R.N., the commander, came with a party of young ladies together with some of the gentlemen belonging to his ship. There was a deluge of rain but the girls did not mind it more than a flock of ducks. They were out for fun.

Time flew fast those days in Australia, and it was December 6, 1896, when the *Spray* sailed from Sydney. The intention of her skipper was to sail around Cape Leeuwin direct for Mauritius on his way home. In those low latitudes the westing would be much shorter. He therefore coasted towards Bass Strait in that direction. On December 17, the *Spray* came in close under Wilson's Promontory, seeking shelter from a hard wind. Receiving directions from the light keeper, she found a good anchorage in Waterloo Bay, about three miles to leeward.

In Waterloo Bay were some interesting characters and very much like those in Australia. They were Captain Young and his crew from a sawmill up the coast; they had a converted ferry boat called the *Mary* and were whaling. The captain of the *Mary* was a genius. Not one of his crew had seen a live whale when they shipped. But they were boatmen and their captain had told them that to kill a whale was no more than to kill a rabbit. They believed him, and that settled it. As luck would have it, the very first one they saw on their cruise was a dead whale. Nothing but whales interested the crew of the *Mary*, and they spent most of their time in Waterloo Bay gathering fuel along the shore for a cruise on the grounds off Tasmania. Whenever the word "whale" was mentioned in the hearing of these men, their eyes glistened with excitement.

340

The two vessels spent three days in the quiet cove, listening to the wind outside. Meanwhile the skippers of the respective craft explored the shores, visited abandoned miners' pits, and prospected for gold themselves. Their vessels parted company

Captain Slocum working the Spray *out of the
Yarrow River, a part of Melbourne Harbor*

the morning they sailed, standing away like sea birds, each on its own course.

The wind for a few days was moderate and with unusual luck of fine weather the *Spray* made Port Phillip Heads on the 22nd of December and was taken in tow by the steam tug

341

Racer and brought into Melbourne. Christmas Day was spent at a berth in the River Yarrow, but the *Spray's* berth was soon shifted to St. Kilda where she remained for a month. St. Kilda was the home of Mr. Shaw, a genuine *Spray* enthusiast. He got her lines and had a duplicate made by a Melbourne boat-builder to be preserved in the Antipodes. January 24, 1897, found the *Spray* again in tow of the tug *Racer,* leaving Hobson's Bay after a pleasant time in Melbourne and St. Kilda.

Ordinarily an east wind could be expected to blow around Cape Leeuwin during the summer months, but owing to a vast amount of ice drifting from the Antarctic, this was all changed, so much so that the south-about way was abandoned. Therefore, instead of thrashing round cold and stormy Cape Leeuwin, the Captain decided to spend a pleasanter and more profitable time in Tasmania, waiting for favorable winds through Torres Strait by way of the Great Barrier Reef, the route he finally decided on.

It was only a few hours' sail from Port Phillip Heads to Tasmania across the strait, the wind being fair and brisk. In Launceston, the *Spray* was berthed on the beach at a small jetty. He then made many journeys among the hills, and rested for the coming voyage on moss-covered rocks at the gorge close by and among the ferns wherever he went. The vessel was well taken care of by the neighbors and he never returned without finding all secure.

The season of fair weather around the north of Australia being yet a long way off, he sailed to other ports in Tasmania, where it is fine the year round; the first of these was Beauty Point. Beauty Point has a shady forest and a road among the tall gum trees. While there, the governor of New South Wales, Lord Hampden, and family came in on their steam yacht. Lord and Lady Hampden paid their compliments to the *Spray* and made a rendezvous with her at the Paris Exposition which was to be held in 1900.

From Beauty Point he made sail for Devonport, an important harbor in Tasmania. Large steamers entered there and carried away great cargoes of farm produce; but the *Spray* was the first vessel to bring the Stars and Stripes to the port, and so it was written in the port records. For this great distinction jams and jellies were put on the *Spray* by the hospitable people—also some bottles of raspberry wine. Tasmania is the fruit garden of the world. The "I.X.L." jam factory is in Hobart and it was a common saying in the British Army that "I.X.L." won World War I.

The *Spray* hauled out on the marine railway at Devonport to be found entirely free of any trace of the destructive teredo, the tropical shipworm that pulverizes wooden ships. As a protection the bottom was coated once more with copper paint, for she would have to sail through the Coral and Arafura seas before refitting again. She weighed anchor April 16, 1897, and again put to sea.

Thursday Island in Torres Strait, twenty-three hundred miles distant, was the next primary objective of the voyage. The season of summer was then over; winter was rolling up from the south, with fair winds for the north. A foretaste of the winter sent the *Spray* flying round Cape Howe. She passed Cape Bundoora the following day, retracing her course northward. This was a fine run and boded good for the long voyage home from the Antipodes. The weather was fine with clear sky the rest of the passage to Sydney, where the *Spray* arrived, for the second time, April 22, 1897, and anchored in Watson's Bay, near the Heads in eight fathoms of water. The harbor, from the

343

Heads to Parramatta, up the river, was more than ever alive with boats and yachts of every class; a scene of animation hardly equalled in any other part of the world.

On May 20, 1897, the *Spray* was at the gateway of the Great Barrier Reef to behold the noble Lady Elliott Light flash up before her path on a dark night in a coral sea. It was a sight for poets.

Near Port Macquarie, the *Spray* made out a modern dandy cutter yacht in distress. It was the *Guinevere* which had sailed from Watson's Bay about three days ahead of her, and she had at once got into trouble. Three jolly tars in white ducks and obvious caps, comprised the crew. They were Mr. Moncton and his two pals on their way from Sydney to Cooktown. My father afterwards told me the amusing story. Mr. Moncton, a true adventurer, was well known both in Sydney and in New Guinea, where he later became a resident magistrate under the administration of Sir Wm. McGregor. Moncton was sometimes a trader on his own account and also did some mining. His first experiment with a vessel was when he chartered a small schooner crewed by kanakas, for Sydney to New Guinea where he secured a cargo of sandalwood and traded it to New Zealand. On returning to Sydney, he began to think of a "reef" in New Guinea which he had sampled and he decided to buy a small vessel to convey his mining gear thither. Someone advised him to get a yacht and the sixteen-ton *Guinevere* was the answer. She was a thoroughbred, sharp, deep and heavily ballasted. She looked good to Moncton but either his good sense or his good angel prompted him to put in a big rotary pump, without realizing how soon it would be before he would owe his life to it. There were no kanakas available for a crew so his two pals Burton and Cox volunteered as far as Cooktown.

The storm signals being up, they came to an anchor in

Watson's Bay, just inside of Sydney Heads, before proceeding. Among other vessels held up by the storm signals was the *Spray*. The *Spray* looked askance at the obvious ducks and fancy gaff-topsails sported by the crew of the *Guinevere* and politely declined an invitation to race to Cooktown. Becoming impatient of the storm signal, the yacht sailed, but as it turned out, the weather man knew best. A southerly "buster" overtook them before night. Not being acquainted with the coast they stood out to sea and as it blew harder no one on board thought about taking in a reef. They should have been close reefed before they sailed through the Heads. Very likely no one on board knew what a reef point was for. Their first big sea washed away their dinghy. Their jib blew away and then the forestaysail. Slacking off the main sheet they managed to get her before the wind, and Moncton steered, lashed to the wheel to prevent being washed overboard. Burton and Cox were shut up down below when Burton, who had crawled out of the scuttle to help Moncton slack off the sheet was washed, by a sea, back down the scuttle instead of overboard. Burton finally stuck his head out of the scuttle and yelled to Moncton that the yacht was filling and that they must pump or sink. Luckily, the handle of the new rotary pump was near the scuttle where Burton could reach it without going out again on deck. He pumped for some hours and kept ahead of the inflowing water. Then the pump choked and the water gained. At this point the mainsail blew out of the roping and they rightly expected that she would broach to and that would be the end of it, water in the hold or no water in the hold. By this time it was black night and they could not understand why they were not rolling in the trough of the sea until, when daylight dawned, it was discovered that the torn sail had jambed between the mast and the rigging to act as a square-sail to give them steerage

345

way. That enabled them to still run before it. With the hold pumped reasonably dry, and totally exhausted, they came to anchor near the Solitary Islands, an exposed berth and foul ground. The *Spray*, to render possible assistance bore down upon them and luffed up under their lee. They were a spectacle of both contempt and pity, the very kind that brings amateur seamanship into disrepute.

"Up anchor and let me tow you into Port Macquarie," shouted the *Spray*, "it's twelve miles from here."

"No," returned the owner, "we'll go back to Newcastle. We missed Newcastle on the way coming; we didn't see the light, and it was not thick, either." That he shouted very loud, looking disgustedly at the other two. The skipper of the *Spray* again tried to persuade them to be towed into a port of refuge so near at hand. It would have cost them only the trouble of weighing their anchor and passing him the end of a line, but they declined even that in sheer ignorance of a rational course.

"What is your depth of water?" the *Spray* inquired.

"Don't know; we lost our lead. All the chain is out. We sounded with the anchor."

"Send your dinghy over, and I'll give you a lead."

"We've lost our dinghy, too," they wailed.

"God is good, or you would be worse off. Goodbye. I will report you."

It was eighteen days before the *Spray* heard of the *Guinevere* again, which was on the 31st of May, when she reached Cooktown. A despatch said:

May 31, the yacht *Guinevere*, from Sydney for New Guinea, three hands on board, lost at Crescent Head. The crew saved.

According to that, it took the three jolly tars three days to lose the yacht, after all.

346

The sloop was now in a protected sea and smooth water—the first she had dipped her keel into since leaving Gibraltar—and a change it was from the heaving of the misnamed "Pacific" Ocean. On second thought, the ocean outside might be rough, but coral rocks are rough as well, besides being sharp and dangerous. The *Spray*, therefore, now trusted to the mercies of the maker of all reefs, keeping a good lookout at the same time for perils on every hand.

Historic Cooktown was the next important stop, being one of the two or three places where the *Spray* came to an anchor. It was much less hard work sailing nights than to hoist the sails every morning to start. Cooktown was one of the places where Captain James Cook stopped to heave down and paint his ship just as the *Spray* had been painted in Devonport. A self-appointed but well-meaning reception committee first showed my father the monument, well inland, which they told him marked the spot where the *Endeavour* had been hove down. Then it was proposed to visit the very spot where the great circumnavigator had been murdered. The visitor was somewhat disturbed by the four-thousand-mile error (the distance from Hawaii), but was relieved by the usual informative youth that is sure to pop up on such occasions:

" 'E wasn't killed 'ere at all, 'e was killed in Hafrica; a lion ate 'im."

It was just as the *Spray* was getting well on toward Cape Claremont that her pasture-oak stem was tested against a coral head; the pasture-oak stem was not greatly damaged. It was on "M" reef, where the beacon was removed for some reason. Anyway, the Captain did not see it before he struck, and he had no time to look for it afterwards. It did not matter then whether he saw it or not.

The first and only Australian canoe he ever saw on the voyage

347

now crossed his bow from the mainland off to an adjacent small island. It was a wretched affair with a rag of a sail.

In this sea of coral a fish that was not a flying fish leaped on board in the night. He was served up by the cook for breakfast. This one was no larger around than a herring, which it resembled in every respect except that it was three times as long, which was so much the better, for the crew of the *Spray* was fond of herring anyway.

Close to Albany Pass, he interviewed the pearl fisherman *Tarawa* whose skipper was an American and the very heart yarn of a sailor. Captain Jones, he was. And during the evening when both vessels were moored to the land they were visited by Mr. and Mrs. Jardine and family. Jardine was a stockman well known throughout the land. Mrs. Jardine was the niece of King Malietoa, and cousin to the beautiful Faamu-Sami ("To make the sea burn"), who visited the *Spray* in Samoa. Mr. Jardine himself was a fine specimen of a Scotsman. The *Spray* noted that with his little family about him, he was content to live in that remote place, accumulating the comforts of life.

During the time of the *Spray's* stay at Thursday Island there was a grand corroboree in honor of the Queen's jubilee which was June 22. For that purpose Mr. Douglas, the resident magistrate, imported four hundred native warriors, together with their wives and children for the event. The corroboree, which is a sort of war dance, took place at night and the performers, painted in fantastic colors, danced or leaped about before a blazing fire. Some were painted like birds and some like beasts, in which the emu and the kangaroo were represented. Some had the human skeleton painted on their bodies, while they jumped about, threateningly, spear in hand, ready to strike down some imaginary enemy. It was a show at once amusing, spectacular, and hideous.

On June 24th the *Spray*, well fitted in every way, sailed for the long voyage ahead—down the Indian Ocean. She had passed nearly all the dangers of the Coral Sea and Torres Strait, and from this point on was plain sailing and a straight course. The trade wind was still blowing fresh, and could be safely counted on down to the coast of Madagascar.

With no wish to arrive off the Cape of Good Hope before midsummer the course was shaped, first, for the Keeling Cocos, atoll islands, distant twenty-seven hundred miles. Timor, an island of high mountains, would be sighted on the way. In the Arafura Sea, for days, there was sailing in water milky-white and purple. It was during the last quarter of the moon, when in the dark nights the phosphorescent light effect could be seen in its greatest splendor. The sea, where the sloop disturbed it, seemed all ablaze, and her wake was a path of fire. Now was the time to crowd on sail. The flying jib made by the Juan Fernandez beauty was bent on and set as a spinnaker from bamboo that Mrs. Robert Louis Stevenson had presented to the *Spray* while in Samoa. With the spinnaker pulling well and the bamboo holding its own, she picked up on her speed.

In the part of the Arafura Sea she came to first, where it was comparatively shallow, sea snakes writhed in the surface of the water, but where the sea became deep they disappeared.

On July 11th, with all sail set and the spinnaker still drawing, Christmas Island came into view. Before night it was abeam and distant two and a half miles.

To Keeling Cocos Islands was now only five hundred and fifty miles, but even in this short run it was necessary to be careful to keep a true course else he would miss the atoll. The first unmistakable sign of land was a visit one morning from a white tern. The tern is called by the islanders the "pilot of Keeling Cocos." The reckoning was up, and from half way up the mast, coconut trees standing half-way out of the water could be seen. The *Spray* had made the landfall dead ahead. Even then her skipper did not touch the helm, for with the current and the heave of the sea, the sloop at the end of the run found herself absolutely in the center of the channel. He then trimmed her sails by the wind, took the helm, and beat up to the harbor landing where he cast anchor 3:30 P.M., July 17, 1897, twenty-three days from Thursday Island. The distance run was twenty-seven hundred miles.

This would have been a fair Atlantic voyage. It was a delightful sail. During those twenty-three days he had not spent more than three hours at the helm, including the time occupied in beating into Keeling Harbor. He just lashed the helm and let her go; whether the wind was abeam or dead aft, it was all the same, she always sailed on her course. No part of the voyage, up to this point, had been so finished as this.

The Keeling atoll was the most beautiful thing the *Spray* had seen. As she left the ocean depths of deepest blue and entered the coral circle the contrast was most marked: the brilliant colors of the waters, transparent to a depth of thirty feet, now violet, now sky-blue, now green; the encircling palm-covered islands, the white-sand shores and the whiter gaps where breakers appeared, and lastly the lagoon itself, seven or eight miles across from north to south and five miles from east to west, was a sight never to be forgotten.

A strong impression made upon the Captain of the *Spray* was that the crime of infanticide had not reached islands. Hundreds of children of all ages and sizes were mustered at the jetty. They first regarded the one-man ship with suspicion and fear. A man had been blown away to sea many years before and they hinted to one another that this might be his spirit returned in the sloop.

On the 22nd of July arrived the H.M.S. *Iphigenia* with

Mr. Justice Leech on board on a circuit of inspection among the Straits Settlements, of which Keeling Cocos was a dependency, to hear complaints and to try cases by law. They found the *Spray* hauled ashore and tied to a coconut tree. Of her, Mr. Leech stated in his report which was transmitted by the Governor of Singapore to Joseph Chamberlain, the Colonial Secretary: "On reaching the landing stage, we found, hauled up for cleaning, etc., the *Spray* of Boston, a yawl of 12.70 gross tons, the property of Captain Joshua Slocum. He arrived at the island on the 17th of July, twenty-three days out from Thursday Island. This extraordinary solitary traveller left Boston some two years ago, single-handed, crossed to Gibraltar, sailed down to Cape Horn, passed through the Strait of Magellan to the Society Islands, thence to Australia, and through the Torres Strait to Thursday Island."

After the sloop was coated with copper paint and made ready for the water, she again found herself the subject of island folklore. When she did not readily launch, the children all clapped their hands and said it was the Kpeting (giant crab) that was holding her by the keel in the sand. Little Ophelia, ten or twelve, suggested that, for a pot of that Tasmanian blackberry jam (which they all found out was on board), the Mohammedan priest might bless the voyage and make the Kpeting let go its hold, which it did, if it had a hold, and she floated the very next tide. To celebrate this occasion, Ophelia wrote in the *Spray's* logbook.

> A hundred men with might and main
> On the windlass hove, yeo ho!
> The cable only came in twain;
> The ship she would not go;
> For, child, to tell the strangest thing,
> The keel was held by a great Kpeting.

351

Admiral Fitzroy of the *Beagle*, who visited here, where many things are reversed, spoke of "these singular, though small, islands, where crabs eat coconuts, fish eat coral, dogs eat fish, men ride on turtles, sea birds roost on branches and rats make their nests in the tops of palm trees." At Keeling is the great and famous tridacna shell. Fishing for some of these man-trap shells nearly cost the Captain his life by drifting in a boat out of the lagoon.

On August 22nd, the sloop swung out to sea under all sail, heading again for home. It was nineteen hundred miles to Rodriguez and for there she headed across the Indian Ocean. For days she ran her course under reefed sails for the trades were fresh. At the end of her computed run, her skipper, as he says, "kept a weather eye lifting for land."

He was rewarded on a midnight by a black object on the horizon, where the evening before he had seen some resting clouds. It was still a long way off, but there was no mistaking that it was the high island of Rodriguez. And on this island there was more folklore of a more serious kind than that which was encountered at the atoll. The good abbé, a few days before the arrival of the one-man ship, had told his people if they were not better, the devil was going to alight on the island some day and get them. When they saw the *Spray* come to, with but a solitary figure about the decks, they cried, "May the Lord help us, it is he, and he has come in a boat!" The more guilty ones locked themselves in their houses.

The governor of the island viewed the commotion at the landing and arranged a meeting of the "devil" with the good abbé of San Gabriel, who royally entertained the governor and his sulphurous companion at the convent. The "devil" and the abbé exchanged compliments, "Captain, I embrace you, and of whatsoever religion you may be, my wish is that you succeed in making your voyage." To that the Captain (no longer the "devil") could only say, "My dear Abbé, had all religionists been so liberal there would have been less bloodshed in the world."

On September 16th, after eight restful days at Rodriguez, the mid-ocean land of plenty, the *Spray* set sail and in three days arrived at Mauritius. But the Satan story was there ahead of him, which served a good turn, for on the strength of it the yarn got out that if anyone should go on board after dark, the devil would get him at once. There was no fear of pilfering at night. Even Mamode Hajee Ayoob, watchman for the first day, could not be hired to watch at night—or even till the sun went down. "Sahib, there is no need of it," he would explain and what he said was true. They wouldn't go near the boat after dark for all the money in Mauritius. The Satan yarn, however, did not prevent the Captain from giving his lecture at the opera house, which was packed to the doors. His Honor, the Mayor introduced the lecturer to His Excellency, the Governor of the island.

While at Mauritius the *Spray* was tendered the use of the military dock free of charge and was thoroughly refitted by the port authorities. Thus well equipped, on 26th October, the *Spray* put to sea. As she sailed before a light wind the island receded slowly, and on the following day the mountain near Moka could still be seen from her deck.

On passing Réunion the pilot came out and spoke her, received a Mauritius paper, and returned to his station leaving the sloop to proceed on her way. From Réunion the course was shaped directly for Cape St. Mary, Madagascar.

As a rule, bad weather may be expected when sailing off any of the great promontories of the world and the *Spray* found no exception as she drew near the southern end of Madagascar.

From the 6th to the 9th of November, in the Mozambique Channel she experienced a hard gale of wind from the southwest, a point from which they blow the hardest in that region. Here the *Spray* suffered as much as she did anywhere save off Cape Horn. The thunder and lightning preceding this gale were very heavy. From this point until the sloop arrived off the coast of Africa, she encountered a succession of windy gales which drove her about in many directions. But on the 17th of November she arrived at Port Natal and met all the members of the Royal Natal Yacht Club. Here the Right Honorable Harry Escombe, premier of the colony, told the Captain he was the kind of a man to go lion hunting with. The Right Honorable, a cribbage player of renown as well as a hunter, even offered to sail the *Spray* around Cape of Good Hope and to play cribbage to pass the time away. The Captain was warned, however, that Mr. Escombe would win the sloop away from him before reaching Capetown.

As could be well imagined the *Spray* had a good time of it in Port Natal, but as all fine things must end, the "crew" swung her dinghy on deck and on December 14, 1897, sailed with a morning land wind which carried her clear of the bar; again she was "off on her alone," as they say in Australia.

The Cape of Good Hope was now the most prominent point to pass. From Table Bay, brisk trades could be counted on, and then the *Spray* would soon be home. The distance from Durban to Table Bay was about eight hundred miles over what might prove to be a rough sea. Gales of wind sweeping around the Cape were frequent enough, one occurring on an average every thirty-six hours, with no more serious result than to blow the *Spray* along her course when it was fair or to blow her back somewhat when it was ahead.

354

On Christmas, 1897, the *Spray* came to the pitch of the Cape. On this day she was trying to stand on her head giving her skipper every reason to believe that she would accomplish the feat before night. After rounding the Cape of Good Hope, the voyage seemed as good as finished to the Captain, for from this time on he knew that it would be nearly all plain sailing. Here was the dividing line of weather. To the north it was clear and settled, while south it was humid and squally and inclined to treacherous gales. From the recent hard weather, the *Spray* ran into a calm under Table Mountain. Here she was picked up by a tug which was out looking for a larger ship, and in lieu of one towed her into port. The sea being smooth, she came to an anchor off the city of Capetown, where the Captain preferred to remain one day alone to quietly enjoy the retrospect of the passage of two great capes.

On the following morning the *Spray* sailed into the Alfred Dry Docks where she remained for three months in the care of the port authorities, while the Captain travelled the country over from Simonstown to Pretoria, being accorded by the colonial government a free railroad pass over all the land. The trip to Kimberly, Johannesburg and Pretoria was a pleasant one.

In Pretoria the Captain met Mr. Krüger, the Transvaal President. His Excellency at first was cordial enough, but when he was told that his caller was sailing around the world he shut up like a clam and just glared. Judge Beyers who introduced the Captain was embarrassed, but the Captain himself was delighted. The incident pleased him more than anything else that could have happened because he was interested in the Boer chief's views concerning the sphericity of the earth, for he had heard while he was in Natal that Krüger believed the world was flat. At first he thought it was a popular canard gotten up to the

355

prejudice of the Dutch. But while he was at Durban he found that three Boers, favored by the opinion of President Krüger, had prepared a work to support that contention.

They came from Pretoria to obtain data from the circum-navigator, and they seemed annoyed when he told them that they could not prove that the world was flat by his experience. With the advice to conjure up the spirit of the dark ages for research, he left the three wise men poring over the *Spray's* track on the chart of the world. It was on Mercator's projection and, of course, "flat." The next morning one of the gentlemen told the Captain, "If you respect the Word of God, you must admit that the world is flat." A pamphlet by these Transvaal geographers was mailed to the Captain before he sailed from Africa on his last stretch around the globe. "The world is flat" theory was a nugget of information quarried out of Oom Paul, but only unthinking people would call President Krüger dull.

Soon after my father's return to the Cape he met many agree-able people including His Excellency, Governor Sir Alfred Milner, who found time to visit the *Spray* with a party. Dr. David Gill, royal astronomer, invited the Captain the next day to the famous Cape Observatory. An hour with Dr. Gill was an hour among the stars. He showed the Captain the great astro-nomical clock of the observatory and he in turn was shown the tin clock on the *Spray*. They went over the subject of standard time at sea and how it was found from the deck of a little sloop at sea without the aid of a clock of any kind.

At the time my father went to sea, lunar observation was not an unusual method of obtaining Greenwich Time for longitude. It was very interesting as it gave the observer a complete inde-pendence of extraneous circumstances, like putting those cups on your ears and listening for electronic advice from the ether

356

—all very well as long as it works. There is still, on cloudless days and nights, the moon going around like a hand on a clock to give you your Greenwich Time. And a sailor who cannot make use of it is not an altogether competent navigator, for independence is a rule of the sea. The clock up aloft was the moon, which together with the sun and several stars whose coordinates were tabulated, furnished the required data. Local time was computed by the usual means of getting the hour angle.

Three observers were generally employed in a "lunar." The senior observer took the angular distance, say, between the moon and the sun. Observers No. 1 and 2 would simultaneously take the altitudes of the sun and the moon. To facilitate the lunar method, her true angular distance from any one of the other available heavenly bodies was given in the Nautical Almanac for the beginning of every third hour, Greenwich Mean Time; the time answering to any intermediate angular distance being arrived at by inspection of a table of proportional parts. The difference between the computed times was the longitude required.

The degree of accuracy to be found in this method depended entirely on the observer's skill in measuring the lunar distance with the sextant. If the observer was sharp enough to make a contact of the two bodies coming within half a minute of arc of the truth, he could compute his longitude thereby within fifteen minutes of a degree. Additional accuracy could be had, however, by taking the mean of a series of angles, both east and west of the moon, being sure to always use the same sextant; in this way, errors caused by both mechanical and personal equation could be made to compensate each other. Results warranted the continuance of this laborious method until the

357

present-day perfection of the chronometer had been reached, together with its invaluable adjunct, the daily Marconi time signal.

The Captain's astronomical conversation with Dr. Gill throws a light on the navigation of the *Spray* which has never been very well understood, owing perhaps to the Captain's purposeful vagueness on this point. Even professional navigators have taken his tin clock joke seriously. My father meant that he employed the same methods in navigating the sloop as he had on all of his former vessels.

To substantiate the reliability of the lunar method, I would here like to make an interesting quotation from the log of the ship *Clive* which in 1859 made a six months' passage without seeing land, from the English Channel to Madras, and sighted the landfall within an hour of the expected time. That could not be beaten at this day. Captain Shaw reported that he checked up his chronometers (which had altered their rates considerably) by lunars. He said he could, by this means, keep to the sea four years, the period of time that lunar tables were published in advance in the Nautical Almanacs.

For "dead reckoning," a check on observations, a rotator log was always towed astern of the *Spray*—even around the world. And she ended the voyage with the identical logline she started out of Boston with; it was none the worse for wear though the rotator came to know the imprint of sharks' teeth in the Indian Ocean. Sights revealed that a fish had at one time altered the pitch of the blades.

The Captain's experience in nautical astronomy was unique; he was proud of the little achievement alone on the sloop. He was in touch with his surroundings. He realized the mathematical truth of the motions of all the worlds, so well known that astronomers compile tables of their co-ordinates through the years and the days and the minutes of a day, with such precision that one coming along over the sea five years later may, by their aid, find the time of any given meridian on the earth.

A pleasant visit from Admiral Sir Harry Rawson of the Royal Navy, and his family, brought to an end the *Spray's* social relations with the Cape of Good Hope. The admiral, then commanding the South African Squadron, and now in command of the great Channel Fleet, evinced the greatest interest in the diminutive *Spray* and her behavior off Cape Horn.

On March 26, 1898, she sailed from South Africa and soon put Table Mountain out of sight. With her new sea-room, the *Spray* again took on her old habit of self-steering. All she needed to keep the course was a glance now and then from her skipper at the lubber's line. Cape pigeons circled above the masthead. Flying fish darted about, and porpoises, who did not mind swimming one hundred and fifty miles a day, kept her company for several days.

St. Helena next appeared on the horizon, at first a mere speck, although it was nearly three thousand feet high and nine miles long. He rounded to and anchored to visit this most historic of islands. He slept in Napoleon's haunted room but did not see his ghost—only a horseshoe nailed over the door, after watching all night. On leaving St. Helena, the *Spray* was entrusted by the governor with royal mail to Ascension, rated in the British Navy as "The Stone Frigate."

After leaving the sea-beaten but interesting rocks of the island of Ascension, on May 8, 1898, the *Spray*, homeward bound, crossed her own outward-bound track. It was where she had been October 2, 1895. She had encircled the globe. A period was made.

She passed Fernando de Noronha at night, going some miles to southward of it. The Captain did not see the dismal island.

But at this point, the *Spray* was still thirty-five hundred miles from home. With a leading wind, and a current which aided her forty miles a day, she was now making one hundred and eighty miles a day (still self-steering) around Cape St. Roque.

At the latitude of the Amazon she had the remarkable experience of meeting up with the Battleship *Oregon*, direct from

The Spray *passed by the* Oregon

the Straits of Magellan herself, and on her way to Santiago to fight the Spaniards.

On passing the *Spray* the *Oregon* displayed a large Spanish flag under the code signal, "Have you seen any men of war?" The *Spray*, who had not yet heard anything about the Spanish-American War, nor even that it had been imminent, guessed the fact, and hoisted the "Negative." As the great sea fortress swept by with turret guns already elevated to fire, the *Spray*,

360

on second thought, hoisted, "Let us keep together for mutual protection." The *Oregon,* however, did not seem to think that was necessary.

A newly graduated ensign who was later to be Commander-in-Chief in China, was on the *Oregon* at the time of her passing

"Reading day and night," which was sketched by Mr. Fogarty on board with the Captain as model

361

the *Spray* in the Atlantic. I refer to Admiral Yarnell whom the writer had the honor of meeting during World War II. Admiral Yarnell told the writer that licking the Spaniards was merely routine, but meeting the diminutive *Spray* in mid-ocean was not. On the contrary, he considered it the top event of his sea life.

The courses of the two ships diverged, the *Oregon's* was to Santiago to fight the Spaniards, the *Spray's* was to Grenada for whence she had mail from Mauritius. There she arrived on May 23rd, forty-two days from the Cape of Good Hope.

The last foreign port to be made on the voyage was that of St. John, Antigua. From there, the *Spray* cleared on June 14, 1898. At the United States Consulate, her license to sail single-handed, even around the world, was handed back to her for the last time.

This license, containing comments upon the nature of the voyage, made by the Consuls of Capetown and St. John, respectively, is now in the files of the Treasury Department, Washington, D. C.

CHAPTER 16

The Disappearance of the *Spray*

AFTER his arrival in his home land and the Presidential reception described in the first chapter of this book, the Captain was encouraged to write an account of his voyage for *Century Magazine*. So, shutting himself up in the quiet cabin of the *Spray,* lying yet in Erie Basin, he went to work on the *Century* articles. The foundation of these (later to appear in book form under the title of *Sailing Alone Around the World*) was a number of syndicated articles which he had sent in from various parts of the world to the *Louisville Courier-Journal,* the *New York World* and the *Boston Globe.* It was the articles and his lectures which had paid his running expenses while at sea. He wrote from the *Spray* in a private letter to the family that the lectures were a great success, for by moving rapidly from place to place he was able to keep ahead of his enraged audiences.

In addition to the newspaper work, he had of course his logbook and a large accumulation of varied documents pertaining to the voyage. Writing was a pleasure to him. He buried himself in it for three months. The manuscript was altogether a sea-going job, for it was both conceived and completed afloat. It was not a new thing for the Captain to write. For many years past he had interested himself in contributing to papers in the various ports he visited. Sailing vessels often had to spend months in the same place, so the Captain took advantage of these opportunities to keep in touch with the journalistic world.

While lying in Erie Basin the *Spray* had a number of unusual visitors. One of these was James Barnes, war correspondent from South Africa. Mr. Barnes brought the compliments of Sir Alfred Milner. Governor Milner said he was charmed by his visit to the *Spray* while she was in Capetown and furthermore he said that her skipper was "the most interesting American" he ever met.

Another reverberation of the world voyage was a visit from Sir Alfred Harmsworth (afterwards Lord Northcliffe), pro-prietor of the *London News*. Sir Alfred was on his way to see the President in Washington but stopped over a day in New York to call on the *Spray*. My brother Garfield rose to the occa-sion by roasting a turkey in the very small coal stove in the fore cabin. The distinguished guest, sitting on a box, said that the turkey was twice as big as the stove and that he never enjoyed one more. He and his press associate were deeply interested in the vessel and examined details of rig and accommodation very closely. They each accepted, as souvenirs, a piece of the logline she had towed across every ocean. For a moment the two gentlemen discussed means of preserving the bits of the line and decided that a glass cigar container would be just the thing.

Soon after the *Century* articles began to attract notice, the Captain became a literary sea-lion. He was sought after and welcomed everywhere. Some painters had him up at the Players

Club, where he met Joseph Jefferson, then president of the Club. He was invited to the Aldine Club and attended there an affair in honor of Mark Twain. At the Twentieth Century Club he was himself the guest of honor (1901) for the Club's Twelfth Night Revel, of which the poet of the occasion wrote in tribute to the guest—

". . . the sunny memory
Of Captain Slocum, whose naive surprise
At his own Yankee wit danced in his eyes
And lighted up his genial kindly face
While he told with such delightful grace
The tale of his lone voyage around the world."

Soon after the Twelfth Night Revel, a review of the book appeared in *The Critic:*

" 'Sailing Alone Around the World' will never win a prize for terse and trenchant titles, yet it is hard to see how it could be briefer and still adequate. As for the story itself, to match it, one must go back to Marryat, and remember that the gallant English captain dealt in fiction, while the American, Captain Slocum, sticks to facts. The skipper of the *Spray* not only officered his little sloop, but manned it—not only manned it but built it.

"The shipbuilders have put a million years between the fleets of Columbus and Magellan and the ocean greyhounds of the year 1900; but Captain Slocum is inspired by the spirit of those early ages and shows himself a close kinsman of the dauntless navigator who discovered America, and of him who made a more marvelous voyage which led to the discovery of the Philippines. All of his experiences were not so terrifying or disheartening as his two cruises through the Magellan Straits, nor yet so idyllic as the run from Australia to the Keeling Islands, when for three weeks not more than sixty minutes were spent in steering.

"A friend of the Captain's connected with The Century Company, who had kept track of the *Spray* on its 46,000-mile adventure, received in November, 1897, a long letter dated, '*The Spray*, tied to a tree at Keeling Cocos Islands, August 7, 1897.' 'Do you think,' asked the modest skipper, 'our people would care for the story of the voyage around?' The answer to the question is the reception the 'story' has had after it appeared in the *Century* where it was planned to run it for three months, the period being extended first to four then to five and again to six months, with a supplement in the seventh number dealing with the structure and rig of the gallant little ship. There is an abundance of salt in this 'personal narrative,' and not all of it is the salt of the sea. Much of it is Attic. The Captain is a stylist as well as a wit."

As *Sailing Alone* became a best seller its author received an increasing number of invitations to lecture. He once had contact with that impresario of lecturers of the time, Major Pond, who, in my father's instance, proved to be a little unreliable about dates, a circumstance that developed some sharp repartee. Pond humorously excused himself on the ground of habitual mendacity from boyhood and even admitted that his father had once "licked" him for lying.

"Major," responded the captain, "that is just where he made a mistake. My father licked me for trying to go to sea."

For the first few summers after returning from the long voyage, the Captain enjoyed sails in New England waters. On one of the trips he landed on Martha's Vineyard and explored the island. Almost in the center and within sound of the surf on South Beach, he bought a small farm on the outskirts of the village of West Tisbury, with several old sea captains for neighbors.

His house was one of the most ancient on the island, a hewn oak-framed dwelling with warped floors, tiny window panes and open fireplaces. Forlorn at first from long disuse it was soon made attractive by a new coat of shingles on roof and sides, and the *Spray* herself made a special voyage to Buzzards Bay to get the shingles.

In a single season the Captain became an enthusiastic agriculturist, proud of his flourishing garden and with the disposition to own and make fruitful all the land round about. He delighted to consider the beauties of the sturdy oak woods which overspread much of the region, the promising condition of the abounding blueberry bushes, the possibilities of the wet hollows for cranberry culture, and of the protective slopes for fruit trees. The only excursion he ever took from garden farming was when some Schoharie County (N. Y.) hop growers came on the Vineyard and got the whole back island excited about hops. They declared that the sandy soil with water close to the top was ideal for the plants. But the water was too near the top and the plants froze the first winter. That ended the hop prospect on the Vineyard even before the poles were put up for the vines. No one regretted the failure to introduce a new and profitable industry "up island" more than the Captain.

Soon after coming to the Vineyard, the Captain began to take an interest in community affairs. On being invited to lecture at the church to help raise money for its repair, he rushed a snapshot of the building to New York and had a slide made for the first picture to show on the screen.

"Why, that's our church," the audience gasped as soon as they saw what it was.

"Yes," chimed in the lecturer, "and it's *got* to be shingled." As the showman, the lecturer was fond of springing a surprise.

It was also his first local public appearance. "Now Captain," said one of the entertainment committee, "of course we are proud to have you with us, but we would like to know just how you happened to pick out West Tisbury to let go your anchor."

"It was the dates on your gravestones," he replied, "and by them I concluded that this was about as healthy a place as I could find."

In 1905, 1907 and 1908, my father, in the *Spray*, made winter cruises to the West Indies, single-handed, as usual. He went, as he put it, "just to save buying a winter overcoat," though the real reason was that he no longer cared for the winter on the Vineyard and that he had become irked by New York life. The great clubs began to bore him, as did spike-tails, white throat seizings and black ties. All of these he exchanged for the jib halyards, and the *Spray* again joyfully buffeted the waves. Her skipper, in talking of one of these cruises, would be as vague as when he was fitting, in the first place, to sail around the world.

Off soundings and free, he would then decide upon detail. Usually he went to Grand Cayman Island, formerly a famous hangout for the English buccaneers, who have left their flavor behind in the present inhabitants of the island. My father loved the Caymaners, for they represented to him the old order of the sea in which he gloried. English surnames still predominate in the island, connoting the wrecks of many English ships upon its shores. The people even talk in an archaic idiom befitting the lineal descendants of the followers of Henry Morgan. The *Spray* just loved to lie at anchor, spread her awning, and listen.

Grand Cayman Island, though important in history, is diminutive in extent, with an anchorage on one side only. Low and unimpressive, it is tucked away near the south coast of Cuba and not far from Jamaica from whence, as a British possession, the island is administered. The present five thousand inhabitants are industrious, being engaged in coconut culture, coir (coconut fiber) rope making, boat building and turtle fishing. They are a happy and interesting sea people, and were well worthy of the Captain's visit.

In 1909 the *Spray* was fitted out at the Herreshoff works in Bristol, Rhode Island, for her customary winter voyage to Grand Cayman. Mr. Herreshoff (the great "Nat") admired his visitor and said she was a good boat. While the *Spray* was in his yard he spent considerable time looking her over and also much time in conversation with her skipper, though Nat was known to be a man who wasted neither time nor words. When the *Spray* left Bristol in the fall of 1909, she was well fitted and provided for, and my father was in the best of physical health.

The events at sea following his departure are matters of conjecture. Anyone's guess is as good as another's. Four things may have happened to the vessel and her skipper: Foundering in a gale, which is unlikely, as there was no seriously bad weather which that pair could not ride out to the sea anchor which was always ready; second, the possibility of fire, a hazard imminent on every vessel everywhere; third, collision at night; and last, shipwreck.

Collision at night has always seemed to me the most likely of any of the things that may have happened, for after the introduction of steamboating, all sailing vessels, great and small, had constantly to be on the alert against collision with a steamer at night, especially in coastal waters. A sailing vessel's running lights, sometimes partly screened by the vessel's own sails, were never entirely depended upon for protection. A flare torch was always kept ready for instant ignition. This was displayed in such manner as to light up the sails and thus warn off a steamer coming on. The *Spray*, like any other sailing vessel, carried a turpentine-filled flare within quick reach in the after companion-way. After clearing Hatteras she would have been reasonably safe from collision for the rest of the passage, but up to that point there were three different great steamship tracks to cross: those out of New York, Philadelphia, and the ports of Chesapeake Bay; all very dangerous at night for small sailing vessels with dim oil-burning side lights. Even a steamer with good lookouts on the forecastle and intense vigilance on the bridge, travelling at eighteen knots, could run down such a small vessel without ever seeing it or feeling the impact. No matter how she was lost, the *Spray* continues to hold her place amongst the historic ships of all time.

In due recognition of the Captain's contribution to the morale of seamen by his own example, the United States Government, during the Second World War, named a Liberty ship the *Joshua Slocum*. She was launched in Portland, Maine, and made many passages between Buenos Aires and India, cutting far to the south as far as the ice fields to avoid German submarines. To have menaced the *Joshua Slocum* seems particularly mean of the Germans, since in 1937 they translated and published the Captain's book in Germany, in an effort to bolster up their own sea morale. *Erdumseglung-Ganz Allein* (Leipzig, 1937) is the title of the German edition. Even the Kaiser, thirty-five years before, had remarked that he liked the *Spray* book because "there was nothing in it about fear."

As the name of Joshua Slocum is remembered through the years as America's outstanding sailor, so is the little *Spray* kept afloat in its many reincarnations by yachtsmen, for successive ships have been built from her lines. To many sailors of the present day her hull is still considered the best for long voyages at sea. Indeed, the key to the first singlehanded voyage around the world can be found in the right little ship and the right man to sail her. It is my hope that this study of both will show that they were well mated.

The Slocums before Joshua

THE earliest Slocums (or Slocombes, to use the original spelling of the name) were English Quakers. It is very likely these peace-loving emigrants, intent upon settling in a new land, were evolved from the horde of sea rovers, who, in the tenth century, had descended on the Northumberland coast from beyond the North Sea. They came first to burn and pillage and later to journey westward to Wessex where they became useful toilers of the soil and workers in iron. It was another literal example of turning swords into ploughshares and spears into pruning hooks. That was a reform which took a number of centuries to effect but such miracles are known to have been.

The first vestiges of any Slocombe (as it was spelled then) on American shores were those of Anthony Slocombe who is credited by reliable genealogists with being the common ancestor of any of the name we may find in the land. Anthony was a colonist from near Taunton, Somerset, England, and an original purchaser of the site of Taunton, Massachusetts. There were

371

forty-six purchasers in the deal and they bought the land from the great Massasoit, Sachem of the Wampanoags. The rate was two shillings an acre, which is an index of real estate values in those parts in 1637.

Several of the white purchasers, with Anthony Slocombe at their head, organized a stock company for the purpose of establishing an iron foundry. That was in 1652. It was the first iron foundry or smelting works to be established on the American continent and a monument to the productive energy of its founder. The works flourished until 1676 when it was demolished by the Indians in King Philip's War against the white settlers. King Philip was the second son of Massasoit, who by this time was deceased.

Anthony had sold out ten years after the establishment of the works and had moved to Dartmouth, which was also destroyed by the savages in the same war which had a very wide range. The war came to an end when one of Colonel Church's men shot and killed King Philip. After that there was comparative security in the land, but the militia was still enrolled and in every settler's house was the long flintlock with its attendant "crookneck" hanging against the panel over the fireplace, ready to be snatched down for instant use. An exciting time to live in, we should say. By the execution of a recorded will and some other documents we learn that Anthony Slocombe lived until he was ninety-five instead of having been both tomahawked and scalped, as he was likely to have been when King Philip was after him.

There is a slight haze over the story of the successions in the Anthony branch of the family because the records were burned in the Taunton fire of 1838. Another fact which has added to the confusion of the antiquarian was the failure of the Quakers, for the first fifty years, to carve names or dates on their gravestones. It was a sparing of shapeless sculpture and uncouth rhyme which has not been conducive to the convenience of vital statistics.

Certain it is, however, that a Captain Simon Slocombe, a coasting mariner of twenty-four, sailed from Baltimore to Boston in his sloop the *Success*. That was in 1701. Twenty-two years later, rated as Master and Pilot, he commanded the Plymouth Colony armed transport sloop *Seaflower*. The *Seaflower* was sixty tons and mounted a battery of four guns. We are not informed of their weight of metal but it is safe to guess that they were six pounders which would have been about all a sixty ton vessel could have stood. Boston did not seem to have any objections to the Captain in a military capacity, besides, they had not hung a Quaker on the Common for nineteen years. The idea might have worn out. He married very soon after arriving in the *Success* and thereafter raised a family of eight children. The eldest of these was Simon 2nd who was to grow up and become a military man like his father, and the youngest son was John who was to marry Experience Healy.

Simon Slocombe 2nd settled in Wrentham, Massachusetts. He first engaged in a mercantile business and at the opening of the 1744-48 War between England and France he was commissioned by Governor Shirley as a Captain in the First Regiment of Militia. Simon 2nd was not opposed to strife and in his actions against French and Indians he certainly displayed a talent for fighting. He participated in Pepperell's expedition to Canada to capture Louisburg, and his company served until after the fall of Quebec. He was in Nova Scotia during the expulsion of the French Acadians. He saw the whole thing through. That he stood well with his superiors is evinced by the success of a "memorial" which he addressed to the Lieutenant Governor and the General Court in Boston in behalf of some

373

of his men who were not getting a square deal from the Government. This was an overtimed guard which had been detailed as a relief of the garrison at Fort Cumberland. "They have farms of their own," he stoutly explained, "and their families at home are uneasy and discontented." Captain Simon was sticking his neck out but he got his men home.

At the opening of the conflict between the Colonies and Great Britain three of the four sons in the family of John and Experience (Healy) Slocombe, enlisted in the Continental Army. The sons were Simon, William, George and John. John, the youngest and twenty-two, dissented from the position of his brothers on the issue of War itself. He just did not want to fight for the Continental Congress, King George or any other agency of Mars. In the days of the Revolution there was no such distinction as Conscientious Objector. It was either fight or get out. John elected to get out. By refusing to bear arms, John drew upon himself the odium of Toryism although he was not a Tory. His stand meant banishment. However, guided by conscience or sentiment, he must have discovered that it took more resolution to keep out of the war than to go along with it. He honored the exhortation by the Society of Friends, of which he was a member: "That they and their children stand clear in their testimony against wars and fighting and the learning to war." That was the doctrine of non-resistance expressed in the quaint Quaker idiom.

In New England especially, loyalism is now almost forgotten, but it is worth a moment's attention. John Adams, in 1776, quite correctly estimated that in the Thirteen States at least one-third of the people were Loyalists of different degrees of saturation. The extremists were opposed to a large majority of moderates who, while they did not approve of England's unwise colonial policy, were yet in hopes that the ills inflicted upon the Colonies

could be adjusted without aggressive action. Congress courageously decided otherwise.

On the evacuation of New York in 1783, General Carleton
found that with his other impedimenta he had 40,000 Loyalist
refugees on his hands, and this great multitude was swelled
by the quotas from other states to a multitude of 60,000 souls
destined to carve out a new empire in a northern wilderness.
After their sufferings, they were eager for a refuge even in virgin forests of pine and spruce and to enter the solitudes of river,
lake and seashore.

The exiles were divided into two main streams, one moving
westward to the region north of Ontario, and the other eastward toward Nova Scotia, or "Nova Scarcity" as they heard
the land of promise derisively alluded to. But if scarcity was not
soon converted to abundance, at least it grew to a frugal com-
petence when the 20,000 began to settle.

In the spring of 1783 eighteen large ships landed 5,000 exiles
on the shores of Shelburne Harbor alone. It was uninhabited
except for an encampment of wandering Micmac Indians. This
contingent was soon followed by another of equal numbers. At
the same time 500 exiles were landed in Digby, on the shores
of the Bay of Fundy, and they all set to work creating new
homesteads and industry. The Digby settlers secured grants of
land from the Crown and among these was John Slocombe of
Wrentham, Massachusetts.

Hardship and a return to first principles made these new
settlers on the shores of Nova Scotia as self-reliant as were the
original settlers of the American Colonies. The exiles represented some of the best of the people of the Colonies: generals,
judges, eminent lawyers, cultured clergy, and the most refined
of the North and the South. When the 20,000 entered Nova
Scotia they formed more than half of the entire population of

whites, of which about 2,000 were French. On the southern coast of Nova Scotia, extending to the east, were already a few sparse settlements of European fishermen who had been voyaging across the Atlantic to work the fishing banks. These pioneers, twenty years before the Loyalists appeared, became well enough established to export their surplus of salted fish and whale oil.

The sudden expulsion of the Loyalists from their already settled homes to a new wilderness was a two-century setback to their colonization. These victims of a war resumed conditions of pioneer hardship forgotten for generations. It inculcated within them a courage, a determination and a perseverance which has been the pride and marvel of their descendants ever since. To be a "Bluenose" meant something. The newcomers braved a rigorous climate. They camped in tents and other temporary shelters until log cabins could be built.

To people used to the refinements of life these were very rude and uncomfortable structures. The typical log cabin was twenty feet long and fifteen feet wide. The walls, made of logs notched at the corners, were but seven feet high. Dirt was the floor and oiled paper took the place of glass in the small openings through the logs called windows. The more ornate log cabins had stone chimneys built outside; others had only a hole through the roof to carry the smoke up from the fireplace or as much of the smoke as could be induced to reach the hole. As fires had to be kept burning all night it can be imagined what that could have been like. Anyway it would have kept the mosquitoes out. Except for the family heirlooms which could be carried on the transports, the furniture was all handmade from materials obtained on the spot. A well-furnished cabin had rough benches, a table and a rope bedstead. An iron kettle hung over the fireplace from a crane and bread was baked in another kettle with fuel piled on top and more underneath in a hole in the ground. Beans were baked the same way, and it was not a bad way either when it came to regular baked beans with salt pork and molasses. There was a frying pan with a three-foot handle for flapjacks. And the same frying pan was good for Johnnycake made of corn meal. The fireplace and the tallow dip were the only sources of artificial light. The dishes, nearly all of them, were birchbark and wood.

Pioneer farming was carried on in a very primitive fashion. At first there were no mills for grinding the corn. It was laboriously crushed between stones or pounded with a pestle in the hollowed top of a tree, the way the Indians did it. The year 1788 became known as "The Hungry Year," due to the crop failure of the year before. In after years, a better management of resources enabled the exiles gradually to surmount the obstacles Nature had placed in their path.

Allocation of the land was very simple. The numbers of the lots were written on small squares of paper and drawn from a hat. Exile John Slocombe, as was his right, drew lands in Digby, but afterwards he was granted a farm of five hundred acres in Wilmot Township, across the ridge called "North Mountain." As soon as a sawmill got into production, he built a comfortable and substantial house which to this day looks from Mt. Hanley across the bay to the blue shore of New Brunswick. He also became the owner of a vessel of sufficient size to be employed as a packet, trading between Port George and St. John. He traded his own produce as well as that of his neighbors. Everything came and went by vessel. John (the exile) was a strong character and as soon as his ship worked off-shore and began to sail on an even keel, he showed leadership. He was a skillful and industrious farmer, and while his ample land holdings had the bold and rocky shore of the Bay of Fundy at their front door, the acreage that went back over the mountain was fertile and productive to a great degree.

The fishing station used by John Slocombe and his neighbors on North Mountain was Reagh's Cove which was lined with hamlets along the shore. The inhabitants made their own fishing gear. There was no such thing as going to a factory for a dory or a web of netting. They were trained by necessity to make their own and they did so. They were versatile and could make a waggon and a pair of ox-bows as well as rig a fish weir. Their thirteen-foot (bottom) dories were of the best type of rough water boat in the world. It had a crew of two and it was pulled by pairs of oars in tholepins. Sometimes they spread a small sail before a fair wind but they depended mainly on their oars. Those robust and husky young fellows were very proud of their strength and endurance. They had been known to pull two hundred miles from a foundered schooner at sea. It was a rugged life on the Bay of Fundy.

Once or twice a year, John was disposed to mount his horse for an extended evangelical tour of the Province. His Quakerism, for which he had made so great a sacrifice, had gradually merged into a type of Methodism that especially appealed to the new settlers of the southern part of Nova Scotia. They were inclined to think that since they had managed, by themselves, to carve out new homes in the wilderness and to solve the problems of *this* world, they were fully competent to formulate their own ideas regarding the next. Nonconformity with the noble ritual of the Church of England, established in Halifax, was in all probability the cause of their leaning toward the more emotional Methodism, which was better adapted to camp meetings. There never was much sympathy anyway between the south of Nova Scotia and Halifax, largely because of the difficulty of travel through the country. Oxcarts had to force their way through the timber, and there was often only a bridle path where an open road should have been. It may thus be seen how the more equalitarian and emotional type of religion preached by the Methodists could have made such progress on the frontier. Their circuit riders brought the comforts of salvation to many a pioneer family and often served as the most important connecting link with the outside world. One devoted father whose little girl was on a visit to Halifax, asked that the minister of grace "pray for his darter in a furrin land." In these days of good roads and autos, it is difficult to understand that honest pioneer's sense of isolation. Halifax seemed to him a thousand miles away.

Journeying through the land John taught and exhorted the people, and as one of the pioneer Methodists of the Province he was noted as an able expounder of the Scriptures. During his tours he carried with him in his saddle-bag, his highly treasured Bible, which was of a very old print and contained considerable Greek, with notes pencilled by his own hand. Nor were his ministrations entirely of the spiritual order, for more often than 'twas known he helped the less fortunate from the store of his own prudence and industry.

Joshua Upham, second son of John the exile, married Elizabeth Farnsworth. It was a step forward to marry into the Farnsworths, for they were a progressive and remarkable family. Joshua and Elizabeth had eight daughters and four sons: Susan, Deborah, Mary Upham, Elizabeth, Lavinia, Angelina, Naomi and Ruth; the sons—John, Joshua, Joel and Samuel. Nearly all of them figured prominently in the early history of North Mountain, and Mt. Hanley in particular.

Joshua Upham, later known as Captain Joshua U., took over his father's bay packet business and continued to carry produce to market. He extended that market from St. John to as far as

New York and Baltimore. Then he had a small brig built for him in Bear River, in which he traded fish products to the West Indies. In Haiti especially he found that the natives liked the salt codfish imported from the north. That salt cod, spiced with condiments, made a hearty chowder which evidently stuck to their ribs.

As soon as Joshua Upham's third and fourth sons, Joel and Samuel, grew old enough to make trips with their older brother, they were not long either in learning the ropes. Samuel afterwards had a packet of his own to ply between Port George and St. John, carrying freight, and he also ran a store at the Port which his wife, Susan, tended while her husband was away on his periodic trips. Brother Joel sometimes took a hand at sailing the packet as well as did their elder brother John, between his spells of leather tanning and boot making. Versatility was a strong point with that particular family.

One anecdote about Captain Joshua Upham was that he always bought a different design or print in dress material for his wife's and each of his eight daughter's gowns, when he visited St. John or Boston on his trading voyages. Many another woman would be seen followed to church by all her daughters in dresses off the same bolt, and how they envied those Slocombes!

Tailors came from St. John to make the men's best clothes; also a furniture maker to fashion the best chairs and tables and other things of the kind for the newly-weds. For each of his eight daughters Captain Joshua Upham had blanket chests made, each with a wreath painted in color on the top or front, and the girl's name stencilled inside. And he had a set of six hardwood chairs with rush bottoms made for each daughter. When Naomi (the eleventh child) went to Boston to live, she divided her best parlour chairs and all of her brass and glass candle-sticks among her sisters.

For sheer versatility, Angelina (the tenth child) probably excelled them all. In later years, on Naomi's arrival back from Boston for a visit, she found Angelina coming out of the farm's carpenter shop. Angelina had just finished building some steps for the front of the meeting house, which she felt must be ready for the next Sunday, and as her boys were too occupied with their own business of building other people's houses and carrying on the farm, Angelina simply did the job herself. Anyone who has ever cut a set of stair horses out of spruce plank with a handsaw will realize what the labor was like, let alone the know-how of installing the risers and treads and mitering the nosings. Angelina's steps were perfect! She came naturally by her enterprise and capability—could work like a man and wasn't afraid to do so. One of her aunts on the Farnsworth side was a doctor who travelled by horse over fences and walls in winter to reach her patients. In fact, all the women were trained in the care of the sick; besides being expert in the dairy and in weaving.

The Slocombe men were noted for being ample providers and their women, grand cooks. The women thought nothing of spelling one another and cooking all night for a big family reunion, when, as fast as one lot of bread and pies and puddings came out of the large brick oven, another went in. A whole sheep would be stuffed with bread and home-grown herbs, summer savory, marjoram, etc., and roasted for the dinner. The sheep, which they raised in great flocks, found the rocky places suited to their nibbling. The family had quantities of tallow candles because of the sheep, and no Slocombe had to resort to a "slut" lamp which the fisher-folk, who had no land to farm, were forced to use in lieu of something better. The fisher-folk lived in "slabtown," name of the little cluster of fishermen's houses between the big farm and Port George, now known as Cottage Cove.

Neat cattle and horses were also raised in large numbers by the Slocombes. Plenty of beef and pork products were put away for household needs and a large surplus sold yearly. This gave them hides from which to make boots and harnesses. Most of the self-sustaining families built cobbler shops alongside their houses in much the same way people do with garages today. There was a cobbler shop at the Farnsworths', the Millers', and the Gates'. There was one on the exile's house. As the Slocombes accumulated an excess of hides, a tannery was built, and then a shoe factory. It was in this "factory" on Mt. Hanley that my own grandfather, John Slocombe, first son of Joshua Upham and Elizabeth Farnsworth, learned to make fishermen's boots, a circumstance which was later to provoke a mutiny in the family.

INDEX

383

INDEX